Africa's World Cup

AFRICA'S WORLD CUP

Critical Reflections on Play, Patriotism, Spectatorship, and Space

Edited by
Peter Alegi and Chris Bolsmann

The University of Michigan Press
Ann Arbor

Copyright © by the University of Michigan 2013
All rights reserved

Published in the United States of America by
The University of Michigan Press
Manufactured in the United States of America
⊗ Printed on acid-free paper

2016   2015   2014   2013   4   3   2   1

A CIP catalog record for this book is available from the British Library.

Library of Congress Cataloging-in-Publication Data

Africa's World Cup : critical reflections on play, patriotism, spectatorship, and space / edited by Peter Alegi and Chris Bolsmann.
    p.   cm.
Includes bibliographical references and index.
    ISBN 978-0-472-07194-4 (cloth : alk. paper) — ISBN 978-0-472-05194-6 (pbk. : alk. paper) — ISBN 978-0-472-02911-2 (e-book)
    1. World Cup (Soccer) (2010 : South Africa)   2. Soccer—Tournaments—South Africa.   3. Sports and culture—South Africa.   4. Sports and society—South Africa.   5. Nationalism and sports—South Africa.   6. South Africa—Social life and customs.   I. Alegi, Peter.   II. Bolsmann, Chris.

GV943.5.2010 A57   2013
796.334'668—dc23

2012047389

To our brothers and sisters of Izichwe Youth Football:

The fame of Izichwe must resound throughout the earth.
Even those who once boasted of the sharpness of their weapons
Shall flee in terror from the fierceness of Izichwe regiment.

Mazisi Kunene, Emperor Shaka the Great: A Zulu Epic

Preface and Acknowledgments

FROM MAY 15, 2004, when the Fédération Internationale de Football Association (FIFA), soccer's world governing body, announced that South Africa would host the 2010 World Cup, South Africans oscillated between collective exhilaration and personal anxiety. In the six years between FIFA's decision and the opening ceremony at Soccer City outside Soweto, South Africans debated the potential benefits of becoming the first African nation to stage what is arguably the most important global cultural event on the planet. In workplaces, schools, markets, streets, taverns, and in the media, ordinary people discussed what hosting the World Cup would mean for a country with extraordinary levels of poverty and inequality stemming from more than a century of colonial capitalism, racial segregation, and apartheid.

As the historic event drew closer, popular debates intensified. Many pundits and knowledgeable fans worried that the national team, popularly known as Bafana Bafana (Zulu for *The Boys*), would exit quickly; other South Africans blinded by patriotic optimism or less familiar with the game, went so far as to predict that their team would win the tournament. When Siphiwe Tshabalala scored to give South Africa the lead against Mexico in the opening game, lingering doubts and fears magically dissipated as millions of South Africans united behind the team. At that moment, the country experienced what no other event, with the exception of the first democratic elections in 1994, had ever achieved: a unified nation, collectively imagining the impossible.

South African sport fans had first tasted this possibility in 1995 when the Springboks won the rugby World Cup on home soil, but it took "the beautiful game"—the national pastime—and a heady infusion of sporting nationalism to make it invitingly real, at least for a few days. This national euphoria partly explains why South Africans readily forgave their team for failing to advance to the second round, the only host nation in World Cup history to have ever suffered such a fate.

What mattered more to South Africans was how the World Cup recast perceptions of their country, altered public spaces in host cities, and how it inspired people across race, class, gender, and age lines to wear yellow Bafana shirts and blow vuvuzelas in fan parks and public viewing areas. After Bafana Bafana's elimination, South Africans supported other teams, with Ghana's Black Stars a popular pan-African choice. Meanwhile, South Africans and foreign visitors alike marveled at the efficient organization and infectious energy. Matches were held in state-of-the-art stadiums without any glitches. To the great satisfaction of the organizers, global media congratulated South Africa for staging a world-class event. The stuff of dreams.

A few days after the lights went down on the 2010 FIFA World Cup, however, South Africa's public sector unions embarked on a massive strike. More than one million disgruntled teachers, nurses, civil servants, and other government workers brought the country to a halt, demanding increases in wages and housing allowances. Two years later, police shot and killed thirty-four platinum miners during a wildcat strike at a Lonmin mine in Marikana. These actions brought home the painful realities that make postapartheid South Africa one of the most unequal countries in the world. As 2012 comes to a close, it is clear that the South African government's and FIFA's promises of tangible economic legacies from the tournament remain largely unfulfilled.

South African football's woes in the international arena continue unabated. At the time of writing (November 2012), Bafana Bafana is ranked eighty-fourth in the world, one rung lower than during the World Cup. To make matters worse, the team tragicomically failed to qualify for the 2012 African Nations Cup. As the final whistle blew after a scoreless draw against Sierra Leone, the South African players danced eagerly on the pitch of the Mbombela Stadium in Nelspruit and smiled for the television cameras, thinking that they had qualified. With South Africa, Niger, and Sierra Leone tied at the top of the group, the tiebreaker was not goal difference, as the South Africans mistakenly believed, but points earned in head-to-head contests. On that basis, Niger qualified instead. A few months later Gordon Igesund replaced an embarrassed Pitso Mosimane as Bafana Bafana head coach. Luckily for the new manager, South Africa automatically qualified for the 2013 African Nations Cup as host country.

The buildup to the upcoming continental competition in South Africa has been markedly different from the country's preparations for the 2010 World Cup. Government investment has been minimal. And despite reasonably priced tickets and a simplified ticketing system, popular excitement and media interest are modest. Bafana Bafana's poor results in 2014 World Cup qualifiers and South African clubs' lack of success against African rivals seem to strengthen the view that local football may have taken one step forward and two steps back since July 2010. For signs of international success, South Africans can turn to the women's national team, Banyana Banyana, which in 2012 competed in the Olympics for the first time and then won silver at the African Women's Championship held in Equatorial Guinea.

South Africa is not alone among nations from outside Western Europe and North America that have recently either hosted or are set to host global mega sporting events. Beijing staged the 2008 Summer Olympics and Delhi the 2010 Commonwealth Games. Brazil is hosting the 2014 World Cup as well as the 2016 Summer Games in Rio de Janeiro. Similarly, Russia acquired the 2014 Winter Games (in Sochi) and the 2018 World Cup. Brazil 2014 organizers, like their South African counterparts several years ago, face intense FIFA scrutiny and media criticism for delays in infrastructure construction projects.

Brazil also shares with South Africa the political goal of using the World Cup to advance their power and influence in their respective continents. There are differences, too. For example, Brazilian security forces have been far more aggressive than South African forces in removing poor communities from favelas in preparation for 2014 and the 2016 Olympics. Placed in this international context, the personal experiences and social analysis presented in this book should thus resonate both locally and globally, and certainly beyond 2010.

THIS VOLUME WAS MADE POSSIBLE by the work and commitment of our South African and international contributors. As editors, we thank you for taking part in the rewarding journey that produced *Africa's World Cup*. We are deeply grateful for the unflinching support of Thomas Dwyer and the excellent staff at the University of Michigan Press. We appreciated the constructive feedback from two anonymous reviewers and Ellen D. Goldlust's meticulous copy editing, which transformed the original manuscript into a fine book aimed at general readers as well as students and specialists working on Africa, sport, and globalization.

Peter Alegi and Chris Bolsmann

East Lansing and London
November 2012

Contents

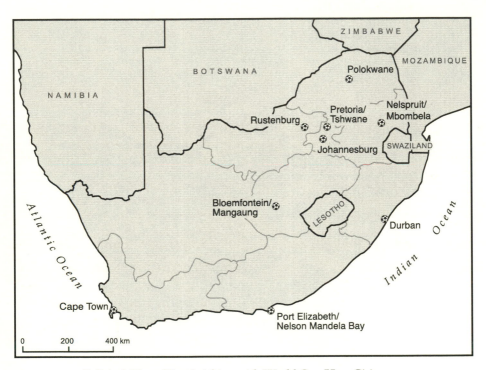

Political Map of South Africa, with World Cup Host Cities, 2010.
(Map by Claudia K. Walters, Dearborn, Michigan.)

Introduction

PETER ALEGI AND CHRIS BOLSMANN

THE WORLD CHEERED IN 1994 when Nelson Mandela became the first democratically elected president of South Africa. It celebrated again in 2010 when the World Cup—the world's most popular sporting event—was successfully staged in the former land of apartheid. After Spain defeated the Netherlands to win the first World Cup played on African soil, global media heaped praise on South Africa for its warm people, high modernist stadiums, tight security, sound event management, adequate accommodation, functional transportation, and telecommunication networks. "The World Cup has been a triumph for South Africa," wrote the *Times* of London; the competition "has soared beyond its problems to deliver one of the slickest tournaments on record [and] has generated a wave of national confidence."[1] The *Wall Street Journal* offered a literary nod to what may be South Africa's most widely read novel, Alan Paton's *Cry, the Beloved Country*, announcing, "Rejoice, the Beloved Country, toot your own vuvuzela."[2]

Self-congratulatory headlines and stories filled South African television, radio, newspapers, and electronic media: "We did it, we showed the world," Mark Gevisser put it in the *Guardian*.[3] South African big business enthusiastically joined the praise singers' bandwagon, taking out full-page advertisements in the country's major dailies: "Today this is the greatest country in the world," declared First National Bank, an official World Cup sponsor; "South Africa: you can be proud," stated the Pick 'n Pay supermarket chain. "Anyone who wasn't thrilled by the World Cup needs to see their psychiatrist," said Nobel Peace laureate Desmond Tutu in an interview with *Time* magazine.[4]

In many ways, of course, Tutu was right. New and revamped stadiums, expanded airports, improved road and rail transport are tangible long-term legacies left by the tournament. Less tangible but at least as important were the emotional and thus temporary legacies of the World Cup: a sharper sense of patriotic unity and pride in a nation still deeply divided along racial and economic lines and a reinvigorated sense of pan-African solidarity. For those of us privileged and fortunate enough to attend matches, visit fan parks and public viewing areas, "do" vuvuzela, and party with thousands of visitors from around the world, the monthlong football fest was a physically exhausting and emotionally draining experience.

This collection focuses on a remarkable month in the modern history of Africa and in the history of global soccer. Having published extensively on South African and African football, including a coedited scholarly collection, we invited an international team of academics, journalists, writers, bloggers, curators, photographers, architects, players, and coaches to write about their lived experiences at the World Cup. Combining essayistic writing with analytical insights informed by the latest scholarship, the authors wrote about matches, fan culture, media coverage, museum exhibits, grassroots football, and political and economic struggles related to the tournament. In so doing, the contributors reflect on what the World Cup meant to them and discuss the 2010 World Cup's wider meaning, significance, complexities, and contradictions, both on and off the field of play.

THE BOOK COMPRISES FOUR PARTS, arranged thematically. The essays in Part 1 consider the ways in which the 2010 World Cup refashioned urban spaces in host cities and the local struggles these changes engendered.[5] At the heart of South Africa's World Cup urban redevelopment initiatives were the stadiums. Municipal, provincial, and national authorities used publicly financed, architecturally impressive new stadiums as centerpieces of place branding campaigns. New stadiums were built in Cape Town, Durban, Nelspruit, Polokwane, and Port Elizabeth.[6] In Johannesburg, Bloemfontein, Pretoria, and Rustenburg, stadiums underwent renovations, while several smaller training venues were significantly upgraded. Soccer City, the venue for the opening match and the final, situated on the road between Johannesburg and Soweto, was almost completely rebuilt and now boasts the largest seating capacity of any stadium in Africa (94,000). Its calabash exterior shell, perhaps inspired by Beijing's Olympic Stadium (aka the Bird's Nest), captured and projected the African symbolism of the tournament. Overall, stadium construction accounted for nearly half of South Africa's total World Cup expenditures.[7]

While FIFA's self-interest partly explains the enormous financial burden placed on South Africa for staging the World Cup, the role of South African boosterist coalitions in putting their stamp on the process should not be underestimated. After South Africa's 1995 rugby World Cup triumph (memorialized in the film *Invictus*, directed by Clint Eastwood) and 1996 soccer victory in the African Nations Cup, megaevent hosting as a strategy for bolstering national unity and triggering economic growth became axiomatic for political, business, and labor leaders.[8] This combination of global and local dynamics, as political economists such as Hein Marais and others have noted, illustrates how structural forces in the global economy are "shaped by shifting balances of forces, and by histories of contesting social forces, as well as the societies in which they operate."[9] The World Cup business is no different.

The essays on Cape Town, Johannesburg, and Durban by Daniel Herwitz, Marc Fletcher, David Roberts and Orli Bass, and Killian Doherty demonstrate the ways in which "in order to compete on a global catwalk for investment and tourism, cities are remaking their physical landscapes and creating new experiential milieus."[10] These chapters shed light on the contradictory ways in which the 2010 World Cup accentuated processes of inclusion and exclusion in South Africa. FIFA's exacting conditions for hosting the World Cup corresponded in intriguing ways with postapartheid city builders' emphasis on "the creation of upscale aesthetic spaces for cultural consumption and visual spectacles of all kinds, all intended to lure tourists in search of exotic adventure, corporate executives on business excursions, and jet-setting conventioneers."[11] After the end of apartheid, Johannesburg and other major cities in South Africa witnessed a proliferation of "security parks" (fortified gated communities) and of city improvement districts and other public-private partnerships. These entities have transformed the social and political geography of cities, creating "an archipelago of extraterritorial sovereign spaces where the ordinary functioning of civil protections under the rule of law is suspended and replaced by the discretionary powers of private ownership."[12] In form and function, these spaces in urban South Africa bear a striking resemblance to FIFA's "exclusion zones," enabled by the South African Parliament's passage of the 2010 FIFA World Cup Special Measures Acts (11 and 12) of 2006. In this light, the Disneyfication of urban spaces and World Cup venues noted throughout this volume was the result of both external pressures (from FIFA and its corporate allies) and forces internal to South Africa.[13]

Set in Cape Town's Long Street on the night of the final, philosopher Daniel Herwitz's essay argues that the World Cup reactivated South Africa's national narrative of the "miracle" of the 1990s: the story of the "negotiated revolution" that ended apartheid and gave rise to democracy and rainbow nationalism. Together, the 2010 World Cup festival and the rainbow nation of the Mandela presidency reveal the importance of such a shared experience of the miraculous to South Africa's sense of imagined community. Fletcher's chapter on Johannesburg shows how many residents' attitudes toward the city improved during the World Cup, mainly as a result of a revamped public transport system, a visible police presence in the central business district, secure parking facilities, and watching matches in private malls. Fletcher points out that this shift in perception occurred in spaces that compartmentalized and circumscribed the World Cup experiences of unusually wealthy fans normally absent from the black working-class culture of South African football. Writing on the coastal city of Durban, academic researchers Roberts and Bass unveil a dynamic similar to that found in Johannesburg. During the World Cup, Durban residents reengaged in positive ways with their city's redeveloped public spaces, including the beachfront. In the process, however, subsistence fisherfolk were banned from the piers and a new set of municipal restrictions against behaviors deemed a nuisance undermined the constitutional rights (freedom of speech, movement, assembly) of informal traders, street children, and activists.

Killian Doherty, an architect by trade, considers World Cup urban improvements in Cape Town and their social impact. He shows how publicly funded renovation and beautification of the airport, main train station, roads, and several downtown areas disproportionally benefited wealthier people and classes at the expense of the city's poor. The new Football for Hope Center in Khayelitsha, a FIFA corporate social responsibility project in a black township on the outskirts of Cape Town, provides additional evidence that megaevent development must be sensitive to local needs and made more equitable and sustainable in the long run. Overall, the essays in Part 1 suggest that the reorganization of public space in World Cup host cities fostered greater social interaction and a more inclusive (and perhaps cosmopolitan) sense of South Africanness, at least in the short run; at the same time, however, these changes reinforced patterns of social exclusion and segregation along race and class lines.

Part 2 focuses on how football, the World Cup, and South Africa were represented in popular art, music, media, and visual culture both locally and abroad. Cultural studies scholar and blogger Jennifer Doyle's essay provides acute insights into the uses of World Cup music. She examines the political and cultural implications of U.S. broadcaster ESPN's soundtrack for its World Cup coverage, Shakira's plagiarism of the official World Cup song, and Coca-Cola's editing of K'naan's song "Wavin' Flag." The emergence and distribution via the Internet of oppositional World Cup music offered an alternative to multinational companies' generic pop jingles. In the next essay, anthropologist Solomon Waliaula explores the paradox of the vuvuzela as both leisure and noise. A plastic horn two to three feet in length, the vuvuzela produces a 100-plus decibel sound in B-flat that sounds like a wailing goat (Mondli Makhanya's description). In South Africa, Freddie "Saddam" Maake claims to be its inventor, but the Shembe Church has pointed out that it has used a similar horn since the 1950s; others believe that traditional kudu horns are the original vuvuzelas. Such competing claims aside, the vuvuzela is an invented tradition of the postapartheid era, and its popularity has expanded greatly in the past decade.[14] Waliaula's ethnographic piece probes the cultural resonance of horn-produced sounds in rituals among the Bukusu people in Kenya and the Acoli in Uganda. The essay makes intriguing if speculative connections between centuries-old agrarian rites of passage and the globalized fan culture of the World Cup. As a joyous and defiant declaration of South African ownership, the vuvuzela is possibly the most enduring symbol of the 2010 World Cup.

Moving away from the aural, the essay by Fiona Rankin-Smith, curator of the *Halakasha!* exhibition at a Johannesburg gallery, focuses on the aesthetics and visuals of football-related art. The carefully contextualized display of material culture, graphic art, and photographs depicting South African and African fans conveys the politics and nationalist sentiment permeating the sport, past and present. Art incorporated blackness more deeply into the World Cup experience in other ways, too. For example, the official logo and poster of the 2010 World Cup encapsulated the pan-Africanism projected by local organizers. The logo featured a player executing an overhead kick superimposed on the map of Africa,[15] while the poster showcased the profile of an African superimposed on the continent, a ball above his head. For Danny Jordaan, CEO of the Local Organizing Committee, this iconography "symbolises the important role of football in the history, tradition and culture of the African continent."[16]

Concerns about bringing out the "Africanity" of this FIFA event extended beyond the organizers. Corporate sponsors such as MTN, the South African telecommunications giant with significant presence in Africa, coined the term *ayoba*, meaning "cool." Adidas, the official technical supplier of FIFA, produced a much-despised match ball named Jabulani after the isiZulu word for happiness. In April 2009, the hotel group Southern Sun introduced "Football Fun Days." Modifying the "casual Friday" tradition, the chain encouraged its six thousand employees to wear soccer shirts to work.[17] This corporate initiative proved popular, and in late 2009, the Local Organizing Committee, the International Marketing Council of South Africa, the Government Communication and Information System, South African Tourism, and the South African Broadcasting Corporation launched "Football Fridays." Like the Southern Sun campaign, this initiative called on South Africans to wear football shirts on Fridays.

Football Fridays sought to generate greater enthusiasm for the World Cup and to mobilize support for the South African national team, which languished as low as number 90 in FIFA's world rankings in May 2010. South Africans were also urged to "wear a *makarapa* [decorated hard hat]. Blow a vuvuzela. Fly the South African flag. Practise singing the South African anthem."[18] Alongside Football Fridays, South African Tourism funded the Diski Dance project. According to Wendy Ramokgadi, choreographer of the dance, "the whole idea was that we needed to come up with something that is truly South African."[19] "Our country's football is rhythmic," she added, "so all the moves that we use in the dance are those same moves that are used on the South African football pitch, moves you can only find in our country."[20]

South Africa's considerable investment, public and private, into this kind of ideological work compensated in part for the overrepresentation of upper-middle- and middle-class South Africans (mostly whites and Indians) inside the stadiums.[21] The blackness of the sporting festival was further diluted by the fact that only 36,000 of the 3,178,856 tickets sold were purchased by "foreign Africans." However, the total number of spectators and average attendance of 49,670 for the 64 matches compare favorably with the total of 3,359,439 spectators and average of 52,491 who attended matches at Germany 2006.[22]

The final essay in this section, by writer John Harpham, serves as a bridge between Parts 2 and 3. It carefully records the sounds and conversations among the patrons watching France's World Cup matches at a bar in the Thirteenth Arrondissement (administrative subdivision) of Paris. As the French national team's insipid play and internal bickering leads to a humiliating early exit from the tournament, Harpham captures how World Cup soccer allows us to think about belonging and identity in contemporary France.[23]

Part 3, the longest in the book, focuses on the complicated relationships among soccer and patriotism, nationalism, and pan-Africanism.[24] World Cups are not only about host nations and how they project their desired images to the world; the competitions are also (even mainly) about the participating countries, players, and fans. With one exception, the essays in this section chronicle supporters who followed their teams abroad. Having invested financially and emotionally in their nation's performance, World Cup fans' lived experiences provide a glimpse into the social construction of identities. These essays humanize the World Cup corporate spectacle and, for good or ill, lend sporting nationalism existential weight.

Historian Craig Waite's essay frames the World Cup fortunes of Ghana, the best African performer in South Africa, within the context of Kwame Nkrumah's rise to power as the country's first president. Nkrumah's government supported the Black Stars (named after Marcus Garvey's shipping line) financially and propelled them to victory in the African Nations Cup in 1963 and 1965 and to a quarterfinal finish at the 1964 Olympics in Tokyo. Among the intriguing connections Waite makes between the Ghanaian teams of the 1960s and the 2010 squad is the tension between local coaches and European coaches, a long-running bone of contention in African football.[25] Next, Chris Bolsmann reflects on growing up in Pretoria, the capital of apartheid South Africa. He connects the importance of soccer to his socialization and political consciousness to broader meanings of patriotism at the World Cup through his ambivalence about singing South Africa's national anthem.

Bolsmann's recollections speak directly to a key theme of the 2010 World Cup: its capacity to articulate a more inclusive South African nationalism. The tournament created a common experience and discourse across race, class, gender, and generation fault lines. The tolerance and civility visible in interactions between South Africans during the event was encouraging and gives hope for the future of the imagined community in South Africa. Support for Bafana Bafana ignited South African national pride. A parade in Sandton on June 9, 2010, drew tens of thousands of South Africans of all backgrounds to the streets to salute the team riding an open double-decker bus. The event was also broadcast live on television. More than ten million South Africans watched the opening game between Bafana Bafana and Mexico on television, "figures which a Springbok–All Black rugby clash can only dream about," said Rob Smuts of RMS Media.[26] Siphiwe Tshabalala's marvelous go-ahead goal in that game detonated a thunderous explosion of collective joy around the country.

The team's disappointing first-round exit quieted rainbow nationalism, but "still, for the first time in South Africa's history, it seemed, patriotism was not a political statement," Mark Gevisser observed. "South Africans were waving flags, and supporting their team out of a sense of joy and belonging, rather than the deficit-driven pride that has fuelled both Afrikaner and African nationalism for so long. . . . 'We won' most of all, because we could finally say 'we.'"[27] Yet the limits of racial integration at the World Cup were clearly visible. Only those of us who could pay the high ticket prices gained access to stadiums and their surrounding exclusion zones (despite the sale of 120,000 tickets priced at 140 rand in South Africa). This exclusionary, gentrifying dynamic is part of the struggle for urban space described earlier, in which racial integration is indeed taking place in contemporary South Africa, but mostly in bourgeois enclaves surrounded by high walls and defended by private security forces.[28]

Among the fans who traveled to South Africa for the World Cup were former activists and supporters of the global antiapartheid movement. Simon Akindes, a former member of Benin's national soccer team and now a professor of political science and law in the United States, went to South Africa with his teenage son. His memoir tackles the role of football in father-son relationships and the vexing contradiction of being a "deterritorialized" fan at the World Cup with allegiance to a club (Arsenal) rather than a nation. Journalist David Patrick Lane chronicles his World Cup travels with fans of Uruguay, the tournament's surprise team. He reveals how and why the Uruguayan team achieved success while dispelling myths about their playing style and supposedly hyperaggressive approach to the game. Andrew Guest, a social scientist with a playing past in Malawi, turns to the meanings of fandom and patriotism among supporters of the United States, one of the largest contingents of traveling fans in South Africa. Pivoting around a paradox intrinsic to team sports, which simultaneously unite and divide, he juxtaposes the binding force of chants, insignia, and paraphernalia among U.S. fans during the game against England with his recoiling at jingoistic nationalism expressed by fans with whom one would never associate outside the World Cup context.

The unusual experiences of a group of English fans in South Africa are the subject of Mark Perryman's essay. For this journalist and author, a journey around South Africa meant a self-conscious distancing from the right-wing nationalism of England hooligans abroad. Countering the British press's sensationalistic coverage of the perceived dangers and concerns related to violent crime and poverty in South Africa, this group of England fans allowed themselves to be transformed by visiting historic places in the liberation struggle, such as the Hector Pieterson Museum in Soweto, where schoolchildren reignited the fight against apartheid in June 1976, and the Robben Island Museum on the grounds of the infamous prison where the regime incarcerated Mandela and many other political prisoners. Mexico, too, had a large contingent of fans in South Africa. A professional ethnographer and recreational footballer in Mexico City, Sergio Varela reveals how Mexican and Mexican American fans, fueled by alcohol consumption and vulnerable to the pressure of commercial spectacles, expressed nationalistic impulses that ignored Mexico's history of strife and division. Borrowing a concept from popular Mexican writer Carlos Monsiváis (who died during the

2010 World Cup at age seventy-two), Varela dubs them "closet Mexicans," arguing that their performances reinforced Mexican stereotypes of sexism, machismo, and banal patriotism. The closing essay in Part 3 is a travelogue by Niels Posthumus, a Dutch reporter, and Anna Mayumi Kerber, an Austrian photographer. In December 2009, the authors set out on a six-month overland journey from Marrakech to Johannesburg, winding their way through the local football cultures of Mauritania and several West African countries (including Ghana and Togo) before arriving in Johannesburg for the World Cup. This essay underscores the resilience of the African game in bleak circumstances and the power of international soccer to showcase the strengths and weaknesses, "the tragedy and hope," of the continent and its people.[29]

Part 4 centers on political discourses and economic rationales of World Cup hosting. South Africa's bids for 2006 and 2010 emphasized the potential economic benefits of hosting the World Cup. In a 2008 survey conducted by the Human Sciences Research Council, "economic growth" and "job creation" were highlighted by three-quarters of South African respondents (along with international prestige) as the main benefits of hosting the World Cup.[30] As preparations got under way, however, South Africa found itself, like past host nations and cities, mired in "a fantasy world of underestimated costs, overestimated revenues, undervalued environmental impacts and overvalued regional development effects."[31]

In South Africa's World Cup, political objectives trumped economic goals. Under the stewardship of three different presidents—Thabo Mbeki (1999–2008), Kgalema Motlanthe (2008–9), and Jacob Zuma (2009–present)—the African National Congress–led government rallied with big business and organized labor around two grand narratives: globally marketing "Brand South Africa" (the image of the country as modern, democratic, technologically advanced, pro-business, culturally rich) and fostering a stronger sense of South Africanness and national pride.[32] With more than 3.2 billion people (nearly half of the world's population) estimated to have watched at least one minute of television coverage, Winnie Mandela acknowledged the resonance of global capitalist football for the nation-state: "The 2010 World Cup is about nation-building, putting us on the global map and making us a nation to be reckoned with."[33]

Political discourses in South African football are not a new phenomenon, as the fierce sporting struggles fought against racial oppression inside and outside the country during the apartheid era clearly demonstrate.[34] As the country began to shed its outcast status following the release of Nelson Mandela and the unbanning of liberation movements, previously antagonistic football associations merged in 1991 to form the South African Football Association (SAFA).[35] Coming more than two years before the first democratic elections, unity in football provided evidence of black-led institutional democratization at a time of political turmoil. Suspended from FIFA in the 1960s and expelled in 1976, South Africa reentered international football in 1992 as the sport boycott ended. As apartheid crumbled, "the game of football captured the nation's euphoria in winning the franchise and acquiring global citizenship, and embodied the seemingly boundless potential of a liberated and united South Africa ahead of the first democratic elections in April 1994."[36]

In 1992, FIFA president João Havelange added to South Africa's growing confidence when he said that South Africa could serve as a future World Cup host.[37] After leading a FIFA delegation to South Africa that year, he wrote a complimentary letter to SAFA: "I was pleasantly surprised by the excellent sports facilities, the administrative installations and by the work you have achieved for the benefit of football in your country."[38] Returning from the 1994 World Cup in the United States, SAFA officials made their hosting intentions known to FIFA: "We hereby formally lodge our bid with your honourable selves to host the 2006 games in South Africa. . . . [W]e have the capability, competence, and skills to manage this great event. We also rightly believe that we are the best qualified country in Africa to host the World Cup for the first time on this great continent of Africa."[39] This one-page letter discovered in the bowels of the FIFA Archives in Zurich reveals not only that local football administrators cast themselves as pan-African representatives but also that they were keen to host a football World Cup prior to the arrival of the rugby World Cup in 1995.[40]

In their essay, historians Albert Grundlingh and John Nauright compare the political meanings of South Africa's hosting of the 1995 and 2010 events. Many South Africans who never entered the stadiums at the rugby and soccer World Cups still celebrated and profited from these global events, sometimes in ways that confounded organizers' agendas while creating rare opportunities for carnivalesque revelry. Grundlingh and Nauright assert that neither 1995 nor 2010 measurably addressed poverty, unemployment, or other critical socioeconomic questions facing postapartheid South Africa.

Novelist and academic Meg Vandermerwe questions World Cup discourse about pan-African solidarity in a society riven by xenophobic tensions. In the wake of xenophobic killings in 2008, rumors began circulating in South Africa that "African foreign nationals" would be attacked if they did not leave the country immediately after the World Cup. African immigrants seem to have become scapegoats for social grievances tied to widening intraracial inequality, a sluggish economy, and the government's limited capacity to improve the lives of the poor.[41]

South Africa's World Cup surrendered key aspects of national sovereignty to FIFA. According to the binding Organising Association Agreement signed by SAFA and FIFA, SAFA "was subject to the control of FIFA, represented by the Organising Committee for the Championship. FIFA has the last and final decision power on all matters relevant to the hosting of the Championship."[42] But unlike the 2006 World Cup in Germany, when private funds paid for 60 percent of stadium construction costs, South African government (national, provincial, and local) subsidies paid for almost all of the stadiums, media facilities, transportation and communications infrastructure, and security arrangements. Stadium construction costs increased from 3 billion rand in the 2003 Bid Book to 14.9 billion rand in 2006 and topped 40 billion rand (about $6 billion) in total World Cup–related infrastructure by 2010.[43] The inequity of South Africa's hosting agreement with FIFA was brought into stark relief by the world body's unprecedented revenue from the tournament: $3.2 billion tax-free, largely through the sale of World Cup television rights and corporate sponsorships.[44] The Local Organizing Committee earned $70–100 million from ticket sales.

The World Cup generated a spike in revenues for South African shopping mall retailers, construction giants, and food and hospitality companies, but the overall impact on GDP in South Africa amounted to between 0.3 and 0.5 percent—roughly one-tenth of the original government estimate.[45] In part, this outcome stemmed from the smaller-than-expected number of tourists who entered the country to attend World Cup matches. Initial projections had predicted 500,000 arrivals, but the final number, according to government sources, was closer to 250,000.[46]

Laurent Dubois's essay cautions against belittling South Africa's

World Cup hosting experience for reproducing patterns of racial oppression and economic inequality. The World Cup is the planet's largest theater, Dubois writes, an escapist narrative that plays out on iconic stages, with unpredictable outcomes, plot twists and turns, and unusual characters in the stands and on the pitch. What exactly thousands of football pilgrims found at the 2010 World Cup in South Africa remains an elusive question.

The book ends with a roundtable that puts forward several South African perspectives on the tournament and its aftermath. Thabo Dladla, a former professional player and founder of the Izichwe Youth Football program in Pietermaritzburg, KwaZulu-Natal; Rodney Reiners, also a former professional player and currently the head soccer writer for the *Cape Argus* newspaper; and Mohlomi Kekeletso Maubane, a freelance journalist in Gauteng, respond to questions about what the World Cup meant to them, the quality of play, FIFA's organizational role, the African character of the World Cup, and the long-term impact of the tournament on South African soccer and society.

NOTES

1. "Sing, the Beloved Country: The World Cup Was a Triumph for South Africa, If Not for England," *Times* (London), July 12, 2010, 2.

2. As quoted in Peter Fabricius, "Journalists Praise SA for Reinventing Itself," *Pretoria News*, July 13, 2010, 4.

3. Angelique Serrao, Nontobeko Mtshali, Thandi Skade, and Kevin McCullum, "Simply the Best! 'Thanks, Mzansi, We Had the Time of Our Lives,'" *Star*, July 12, 2010; "What a Show!," *Sunday Times*, July 11, 2010; Mark Gevisser, "We Did It, We Showed the World," *Guardian*, July 10, 2010.

4. Alex Perry, "Retiring from Public Life, Desmond Tutu Reflects on Good and Evil," *Time.com*, October 7, 2010, http://www.time.com/time/world/arti cle/0,8599,2023562,00.html, accessed October 31, 2010.

5. See also Udesh Pillay, Richard Tomlinson, and Orli Bass, eds., *Development and Dreams: The Urban Legacy of the 2010 Football World Cup* (Cape Town: HSRC Press, 2009); Collette Schulz-Herzenberg, ed., *Player and Referee: Conflicting Interests and the 2010 FIFA World Cup* (Pretoria: Institute for Security Studies, 2010); Christopher Merrett, "From Non-Racial Sport to the FIFA World Cup: A Tale of Politics, Big Business, and Hope Betrayed," in *Sport versus Art: A South African Contest*, ed. Chris Thurman (Johannesburg: Wits University Press, 2010); Ashwin Desai, ed., *The Race to Transform: Sport in Post-Apartheid South Africa* (Cape Town: HSRC Press, 2010).

6. For case studies on World Cup stadiums in South Africa, see Peter Alegi, "'A Nation to Be Reckoned With': The Politics of World Cup Stadium Construction

in Cape Town and Durban, South Africa," *African Studies* 67, 3 (2008): 397–422; David Roberts, "Durban's Future? Rebranding through the Production/Policing of Event-Specific Spaces at the 2010 World Cup," *Sport in Society* 13, 10 (2010): 1486–97; Sam Sole, "Durban's Moses Mabhida Stadium: Arch of Hope or Yoke of Debt?" in *Player and Referee*, ed. Schulz-Herzenberg, 169–201; Peter Alegi, "The Political Economy of Mega-Stadiums and the Underdevelopment of Grassroots Football in South Africa," *Politikon* 34, 3 (2007): 315–31; Karen Schoonbee and Stefaans Brümmer, "Public Loss, FIFA's Gain: How Cape Town Got Its 'White Elephant,'" in *Player and Referee*, ed. Schulz-Herzenberg, 133–67; Dale T. McKinley, "Mbombela: Corruption, Murder, False Promises, and Resistance," in *South Africa's World Cup: A Legacy for Whom?*, ed. Eddie Cottle (Scottsville: University of KwaZulu-Natal Press, 2011), 281–311.

7. Due to the pervasive secrecy and lack of transparency of megaevent planning and decision making, it is extremely challenging to find precise expenditure figures for South Africa 2010. According to an official source, construction costs for the five new stadiums and the substantially rebuilt Soccer City amounted to 15.5 billion rand, a figure that does not include the costs of renovating four other venues; see *The 2010 FIFA World Cup Official Guide Book* (Paarl: Touchline, 2010), 105–24. On the tournament's economic impact, see Ramos Mabugu and Ahmed Mohamed, *The Economic Impacts of Government Financing of the 2010 FIFA World Cup*," Stellenbosch Economic Working Papers 08/08, http://www.ekon.sun.ac.za/wpapers/2008/wp082008/wp-08-2008.pdf, accessed December 15, 2011; Schulz-Herzenberg, *Player and Referee*, 204–13; Patrick Bond and Eddie Cottle, "Economic Promises and Pitfalls of South Africa's World Cup," in *South Africa's World Cup*, ed. Cottle, 39–71.

8. Alegi, "'Nation to Be Reckoned With.'" On corruption, dirty tricks, and protests, see McKinley, "Mbombela," 281–311.

9. Hein Marais, *South Africa Pushed to the Limit: The Political Economy of Change* (London: Zed, 2011), 137.

10. Monica Degen, "Fighting for the Global Catwalk: Formalizing Public Life in Castlefield (Manchester) and Diluting Public Life in El Raval (Barcelona)," *International Journal of Urban and Regional Research* 27, 4 (2003): 879.

11. Martin J. Murray, *City of Extremes: The Spatial Politics of Johannesburg* (Durham: Duke University Press, 2011), xii.

12. Ibid., 278. On gated communities in Johannesburg, see Derek Hook and Michele Vrdoljak, "Gated Communities, Heterotopia, and a 'Rights' of Privilege: A 'Heterotopology' of the South African Security-Park," *Geoforum* 33 (2002): 195–219.

13. For additional commentary on this issue, see *Africa Past and Present*, "Episode 43: Reflections on Africa's First World Cup," podcast, July 22, 2010, http://afripod.aodl.org/2010/07/episode-43-reflections-on-africas-first-world-cup/, accessed July 23, 2010.

14. On the history of vuvuzelas, see Sean Jacobs, "Vuvuzelas Originate in the United States," June 24, 2009, http://www.footballiscominghome.info/the-hosts/the-vuvuzela/, accessed September 14, 2011; Rob Palmer, "The Vuvuzela as Cultural Artifact," *New York Times*, July 2, 2010. While broadcasters and many fans disliked the deafening blare of thousands of vuvuzelas, FIFA president Sepp Blatter tweeted his approval: "I have always said that Africa has a different rhythm,

a different sound" (quoted in BBC, "World Cup 2010: Organisers Will Not Ban Vuvuzelas," June 14, 2010, http://news.bbc.co.uk/sport2/hi/football/world_cup_2010/8737455.stm, accessed June 16, 2010).

15. Chris Bolsmann, "Representation in the First African World Cup: 'World-Class,' Pan-Africanism, and Exclusion," *Soccer and Society* 13, 2 (2012): 156–72.

16. BuaNews, "2010 Poster a Symbol of Africa," November 26, 2007, http://www.southafrica.info/2010/2010poster.htm, accessed December 12, 2011.

17. "Southern Sun Redefines Fridays to Football Fun Days!," April 24, 2009, http://www.southernsun.com/media/press-releases/2009/pages/southern-sun-redefines-fridays-to-football-fun-days!.aspx, accessed December 12, 2011.

18. "Play for Team SA on Football Fridays!," n.d., http://www.southafrica.info/2010/footballfridays.htm, accessed May 9, 2010.

19. 2010 FIFA World Cup South Africa Organizing Committee, "Diski Dance: Rhythm of SA 2010," December 24, 2009, http://www.southafrica.info/2010/diski-201109.htm#ixzz1g807Gdim, accessed January 6, 2010.

20. 2010 FIFA World Cup South Africa Organizing Committee, "Diski Dance: Rhythm of SA 2010," December 24, 2009, http://www.southafrica.info/2010/diski-201109.htm#ixzz1g807Gdim, accessed January 6, 2010.

21. For an insightful ethnographic study of South African fans, see Marc Fletcher, "'You Must Support Chiefs: Pirates Already Have Two White Fans!': Race and Racial Discourse in South African Football Fandom," in *South Africa and the Global Game: Football, Apartheid, and Beyond*, ed. Peter Alegi and Chris Bolsmann (London: Routledge, 2010), 79–94.

22. FIFA Technical Study Group, "2010 FIFA World Cup South Africa, Technical Report and Statistics," http://www.fifa.com/mm/document/affederation/technicaldevp/01/29/30/95/reportwm2010%5fweb.pdf, accessed September 1, 2011.

23. For more on this topic, see Laurent Dubois, *Soccer Empire: The World Cup and the Future of France* (Berkeley: University of California Press, 2010).

24. On South Africa's role in Africa, see Adekeye Adebajo, Adebayo Adedeji, and Chris Landsberg, eds., *South Africa in Africa: The Post-Apartheid Era* (Scottsville: University of KwaZulu-Natal Press, 2007).

25. For more on playing styles in Africa, see Peter Alegi, *African Soccerscapes: How a Continent Changed the World's Game* (London: Hurst; Athens: Ohio University Press, 2010), esp. chapters 2, 5. On European coaches in Africa, see Bea Vidacs, *Visions of a Better World: Football in the Cameroonian Imagination* (Berlin: LIT, 2010), esp. chapter 6.

26. Tony Koenderman, "'Amazing' World Cup TV Audiences," July 7, 2010, http://m.news24.com/fin24/AdReview/News-that-Matters/Amazing-World-Cup-TV-audiences-20100707, accessed August 27, 2011.

27. Gevisser, "'We Did It.'"

28. Hook and Vrdoljak, "Gated Communities."

29. The phrase is borrowed from Howard W. French, *A Continent for the Taking: The Tragedy and Hope of Africa* (New York: Knopf, 2004).

30. HSRC Media Release, "Consolidation of Positive Attitudes towards 2010, but Expectations Must Be Addressed," February 27, 2008, http://www.hsrc.ac.za/Media_Release-345.phtml, accessed September 15, 2009.

31. Bent Flyvbjerg, "Macchiavellian Mega Projects," *Antipode* 37, 1 (2005): 18.

On sporting megaevents, see David R. Black and Janis van der Westhuizen, "The Allure of Global Games for 'Semi-Peripheral' Polities and Spaces: A Research Agenda," *Third World Quarterly* 25, 7 (2004): 1195–1214; Maurice Roche, *Mega-Events and Modernity: Olympics and Expos in the Growth of Global Culture* (London: Routledge, 2000).

32. Alegi, "'A Nation to Be Reckoned With'"; "Finals Had over 700 Million TV Audience," *OneIndiaNews*, July 13, 2010, http://news.oneindia.in/2010/07/13/fifa-world-cup-2010-finals-spain-holland-tv-audien.html, accessed July 22, 2010.

33. "Almost Half the World Tuned in at Home to Watch 2010 FIFA World Cup South Africa," July 11, 2011, *FIFA.com*, http://www.fifa.com/worldcup/archive/southafrica2010/organisation/media/newsid=1473143/index.html, accessed December 21, 2011; Winnie Mandela quoted in the *Mercury*, March 16, 2007.

34. On football, see Peter Alegi, *Laduma!: Soccer, Politics, and Society in South Africa: From Its Origins to 2010* (Scottsville: University of KwaZulu-Natal Press, 2010). On other aspects of South African sport history, see John Nauright, *Sport, Cultures, and Identities in South Africa* (London: Leicester University Press, 1997); Douglas Booth, *The Race Game: Sport and Politics in South Africa* (London: Cass, 1998); Bruce Murray and Christopher Merrett, *Caught Behind: Race and Politics in Springbok Cricket* (Johannesburg: Wits University Press; Scottsville: University of KwaZulu-Natal Press, 2004).

35. Peter Alegi and Chris Bolsmann, "From Apartheid to Unity: White Capital and Black Power in the Racial Integration of South African Football, 1976–1992," *African Historical Review* 42, 2 (2010): 1–18; Chris Bolsmann, "White Football in South Africa: Empire, Apartheid, and Change, 1892–1977," *Soccer and Society* 11, 1–2 (2010): 29–45.

36. Alegi and Bolsmann, "From Apartheid to Unity," 18. See also Ivor I. Chipkin, *Do South Africans Exist? Nationalism, Democracy, and the Identity of "the People"* (Johannesburg: University of the Witwatersrand Press, 2007).

37. Peter Alegi, "'Feel the Pull in Your Soul': Local Agency and Global Trends in South Africa's 2006 World Cup Bid," *Soccer and Society* 2, 3 (2001): 1–21.

38. João Havelange to Solomon Morewa, April 14, 1992, South Africa Correspondence, FIFA Archives, Zurich, Switzerland.

39. SAFA to FIFA, "Bid for World Cup 2006," September 16, 1994, South Africa Correspondence, FIFA Archives.

40. Scarlett Cornelissen, "Sport Mega-Events in Africa: Processes, Impacts, and Prospects," *Tourism and Hospitality Planning and Development* 1, 1 (2004): 39–55; Justin van der Merwe and Janis van der Westhuizen, "The Branding Game: The Role of Sport in South African Foreign Policy," *Global Insight* 67, 1 (2006): 1–3.

41. See Jeremy Seekings and Nicoli Nattrass, *Class, Race, and Inequality in South Africa* (New Haven: Yale University Press, 2005), esp. 307–8; Marais, *South Africa Pushed to the Limit*, esp. 123–75. For a penetrating analysis of globalization and resistance, see Ashwin Desai, *We Are the Poors: Community Struggles in Post-Apartheid South Africa* (New York: Monthly Review Press, 2002).

42. Organising Association Agreement in South Gauteng High Court, "Judgement," June 8, 2010, http://mg.co.za/uploads/2010/06/09/mg-v-fifa-loc-judgement-8-may-2010.PDF, accessed October 3, 2011.

43. Bond and Cottle, "Economic Promises and Pitfalls," 45. This figure does

not include the Gautrain high-speed train link between Johannesburg and Pretoria or Durban's King Shaka Airport, megaprojects included in the national transportation development plan independently of the World Cup. See Janis van der Westhuizen, "Glitz, Glamour, and the Gautrain: Mega-Projects as Political Symbols," *Politikon* 34, 3 (2007): 333–51.

44. Natasha Marrian, "World Cup: FIFA to Rake in Billions," *Mail and Guardian Online*, June 18, 2010, http://mg.co.za/article/2010-6-18-world-cup-fifa-to-rake-in-billions, accessed July 10, 2010. See also AFP, "The 2010 World Cup Helped Raise FIFA Profits to $631 Million," *New York Post*, March 3, 2011, http://www.nypost.com/p/blogs/soccerblog/the_world_cup_helped_raise_fifa_JFlGZ RqZ73lFn09EQ2YPlI, accessed December 15, 2011.

45. Bond and Cottle, "Economic Promises and Pitfalls," 45.

46. South African Tourism claims that 309,554 tourists arrived "for the primary purpose of attending the 2010 FIFA World Cup." Given that only 11,300 foreign Africans bought World Cup tickets and that only 5 percent of tourists visited African countries other than South Africa, the total arrival figures appear flawed. The official figures also include 24,483 from Mozambique, 19,593 from Swaziland, 16,387 from Botswana, 12,733 from Lesotho, and 10,351 from Zimbabwe, representing the improbable figure of 32 percent of all World Cup foreign visitors. Figures cited in South African Tourism, "Impact of the 2010 FIFA World Cup," December 2010, http://www.tourism.gov.za:8001/PublicDocuments/2010_12_06/World_Cup_Impact_Study_v8_report_03122010.pdf, accessed August 2, 2011. For a critical study of the 2010 World Cup's projected impact on community-based tourism, see Andrea Giampiccoli and John Nauright, "Problems and Prospects for Community-Based Tourism in the New South Africa: The 2010 FIFA World Cup and Beyond," *African Historical Review* 42, 1 (2010): 42–62.

PART 1

Refashioning Urban Spaces and Local Struggles in Host Cities

World Cup Finale on Long Street

DANIEL HERWITZ

IT IS JULY 11, 2010, the moment of victory for the Spanish team. Spain has put unrelenting pressure on the Dutch goal with elegant passing across midfield and shot after shot on goal until 116 minutes into the game, Andres Iniesta scores. It is a victory of decency over roughhouse. The Dutch have played a kick-bite game, with seven players earning yellow cards and Heitinga sent off; they have clawed their way to possession, but Spain has retained civility on the field and won. The game has been a parable about clean versus brutal. The best team has won out by holding the high moral ground and proving themselves. In an event replete with contingency, disappointment, mistakes, accidents, yellow cards, and other disasters, the finale has the feel of a storybook ending.

By midnight, twenty thousand youths are dancing down Long Street in central Cape Town, glowing in the illumination of moon, stars, and flat-screen TV. They spill from bars, cafés, and restaurants in a river of unfurled flags and vuvuzelas. The street that has hosted the fan walk, part of the ritual approach to Green Point Stadium from the (Dutch East India) Company Gardens prefacing World Cup matches in Cape Town, is tonight medieval; its mosques, government buildings, clothing shops, old bookstores have disappeared behind courtiers draped in the red and yellow colors of Spain. French hug Ghanaians who down beer with English who carouse with Mexicans who sing with Senegalese. South Africans of every color are merged into the crowd, for an instant reveling in this international suspension of human division as a metaphor of themselves. Tonight, social strife and division have been red-carded. There is only the shared splendor of success, the euphoria that the country has pulled it off, neither glass nor bones have been broken, tourists have not been assaulted, the games have proceeded like clockwork in beautiful stadiums—the best World Cup ever, some announcers have said.[1] South Africa has announced itself as safe as Britain, as orderly as Germany. It profiled itself as capable of pulling off a major signature event, branded itself for the global marketplace.[2] By some irony, it has taken the gaze of the world and a global congregation in stadium and city to get South Africans to dance together. The last time South Africans occupied a unified space with this degree of pleasure was when the entire country stood in line to vote in the first democratic election of 1994. The World Cup has offered a second chance at the miraculous. They are happy to fall into a dreamlike belief that their feeling of fellowship is sustainable and their future assured. A taste of the Cape and every European will want to invest in property and tourism, even if it has been raining during many of the games and the glorious Table Mountain has been invisible through the fog. After a ten-year hiatus, the World Cup has reactivated South Africa's national narrative, which the country inhabited as if in a trance during the 1990s.

Cut to 1994, to the first "miracle," which this World Cup reactivated in spirit, a "negotiated revolution" that took place out of a spiral of economic collapse and increasing violence that had accompanied the demise of the apartheid state.[3] South Africa's transition to democracy between 1990 (when Nelson Mandela was released from prison) and 1994 proved the so-called miracle that nobody believed could happen, even while it was happening.[4] In December 1991, Mandela and state president F. W. De Klerk began formal negotiations to hammer out the terms for a new state. The Convention for a Democratic South Africa (CODESA) Talks between them and their parties were fraught with instability but continued on. These talks took place in a climate of fear and conflagration: Zulu nationalists of Inkatha aiming for provincial autonomy, aided and abetted by a shadowy "Third Force" made up of elements of the South African security establishment, fought the African National Congress, resulting in more than twelve thousand dead in the area today known as KwaZulu-Natal. And yet the talks led to the interim constitution (1993). That interim constitution, with its preamble about reconciliation, mandated the first free and democratic elections in the country's history, the terms of the Truth and Reconciliation Commission, and the pathway to the writing of a final constitution. Even with that document completed, it was widely expected that the 1994 elections would fail to come off. Whites bought long-life milk and hoarded canned goods in expectation of anarchy, the Inkatha Freedom Party boycotted the elections until a week before they took place, and the Pan Africanist Congress split into factions as a consequence of a dispute about whether to participate. Yet these elections constituted a milestone in South African history, a setting of the wheels of democracy in action, the beginning of national democratic process. Madiba (Mandela) became the first president of the new country: an international moral icon assumed power.

This miraculous beginning continued into 1996 with the proceedings of the Truth and Reconciliation Commission (TRC). Above the commission each and every day was its banner, which read, "Truth, the Road to Reconciliation." The TRC was the first commission of inquiry into human rights abuses that offered the unlikely feature of qualified amnesty. Qualified amnesty emerged from the CODESA talks as a compromise formation: The African National Congress wanted outright punishment for crimes; the National Party wanted blanket amnesty (as in the Chilean Truth and Reconciliation Commission, which was in certain other respects a model for the South African one). Qualified amnesty was so controversial that it was added only as a postscript to the 1993 interim constitution. What was offered was amnesty in exchange for two things: complete and true testimony by perpetrators (something hard enough to measure) and proof of "proportionality." Proportionality is in one sense an absurd criterion, since gross human rights violations are by definition out of proportion to their motivating circumstances. But the idea was to refute crimes clearly adjunct to the "war" between the apartheid state and those desiring its downfall, such as the rape of children, the killing of old people who happened to be nearby, and so on.[5]

The year 1996 also saw the adoption of the country's final constitution of the country was adopted. Beginning from a concept of the dignity of the individual, that document goes on to flesh out what human dignity means in terms of among the richest panoply of human rights yet offered by any state constitution. The rights mandated by the final constitution include a panoply of civil and political rights as well as substantive rights such as the right to health care, jobs, and housing. So that all South Africans may take advantage of their right to an education, the constitution prescribes primary education in all of the country's eleven official languages. This emphasis on linguistic diversity institutionalizes cultural diversity as central to dignity; preservation of this diversity through language is therefore a right. The constitution also reserves a place for "customary rights," although they are eclipsed by individual rights when customary law comes into irreconcilable conflict with individual rights. Perhaps most important, Article 39B mandates that every constitutional judgment be made with respect for the spirit of the constitution as a whole, thus prescribing a regime of continuous philosophical and social reflection on what dignity means and how that notion is to be maintained under shifting human circumstances. Put another way, Article 39B prescribes that each judgment be a new beginning, rewriting the terms of justice in however great or small a way.

These events were refracted in a radiant play of images over the South African media and in a radiant set of performances by President Mandela. His colorful shirts made him look like David after the defeat of Goliath, wearing Joseph's coat of many colors in a vast biblical extravaganza restaged in Africa. It felt that way at what was then the University of Natal, Durban, at a moment when universities were rapidly transforming their European heritages, opening themselves to a mass of formerly excluded populations, rapidly globalizing for the knowledge economy, and caught in a frenzy of debate about what it was to be an African. While Africa became a joyous question mark, Mandela was busy taking tea with Betsy Verwoerd (widow of Hendrik F. Verwoerd, a main architect of apartheid), declaring his entrance in Afrikaner life by playing with the rugby ball, busy being feted by the likes of Princess Diana, becoming moral exemplar-cum-celebrity.

Tremendous positive energy was released in South Africa through the world's rapt gaze. In a six-year period, South Africa went from global pariah to the Mandela years, from white supremacy defended by martial law to democracy bolstered by the TRC. South African images circulated everywhere, and the country was quick to attempt to capitalize on that profiling. In 1996, a television commercial widely broadcast during Cape Town's bid to host the 2004 Summer Olympic Games featured a former prisoner from Robben Island recalling the importance of intramural games for prisoner morale during the terrible days of his imprisonment, while a camera lovingly lingered on the now empty site of the prison. The commercial sought to sell the idea of having the games in Cape Town under the banner of South African liberation, recruiting painful history and its moral achievement to the twin purposes of nationalism and global branding. Proponents of the Olympic bid were attempting to persuade the world that the high moral road deserves recognition in all forms, especially that of the Olympics, with its roots in the birth of civilization and its avowed purpose of game-driven civility. But even moral recognition is a matter of global competitiveness, and the birthplace of the Olympics won out: The 2004 games were held in Athens.

Postapartheid South Africa conflated international recognition on moral grounds with competitiveness in the global marketplace, assuming that the Mandela brand could bring business—that and a local version of the World Bank's Structural Adjustment Program, the 1996 Growth, Employment, and Redistribution Strategy (GEAR). Thus, Treasury minister Trevor Manuel codified a neoliberal turn in South African economic policy in the form of GEAR. It artificially tailored the South African economy to fit the stringent suit of structural adjustment to achieve target goals of an annual GDP growth of 6 percent or more by 2000 and the creation of four hundred thousand new jobs each year through foreign investment and internal economic efficiency. What happened instead was that the global market turned to China, leading to little foreign investment and the real loss of two million jobs in South Africa. South African manufacturing began to outsource to China as well as to other regions of Africa (Malawi, for example), where labor costs were lower and unions weaker. Instead of economic and job growth, close to 40 percent of the country's workforce found itself unemployed (depending on who did the measurement and what was counted as "informal work"). The policy of black economic empowerment simultaneously generated a small elite black African capitalist class but did little more than deracialize the business elite.[6] As a result of these economic trends, South Africa's Gini coefficient (differential between rich and poor) remained among the highest in the world.

Then the moral capital began to depreciate in value through a number of global and internal recognitions: (1) Crime was out of control, with policing a failure in the newly weak (that is, no longer authoritarian/fascist) state; (2) No public works programs were being properly instituted to drive the country toward the noble human rights goals set forth in the constitution; (3) "Racialized" practices were deeply ingrained in the new regime, including some that had been subdued during the apartheid regime between black African, coloured, Indian, and so on.

In 1999, the country also found that it could also no longer hold off acknowledging the HIV/AIDS pandemic. The province of KwaZulu-Natal was the epicenter of the pandemic, with some figures showing a 39 percent HIV-positive rate among adults. In South Africa overall, the rate of infection skyrocketed to between 12 and 20 percent.[7] In response to this crisis, President Thabo Mbeki articulated and held to a policy of denying AIDS, leading to significant depreciation in South Africa's global image and a crisis of governance. Opposition groups of scientists, the Medical Research Council of South Africa, and others engaged in fierce debate against the government, whose stance became increasingly recalcitrant. Postcolonial rhetoric took on the guise of irrationality; the "African Renaissance" philosophy disappeared from view. South Africa quickly became rebranded as the AIDS capital of the world rather than the moral capital.

Thus, by the end of the first decade of the South African transition, the experience and narrative of the miraculous had collapsed. In real terms, however, the society began to marshal its resources toward addressing at least some of its problems. The power of the constitution was invoked as corrective to both the housing crisis (in 2000) and the health crisis (in 2002). In a pair of landmark decisions that went against the government, the Constitutional Court established and confirmed the rule of law. The first decision concerned a Mrs. Grootboom, who had been living in a shack on the Cape Flats, a flimsy lean-to built on sand without electricity, running water, or sewers. Millions of other South Africans were living in similar conditions, and she chose to sue for her right to housing. The Constitutional Court ruled in her favor, declaring that the South African state had failed in its constitutional obligation by not having made a "reasonable effort" to satisfy the right to housing that she and many others possessed. This decision prompted a program in which more than two million houses have been built, with informal settlements, provided with electricity, running water, and municipal services. The results have been both dramatic and inadequate.

The second case against the government was brought in 2002 by the Treatment Action Campaign, an HIV/AIDS activist group that sued on the grounds that the government had failed to make the reasonable effort mandated by the constitution to institute the right to health care. The Constitutional Court forced the government to roll out antiret-roviral drugs, which became affordable as a consequence of a second lawsuit by the Treatment Action Campaign against two pharmaceutical companies producing the drugs. Nevertheless, about a thousand South Africans a day are still dying of HIV/AIDS.

One problem that was not addressed was that of the absence of a genuine multiparty democracy. The Mbeki regime's crisis of gover-nance regarding HIV/AIDS was connected to that failure. Over the past ten years, the African National Congress has morphed into a kind of Peronist party, a catch-all of communists, trade unionists, corporate CEOs, moderates, and others who are unified not by policy and posi-tion (How could they be?) but instead by the party's role as a conduit between government and big business. The African National Congress is increasingly the route to tender (government contract), corruption, and the gravy train.

Despite such problems, South Africa had hardly lost all its moral and economic capital. The South African rand remained a reasonably stable currency throughout this period, and the country won its bid to host the 2010 World Cup. FIFA's decision put South Africa in the posi-tion of continental exemplar. The World Cup would enable the coun-try again to make its case for greater foreign investment, this time in the form of tourism (at least primarily). A successful World Cup would demonstrate state efficiency, thus reestablishing trust in this African state; it would demonstrate that South Africa could offer safe travel for international fans and players, journalists, celebrities, and digni-taries; and it would prove the world-class character of the country's landscape, hotels, spas, game parks, cities, and cuisine. The World Cup represented an elaborate tourist opportunity and a unique marketing or branding opportunity. If GEAR was about exploiting South Africa's moral capital and structural readiness (according to World Bank/IMF criteria), then the 2010 remake of GEAR would be about exploiting South Africa's aesthetic capital by beautifying cities, building hotels, readying roads, and offering world-class trips to the desert, the sea, and game parks. The point was to create a visual encomium in which travel, accomodation, cuisine, city, point of view, and face-to-face contact with locals would generate future capital. The world would surely be convinced that South Africa had First World status and in particular that its beaches, sunshine, game parks, mountains, wineries, and condominiums are competitive with those in Costa Rica, Tuscany, Phuket, Sydney, and Rajasthan. The country would be profiled through journalists, TV cameras, and the eyewitness accounts of foreign tourists. This emphatic set of lenses meant that new airports and infrastructure had to be efficient and carry the visual splendor of world-class sites. The stadiums for the World Cup had to gleam with newly wrought beauty. The roads must be free of potholes, chaos, and the ugliness of violence and impoverishment.

And so the Green Point Stadium in Cape Town was designed by the German architectural firm GMP Architects and built by South African construction firm Murray and Roberts at the cost of 4.5 billion rand (nearly $600 million).[8] This major expenditure represented a gamble on the economic future since this amount of expenditure could have been used otherwise to significantly solve the problems of housing or education in the Western Cape. Many critics pointed this out at the time of construction.[9] Why was Green Point chosen for the site of the stadium? Many observers thought that the decision sought to break the ghettoized nature of Cape Town by opening up a privileged enclave of the city to the general South African population. I believe that the location was chosen to ensure that the Cape Town games took place on visually superb and socially cloistered ground. Green Point is among Cape Town's most elegant spaces, fronting the Atlantic Ocean and next to the Victoria and Albert Waterfront mall. In preparation for the event, the Green Point seafront was also remodeled. Where international visitors were forced to pass townships—for example, along the main arteries from the Cape Town International Airport to the city—government housing was strategically built so that international tourists would arrive and depart with a rosy picture of South African social development. Were these World Cup visitors to have slowed their taxis and studied the government-constructed plots more carefully, they would have noticed humble lean-tos behind the new structures: Lack of employment has caused recipients of government beneficence to rent out their dwellings and live in shacks jury-rigged at the back of their properties.

And so the fan walk served the purpose not only of merging congregants/fans together in an ecstatic ritual prefacing the games but also of controlling their circulation within strict visual/urban parameters. These parameters were efficient, safe, and a matter of visual profiling in the hope/expectation of future investment. From fan walk to the finale on Long Street, the city was treated as a strict tourist container. Large, anarchic taxis were prohibited from entering except at controlled points; security guards and then the police (after the security guards went on strike) closely monitored the relevant urban space to ensure that the fan walk highlighted Cape Town's best urban experiences. These goals were not devious or even inauthentic. They were about bringing off the World Cup well, safely, and in a way that would reactivate South Africa's earlier goal of foreign investment, this time through the sensuous branding of the country as tourist, property-owning destination.

In the sweep of the spectacle, most if not all criticism of the World Cup disappeared. The pleasure of finding again a shared national consciousness ("We did it! The world again notices and loves us!") was overwhelming. But the day after the finale on Long Street, this "we" woke to a hangover, unsure how to return to the banality of ordinary life, the disillusionment of daily problems, the discarded remains of the unfurled flags and broken vuvuzelas on the streets and in the doorways. Shortly after the tournament, massive strikes shut down the country's schools and hospitals. The World Cup had been a genuine national achievement and something to be proud of. But the world quickly moved on, as it always does in neoliberal society, and South Africans soon realized that no dreamlike fix would follow, that there would be no immediate payback for the cost of the stadiums through investment in property, increased tourism, or anything else. The European Union is at the moment in economic crisis. The price of housing in the Cape continues to fall. The fate of stadiums like Green Point is unclear. Authorities do not seem to know what to do with them.

The year 1996 was about the fantasy that South Africa's moral capital would translate (with the help of structural adjustment) into economic development. The year 2010 was about the fantasy that the country's aesthetic capital would translate into a second tier development. Both may yet happen; however, the fixation on such alchemical forms of panacea ought to be reconsidered. The next site of the World Cup is Brazil (2014). Perhaps South Africa ought to follow Brazil's lead and learn to go it economically alone far more than is currently the case, taking greater responsibility for good governance, employment, development, and the like. Given the capriciousness of markets, the strategy of readying the country for foreign investment is not sustainable. Growth must also be internally stimulated, equity internally mandated. And there is a related point about national consciousness and fellowship. The Rainbow Nation and the finale on Long Street showed that South Africa's sense of imagined unity depends on a shared experience of the miraculous. The miraculous is always temporary. Hence, the sense of national unity and purpose is insufficiently articulated; the country has yet to discover—or create—more sustainable forms of national consciousness. The finale on Long Street signals a need to begin.

NOTES

1. "The Day We Won Respect," *Sunday Independent*, June 13, 2010, 6–7. See also Guy Berger, "Image Revisions: South Africa, Africa, and the 2010 World Cup," *Ecquid Novi: African Journalism Studies* 31, 2 (2011): 174–90.

2. Chris Bolsmann, "Representation in the First African World Cup: 'World-Class,' Pan-Africanism, and Exclusion," *Soccer and Society* 13, 2 (2012): 156–72; Justin van der Westhuizen and Kamilla Swart, "Bread or Circuses?: The 2010 World Cup and South Africa's Quest for Marketing Power," *International Journal of the History of Sport* 28, 1 (2011): 168–80.

3. Hein Marais, *South Africa: Limits to Change—The Political Economy of Transition* (Cape Town: University of Cape Town Press; London: Zed, 2011); Patrick Bond, *Elite Transition: From Apartheid to Neoliberalism in South Africa* (London: Zed, 1999).

4. Allister Sparks, *Tomorrow Is Another Country: The Inside Story of South Africa's Negotiated Revolution* (Johannesburg: Struik, 1994).

5. South Africa, Truth and Reconciliation Commission, *Truth and Reconciliation Commission of South Africa Report*, 5 vols. (Cape Town: Juta, 1998); Deborah Posel and Graeme Simpson, eds., *Commissioning the Past: Understanding South Africa's Truth and Reconciliation Commission* (Johannesburg: Wits University Press, 2002).

6. Roger Southall, "The ANC and Black Capitalism in South Africa," *Review of African Political Economy* 31, 100 (2004): 313–28.

7. Mark Hunter, *Love in the Time of AIDS: Inequality, Gender, and Rights in South Africa* (Bloomington: Indiana University Press, 2010).

8. Peter Alegi, "'A Nation to Be Reckoned With': The Politics of World Cup Stadium Construction in Cape Town and Durban, South Africa," *African Studies* 67, 3 (2008): 397–422; Karen Schoonbee and Stefaans Brümmer, "Public Loss, FIFA's Gain: How Cape Town Got Its 'White Elephant,'" in *Player and Referee: Conflicting Interests and the 2010 FIFA World Cup*, ed. Collette Schulz-Herzenberg (Pretoria: Institute for Security Studies, 2010), 133–67.

9. Peter Alegi "The Political Economy of Mega-Stadiums and the Underdevelopment of Grassroots Football in South Africa," *Politikon* 34, 3 (2007): 315–31.

Integration, Marginalization, and Exclusion in World Cup Johannesburg

MARC FLETCHER

IN OCTOBER 2008, Bafana Bafana played an international friendly against Malawi at Germiston Stadium, east of Johannesburg. The eighteen-thousand-capacity ground appeared to be less than a third full at kickoff, but twenty minutes later, hundreds of ticketless fans were let in for free. My colleague, Dan, and I were two of a tiny number of white spectators in the crowd. While it was a midweek match of little competitive significance, the understated feel of the game was a sad testament to the national team's inability to capture the public imagination eighteen months before South Africa was to host the World Cup. However, in May 2010, Bafana's World Cup warm-up matches sold out in advance in much bigger stadiums than Germiston (despite higher ticket prices). The crowds in 2010 were not only larger but far more reflective of South Africa's Rainbow Nation, with a large minority of white, coloured, and Indian spectators wearing yellow jerseys, blowing vuvuzelas, and waving South African flags. In a relatively short time, Bafana had metamorphosed from a sporting embarrassment to a focal point for national euphoria. Yet this transformation subtly and perhaps inadvertently masked the exclusionary character of the World Cup and the social divisions it reinforced in metropolitan Johannesburg.[1]

I had spent the 2008–9 football season following the Johannesburg branches of the Kaizer Chiefs and Manchester United supporters' clubs as part of my doctoral dissertation fieldwork. At local games, I had become used to being one of a small number of white fans—sometimes the only one in a crowd of thousands. Throughout my research, the largely black, working-class supporters often expressed surprise at my presence at stadiums. I was asked to pose for photos with various fans, many of whom I had never before met. Within the organized support-ers' group, I was often claimed as their "white fan" and used as a walk-ing billboard to attract other white fans to sign up. Conversely, the Manchester United supporters were predominantly white, middle-class South Africans or European expatriates. Overall, I found that racial and class divisions were entrenched in South African football culture. Fans attending domestic league fixtures regularly constructed the local game as an "Africanized" space that stood in dramatic contrast to the con-sumption of European football in the pubs and bars of the city's afflu-ent (and mainly white) northern suburbs.[2] While this dichotomy does not capture the complex nuances of football fandom in Johannesburg, it did make me skeptical of Nelson Mandela's claim that "the World Cup will help unify people and if there is one thing in this planet that has the power to bind people, it is soccer."[3] The use of football to forge and maintain an inclusive national identity would have to overcome the profound divisions that have characterized the game's history and culture in South Africa.

ON WEDNESDAY, JUNE 9, 2010, the streets of Johannesburg's commercial center, Sandton, in the northern suburbs, swelled and swayed with crowds of black, brown, and white South Africans wearing football shirts, waving national flags, and blowing vuvuzelas. Two days before the World Cup, courtesy of the Southern Sun hotel chain, a public show of support for the national team unfolded under the catchphrase "*Sisonke* [togetherness] in hosting Bafana." Between 25,000 (according to the *Sowetan*) and 100,000 (said the *Star*) people congregated along the route taken by the open-top double-decker bus carrying the Bafana squad. Millions watched the parade live on television. By 10:00 a.m., traffic in the area had ground to a standstill. Television and radio en-couraged people unable to make it to Sandton to leave work between noon and 2:00 p.m. to blow their vuvuzelas in support of the national team. I witnessed this crowd while stuck in city traffic. Within two minutes after midday, people had rushed out onto the streets and were making raucous noise.

As I traveled through Johannesburg for the next hour or so, it became apparent that this street festival was widespread. The city suddenly was transformed into a place of celebration and carnival rather than the home of crime, poverty, and inequality. The following morning, the local papers gleefully reported how this event had unified all South Africans. The *Sowetan*, a daily aimed at township readers, believed that "the whole country stood four-square behind one cause," while the *Star* claimed that "we finally have national pride." National sentiment expressed as flag-waving saturated the city in the buildup to the tournament's kickoff and beyond. Flags flying from buildings, flags on advertising boards, and the new trend of national flag car side-mirror covers reminded all South Africans to support "the Boys."

On the morning of the opening game, I was awakened at 5:45 by people enthusiastically blowing their vuvuzelas. The early morning drive through central Johannesburg to my office looked like nothing I'd ever seen: revelers on their way to work, briefcase in one hand, vuvuzela in the other. The journey from my office to the Soweto fan park revealed an inner-city Johannesburg that did not match what I had come to expect. Walking past the Noord Street taxi rank, a reputedly dangerous area in the central business district (CBD), the sight of two white men with Bafana shirts and vuvuzelas caused consternation among passers-by. Central Johannesburg had been designated for whites only under apartheid. In 1986, the repeal of the hated pass laws that enforced segregation and tightly restricted the movement of blacks triggered white flight to places such as Sandton as well as an influx of black people into downtown areas. Yet my colleague and I were not the only people challenging urban flows and commonly held perceptions about who belonged in which neighborhood. Groups of foreign tourists walked the streets openly snapping photographs with their digital cameras, an unthinkable act that a few weeks earlier would have invited muggers to attack.

The bus to the Soccer City Stadium and fan park seven miles away was packed full of supporters, both Mexican and South African, singing loudly. Mexican fans looked on in bemusement as the South Africans (including me) belted out choruses of *Shosholoza*, a migrant workers' song that is a sort of unofficial second national anthem. The Mexicans passionately responded with chants of "Olé!" On the bus and in the Soweto fan park, the buzz of the atmosphere crescendoed as kickoff approached. It was a predominantly black crowd (unsurprising given the location), but there was a noticeable contingent of other South African fans as well. Traveling from the mostly white suburbs to the outskirts of the country's largest black township was symbolically significant: It challenged the city's de facto segregation. With people waving flags and singing the national anthem, this was a rare moment in which Bafana fans, regardless of race, class, gender, or age, could temporarily forget the travails of everyday life and support the same team. It can be tempting to sit in our metaphorical armchairs and downplay the national euphoria generated by such global sporting events, but being there bestowed a different perspective.

When Siphiwe Tshabalala scored for South Africa ten minutes into the second half, the fan park erupted in hysteria. People of all races and ethnicities jumped around in jubilation, hugging each other. Imagining similar scenes of spontaneous rainbow nationalism happening across the country was intoxicating. While Bafana's next game against Uruguay proved deeply disappointing (a 3–0 hiding), their final group game against France produced another popular groundswell of thoroughly irrational yet irrepressible sense of hope. Watching the game in the fan park in Mary Fitzgerald Square in Newtown, Johannesburg, thousands of South Africans were yet again jubilant as Bafana quickly went ahead 2–0. More cheering and hugging ensued with murmurings of possible qualification from the group stage growing louder. Alas, Bafana's inability to convert on chances and capitalize on the man advantage made them fall short of qualification. The 2–1 victory was anticlimactic, and a muted crowd left dreaming of what could have been.

The World Cup affected residents' attitudes toward Johannesburg and changed how some people traveled through it. The increased police presence on the streets was a major factor in creating a cocoon of safety. It allowed a reinterpretation by those who had previously seen such an area as a no-go, crime-infested place. In addition to the added security, the Johannesburg City Council encouraged match ticket holders to use public transport to attend games to alleviate traffic congestion, while Metrorail, the commuter train operator, offered free transportation for ticket holders.

Heading to Park Station, the central station, to catch the train for the Ghana-Uruguay quarterfinal, the car park's capacity proved woefully inadequate, forcing fans to park on the streets. This prospect would usually have been met with apprehension and in some cases outright refusal for fear of mugging or car theft. But the World Cup had dampened such fears. Watching throngs of men, women, and children of all skin colors from all walks of life trawling the streets of the CBD at night, talking and laughing, was extremely unusual. People seemed content to leave their cars on the streets while informal car guards happily pocketed a few rand for their services.

Crammed onto the train to Soccer City, the unusual experience continued. I was struck by the number of white and Indian middle-class fans adopting a form of transportation typically used by the black working class to commute from the townships to work in the city. This odd pattern continued throughout the tournament. Bourgeois fans taking trains, minibus taxis, and buses to a stadium on the outskirts of Soweto was proof that people were reengaging with Johannesburg in a way that would have been almost impossible to fathom before the World Cup.

However, underneath the euphoria and rhetoric of unity lay a different reality. Many of the usual domestic black African supporters (mainly working class) were absent from the seven World Cup matches I attended. Although FIFA had made 3 percent of tickets available exclusively to South African residents at a reduced price of 140 rand ($20), it seemed that few of these Category 4 tickets were going to the target population. Various discussions with my Kaizer Chiefs friends and informants indicated that few of them had tickets to World Cup matches. Cost was a major obstacle. While 140 rand seemed inexpensive to me, it amounted to about 10 percent of an average monthly salary for black workers. Making matters worse, the byzantine ticket-buying process devised by FIFA confounded local fans. While the most convenient method of application was online, the vast majority of my Chiefs informants lacked Internet access at home, although a few did have access at work. And almost no one had a credit card, which was required to buy tickets through FIFA's centralized online ticketing system.

This situation meant that working-class South Africans were limited to applying in person at branches of First National Bank, an official tournament sponsor. This alternative posed three problems. First, the application booklet was in English only. The legalese of the small print at times baffled me, a native English speaker, yet English was the second, third, or even the fourth language for many local fans. Second, the bank's computer system crashed on numerous occasions, frustrating applicants. Finally, the concept of an application process months before matches did not take into account the local culture of fans, who tend to buy tickets at the stadium on match day. Thousands of black fans did attend games, of course, but they did so in spite of the ticketing system. An acquaintance of mine received a second-round ticket by his employer; another received a ticket from his cousin; and another had received a semifinal ticket from a group of foreign tourists whom he had been driving around the country. A couple of people I knew had won multiple tickets in a competition organized by one of the tournament sponsors. But for the most part, traditional fans of South African soccer were consigned to watch the games on television or in the fan parks.

Conversely, most South African supporters of Manchester United had both easy Internet access and credit cards. While a few deliberately chose not to attend games, many spent thousands of rand buying tickets. For example, a small number of local Red Devil fans bought ticket packages that included the final, spending between 3,350 rand ($478) and 19,096 ($2,728). Not only was this far more expensive than the usual price for most domestic club games and Bafana games prior to 2010 (usually 30 rand or less), but most local fans found the total cost of attending a match prohibitive. Within the World Cup stadium zones, concessions and merchandise were also far more expensive than at typical domestic league matches. A bottle of beer, for example, sold for 30 rand ($4.28) but cost 10–15 rand in a *shebeen* (tavern); hot dogs cost 20 rand; and other items were similarly expensive . The World Cup stadium experience was clearly accessible only to people with sufficient disposable income, not the typical constituents for football in South Africa.

Without many regular South African soccer fans, the match-day experience lacked authentic local flavor. The local hawkers and traders who sell soft drinks, *pap-and-vleis* (stiff cornmeal and roasted meat), and barbecue chicken, a common sight at domestic games, were absent or obscured at World Cup venues. FIFA sterilized the stadium experience, allowing only official merchandise and vendors within the perimeter of the stadium precinct to protect the investment of the tournament's major sponsors. This exclusionary practice disenfranchised local vendors, who believed that the World Cup was a glorious opportunity to make some extra money from the global soccer festival. Some street entrepreneurs had become disillusioned. During a conversation with David, one of my key Chiefs informants, such frustration became apparent when he asked me how much vendors in the stadium were selling *pap* for. When I told him that no one was selling *pap*, he snapped back, "But this is South Africa! They must have *pap* there! Why is there no *pap?*" When I explained that only FIFA sponsors' products were allowed, David retorted, "But this could be Brazil or Germany or anywhere!"

David and his business partner set up a food stall just outside the perimeter of Johannesburg's Ellis Park Stadium for the duration of the tournament. They regularly lamented that they were making little profit, believing that tourists were unwilling to try local cuisine although they also admitted that the cost of renting the cooking equipment from a local entrepreneur had cut into their margins. The major gripe was that they were unable to charge what they wanted. On several occasions when I went to such stalls, the vendors claimed that FIFA was controlling prices. Similarly, homeowners who had spent their savings to renovate their homes to accommodate overseas tourists were frequently disappointed with World Cup business. Linda, one of my Chiefs' respondents in Naturena, Soweto, for example, showed me around her home. I was told that her family had been instructed by Match, FIFA's hospitality arm, to make numerous costly improvements to meet its standards; these changes included installing a security system and buying new linen, crockery, and cutlery. Linda explained how Match told her to take a hospitality course at her own expense to learn how to make a cappuccino, among other things. Having spent thousands of rand on such improvements (she declined to tell me exactly how much), one week prior to the World Cup, she had still not heard from Match and FIFA about whether she had been allocated a foreign visitor to host.

Other Chiefs supporters had repainted rooms and bought new furnishings in hopes of making money. But their refusal to sign up with Match to advertise their properties to foreign tourists (due to perceived high fees and unfair conditions) greatly limited their chances of welcoming deep-pocketed guests into their homes. In fact, most were left empty-handed. Irvin Khoza, the chair of the Local Organising Committee, claimed that the World Cup was for "all of the 44 million South Africans." However, the giant image of Cristiano Ronaldo in a motor oil advertisement emblazoned on the side of a high rise towering over the public viewing area in Newtown served as a constant reminder of the corporate stranglehold on the tournament, much to the detriment of local entrepreneurs.

If the World Cup had pushed many South Africans to the margins, the calls for national unity also became similarly divisive. The Football Friday initiative, which took off early in 2010 with the blessing of the government and business community, encouraged all South Africans to wear Bafana jerseys to work on Fridays leading up to the World Cup. This boosterism was designed to foster nationwide support for Bafana, but it paradoxically also reinforced divisions. Made by Adidas, the official kit manufacturer of Bafana, the replica shirt retailed at 600 rand ($85) despite omitting the national symbol of King Protea (which would have required the South African Football Association to pay royalties to the Department of Sport for the use of the emblem). Fans wanting the full shirt (which came in a presentation case) would initially have to fork out approximately 1,500 rand, although the dispute was later resolved and an iron-on Protea badge costing 20 rand was released to attach to the replicas. Football Fridays equated being a good South African with wearing the national shirt, yet many citizens simply could not afford to do so. Being a good South African was reinscribed along middle-class lines. The working poor, ever resilient and resourceful, turned to *fong kong* (fake, "Made in China" in local slang) shirts to show their patriotism, thereby creating a second, lower tier of patriotic soccer supporter. I had encountered the issue of authenticity of football shirts and the importance of official merchandising to the self-definition of a "proper" supporter during my fieldwork. It exposed a class cleavage in my Chiefs case study between those who could afford to consume branded merchandise and those who could not. (Of course, some fans did not care about authenticity and chose pirated products instead.)

While at one level, the 2010 World Cup in Johannesburg transformed attitudes toward space in the city, this shift took within sanitized spaces. Middle-class fans reengaged with the city but did so primarily because of visible police presence on the streets and in the stadiums and because it was a FIFA-organized tournament and therefore free of the allegations of corruption and mismanagement that are often linked to the South African game.

But at a different, perhaps deeper level, residents' pre–World Cup attitudes toward the city were reinforced. The movement of people during the tournament was artificially compartmentalized, neither fluid nor organic. Tourists were taken in relative comfort and security from their accommodations to the match and back again, driving (or riding) through the city but unable to interact with it. Walking the streets of Joubert Park and Doornfontein, just east of the CBD, and heading to Ellis Park Stadium for the Spain-Paraguay quarterfinal, the landscape was eerily empty. It was difficult to tell such a big match was about to take place. No crowds of people were making their way to the stadium; there was no buildup of anticipation. This awkward scene encapsulated the daily reality of life in Johannesburg, where the streets are almost empty at night because people are afraid of leaving the relative safety of their homes. The park-and-ride buses brought fans close to the stadiums without affording them an opportunity to interact with residents of the inner city; the park-and-walk locations fared little better. Anecdotal evidence suggests that many European fans at games I attended seemed baffled by the disjointed nature of the World Cup's urban experience.

Melrose Arch encapsulated this compartmentalized movement of people. Set behind huge walls and electric fences near Sandton in the northern suburbs, this mixed-use commercial and residential space aims to re-create the feeling (not the reality) of a cosmopolitan town center, with restaurants and shops lining its streets and piazzas. It is in essence a town within a city. "Open spaces replace the cage and cocoon. Life pulsates on the streets once again," is how the website advertises it.[4] But the cage is still there; it is just less readily apparent. The fortifications around Melrose Arch prevent the surrounding city from encroaching; its "street life" was accessible only to the socially mobile middle classes with plenty of disposable income. On the afternoon of the final match, Melrose Arch was full of a mixture of tourists and well-heeled South Africans enjoying the buildup, removed from much of city life. In short, just because the national and international bourgeoisie used taxis and trains a few times during four memorable weeks in June and July 2010 did not mean that this practice became entrenched in everyday lives after the tournament ended. After all, Metrorail served the southern half of the metropolis—specifically, the poorer suburbs and black townships—and therefore had little relevance for people who lived and worked in the affluent northern suburbs.

The juxtaposition of the Soccer City Stadium and a nearby informal settlement on the outskirts of Riverlea served as a grim reminder that very little had fundamentally changed in South Africa. The search for greater social cohesion in the World Cup was very much a middle-class agenda, a feel-good device that allowed people living, working, and playing behind high walls, behind fences, and in gated communities to wave national flags and be proudly South African together with the working poor majority. Yet while township inhabitants may have been equally eager to tap into this temporary unity, the pressing concerns of day-to-day life were not far away.

Soon after the tournament ended, "Football Fridays" were recast as "Fly the Flag Fridays" in an attempt proudly to celebrate South Africa's successful hosting of the event. Newspapers and billboards were saturated with self-congratulatory messages such as "We've shown the world what a nation united can do" and "This is the greatest country in the world." Popular and media discourse almost immediately shifted to the question of whether post–World Cup national unity could be sustained. Two key football events in the immediate aftermath of the World Cup suggested that the Johannesburg soccer landscape had altered very little: the Telkom Charity Cup, the annual curtain raiser to the domestic football season, and the South Africa–Ghana international friendly, both staged at Soccer City.

A total of 87,000 fans attended the one-day Charity Cup tournament featuring the Kaizer Chiefs, Orlando Pirates, Mamelodi Sundowns, and Amazulu, breaking the stadium attendance record set during the World Cup. If the Charity Cup was a litmus test for whether the World Cup had challenged the perceptions of the domestic game as a "black game" among middle-class South African football fans, then it did not appear to have done so. The Premier Soccer League had catered for these new fans with an allocation of tickets for a self-contained family zone separated from the commotion of the rest of the stadium. The Rainbow Nation on display in the stadiums during the World Cup was conspicuously absent. At first glance, there were extremely few white, Indian, or coloured fans in attendance; instead, the usual constituency of black African working-class fans were back with their unconventional costumes, elaborate *makarapas* (decorated hard hats), handmade accoutrements, and banners. Trapped in the unruly crowd at the bar, one fan claimed that now that the World Cup had ended, the football authorities were "treating us blacks bad." Throughout the day, other fans came to me to say how happy they were that "whiteys" had come to watch "our" football, adding that there were still too few.

The South Africa–Ghana friendly on a freezing August 2010 night was supposed to reignite the national feel-good effect of the World Cup. It did not happen. While Bafana ticket prices had already increased in the buildup to the World Cup, the South African Football Association decided to raise tickets to 100–150 rand, virtually ensuring that many usual supporters would choose to watch the contest between Bafana and the Black Stars in the warmth of their homes or at neighborhood watering holes. The gigantic stadium was half empty (or half full, depending on your disposition), creating a deadened atmosphere. A strangely quiet and electronically generated backing track facilitated a limp and lifeless rendition of the national anthems, amplified not by the stadium's public address system but by a set of portable speakers on the pitch. Although Bafana won 1–0, Katlego Mphela's goal was a rare moment of excitement in a dull, cold affair. The enthusiasm and optimism of the World Cup had all but disappeared.

ON THAT CHILLY 2008 evening in Germiston, it was hard to imagine that Bafana would soon become a focal point for the outpouring of sporting nationalism and patriotic euphoria, but the 2010 World Cup did just that. In the end, however, the undertones of such a nation-building rhetoric belied the reality of marginalization and exclusion in the everyday lives of many Johannesburg residents. While the haves participated in the carnival of the World Cup, the traditional constituency of South African soccer supporters struggled to join the party as a consequence of the high cost of tickets and merchandise, and they remained largely on the margins of the event. While at first glance the tournament seemed to have altered the flows of people in Johannesburg, on further inspection, little had fundamentally changed.

NOTES

1. For further analysis, see Martin J. Murray, *City of Extremes: The Spatial Politics of Johannesburg* (Durham: Duke University Press, 2011).

2. Marc Fletcher, "'You Must Support Chiefs: Pirates Already Have Two White Fans!': Race and Racial Discourse in South African Football Fandom," in *South Africa and the Global Game: Football, Apartheid, and Beyond*, ed. Peter Alegi and Chris Bolsmann (London: Routledge, 2010), 79–94.

3. Bathandwa Mbola, "The Game That United a Nation," July 5, 2011, http://www.buanews.gov.za/rss/11/11070512051001, accessed August 8, 2011.

4. See http://www.melrosearch.co.za/index.html, accessed October 15, 2012.

The World Cup Geography of Durban

What Will Endure?

DAVID ROBERTS AND ORLI BASS

IN THE WEEKS LEADING UP to the 2010 World Cup, the quality and texture of urban space in Durban, as elsewhere in South Africa, began shifting. In the country's second-largest city and the continent's busiest commercial port, flags rapidly began to sprout from the windows, walls, and balcony railings of apartment blocks, houses, and office buildings as well as cars and minibus taxis. As in other South African cities, the staccato drone of the vuvuzela became an integral part of the soundscape. Many of Durban's three million residents felt a tangible individual and collective sense of excitement at hosting the world's largest football tournament. For one memorable month, a laid-back and sports-loving population engaged with the public spaces of the city and with each other in uncommon ways.

That the World Cup facilitated and inspired new engagements with and in public spaces speaks to potential new ways to think of post–World Cup Durban. The encouraging ways in which members of the city's culturally and economically diverse population interacted in and used public space are now part of collective memory. Yet the long-term impact of the World Cup on Durban's social geography is tempered by the tournament's short duration (four weeks) and by its highly orchestrated probusiness and protourism focus. Moreover, Durban's hosting experience was a complex and in some ways contradictory process. On the one hand, World Cup public viewing areas and the new Moses Mabhida Stadium brought together locals and outsiders in new and unusual ways; on the other hand, subsistence fisherfolk, social justice activists, and any individual deemed by the authorities to be a "public nuisance" were kept away from these and other "World Cup spaces." Even Moses Mabhida's construction was not without controversy: It was built literally across the street from the King's Park Rugby Stadium, which FIFA had deemed adequate, with a few upgrades, to host matches, including a semifinal. Yet in the pursuit of a structural landmark that might set the stage for an Olympic bid, the municipality decided to invest a considerable sum (of taxpayers' money) in the construction of a new stadium.

As urban geographers based in Durban during the 2010 World Cup, we bring a critical perspective to bear on how the city's official fan zones and stadium were constructed and influenced by the local municipality, FIFA, the Local Organizing Committee, and fans as well as how those locales were experienced. We are also interested in how these spaces simultaneously fostered inclusion and exclusion.[1] Our own positionality obviously influences this analysis, weaving between the binaries of detached, empirical researchers and partisan and emotionally involved fans. In this vein, our reflections on Durban's hosting of World Cup matches pivot around the contradiction of progressive (or positive) evolutions of the use of public space facilitated through mechanisms of social exclusion and control. Events during the World Cup in June and July 2010 were not by any means a fully spontaneous or even a haphazard emergence of new lived geographies in Durban; rather, private business interests, planners at all levels of government, FIFA officials, and others had a hand in shaping public responses to the World Cup. We are interested in how the sense of individual buoyancy, combined with structured planning around public space, became translated into a set of unique experiences and negotiations of public (and private) space for the duration of the tournament.

In the run-up to the World Cup, local fans scrambled to obtain tickets to see matches at the new 3.2 billion rand (approximately $457 million) Moses Mabhida Stadium to experience the World Cup in person.[2] However, although organizers reserved a small number of tickets exclusively for South Africans and priced those tickets at around $20 (the lowest price for a World Cup ticket in recent memory), many Durbanites still could not afford to go. Being priced out of the stadium did not preclude people from joining in the official celebrations as Durban played host to an official fan park on the beach and other viewing areas with large television screens, including some areas located in the apartheid-era townships surrounding the city. While these fan venues, like the Mabhida Stadium, represented a tightly controlled and heavily policed environment, free entry made them far more accessible and inclusive than the stadium. The result was that public viewing areas in greater Durban (as in other host cities) had a different texture that seemed slightly more organic than the highly corporate and exclusive stadium experience.

The beach area, with its official fan zones, underwent a significant remodeling prior to the World Cup. This revamped public space attracted huge numbers of people (by the sixth day of the tournament, two hundred thousand people had flocked to the beach fan park),[3] drawn by the World Cup–themed activities and the opportunity to view the matches live in a public and interactive setting. The atmosphere was electric, and the city was buzzing about it, with Durbanites trading anecdotes and photographs as well as planning future activities. The official park was such a magnet that at times it reached capacity and had to turn away fans. Matches were broadcast on a giant screen, and entertainers were on hand to jolly the crowd along in breaks and down times, not that there were many of these with spectators in full fan mode and constantly blowing their vuvuzelas. The sheer number of people mingling on the beach, in the food zones, and along the promenade was invigorating. The first day of the year has traditionally attracted large crowds to the beach, and the beachfront has long featured a range of uses and users; however, the combination of factors associated with Durban's role as a host city and of course the excitement of the World Cup itself contributed in some senses to a unique atmosphere. Many of the culturally and ethnically diverse communities that make up Durban came together to celebrate and enjoy the city and each other as much as the soccer on the big screens. But the concentration of humanity in this context was different in a variety of ways.

One of these ways was how people used the World Cup beach spaces as well as the fact that they flocked to the beach at night. The shift cannot be ascribed solely to the orchestration of FIFA, the Local Organising Committee, and the various locally based authorities: Durbanites embraced the World Cup as their own. With large numbers of police officers and private guards providing security, the gigantic television screen attracted huge numbers of viewers from different segments of the city. It seemed appropriate for the country's surfing capital to have surfers, boards in hand, watching the match between the United States and Ghana in the round of sixteen.[4] Conceding a goal early in the match, as had become the team's hallmark in the 2010 tournament, the United States equalized in the second half and held on to send the match into extra time. The crowded beach erupted with joy when Ghana's Asamoah Gyan scored what turned out to be the winning goal as the Black Stars booked a ticket to the quarterfinals, matching the exploits of Cameroon in 1990 and Senegal in 2002. On the beach alongside the Indian Ocean, it was a moment of indefinable euphoria for this South African city, an example of the sentiments and experiences that spatial planning sometimes generates. It is difficult to think of anything other than football generating a comparable shared experience on such a massive scale.

The embrace of Ghana as the team that Durbanites supported after Bafana Bafana's elimination was felt countrywide. Ghana represented the last hope for an African country to win the World Cup on African soil. Having South Africans embrace Ghana also fit nicely with the government's marketing of the tournament as Africa's (not just South Africa's) World Cup. This support must, however, be situated within South Africa's recent history of xenophobic violence targeting non–South African Africans. Following the eruption of May 2008 xenophobic riots that killed at least sixty people and injured hundreds of others, there have been concerns and rumors, especially among African foreign nationals and refugee communities in Durban and elsewhere, that it is only a matter of time before violence against non–South African Africans again explodes.[5] So, although the unique politics of World Cup enjoyment certainly did not permanently alleviate these concerns, it temporarily reconfigured some geopolitical imaginations. A thunderous elation would most likely have gripped the fan parks had Ghana not suffered an undeserved ouster from the tournament at, quite literally, the hands of Uruguay.

That many of the evening matches drew crowds to the beachfront is significant. As with many places in South Africa, concerns about safety have left the beach and other parts of the central business district relatively deserted during the evening hours. The added World Cup policing, in conjunction with the mass of people using public space, countered these fears and allowed for areas potentially perceived as no-go prior to the event to become spaces of celebration and community interaction.

This is not to say that the beachfront fan park was a completely inclusive space— in fact, in the run-up to the World Cup, the eThekwini (metropolitan Durban) Municipality, in conjunction with FIFA's guiding hand, did much to ensure that the fan parks and other open public spaces fit the image of the safe, warm, and tourist-friendly city that organizers sought to project to foreign visitors and the billions of television viewers from around the world.

As part of FIFA's requirements for host cities, Durban passed a new assortment of municipal bylaws to regulate "nuisance" behaviors in public space.[6] These bylaws prohibited the use of "abusive or otherwise objectionable language" and made it illegal to "lie, sit, stand, congregate or walk as to cause a willful obstruction, or otherwise cause any obstruction, of any nature whatsoever in a Public Space." The use of vague language resembles "civility laws" that have become commonplace in other cities throughout the world; these laws are often used to justify the enforcement of exclusionary practices against the urban poor. In Durban, for example, the World Cup bylaws included new restrictions on informal markets and the selling of goods on the street in certain areas. New legal mechanisms of control were made possible by a significant increase in policing. Given the prominence of the beachfront in the cultural geography of Durban's World Cup, it should not be surprising that the official fan park and surrounding areas witnessed an aggressive crackdown on "nuisance" behaviors. For example, local academic and civil society activist Patrick Bond was detained on two occasions for distributing flyers critical of FIFA in the official beach fan park.[7]

A major aspect of planning for the World Cup was a comprehensive local policing strategy that targeted behavior deemed antithetical to the official imagination of the appropriate use of Durban's public space. Subsistence fisherfolk who use (and in some cases live on) Durban's piers were banned from those piers for the duration of the construction activities that revitalized the waterfront areas in the buildup to the World Cup. However, these bans continued after the facelift was completed. Durban's piers have long been shared but contested spaces, especially between subsistence fisherfolk and recreational surfers as well as tourists and others. The competing usage of the piers involves a complex negotiation of class in and through the use of public space, where middle-class leisure and corporatized/commercialized activities are facilitated and condoned and survival strategies are made invisible or less visible. The municipality sees subsistence fishing and its role in making visible aspects of urban poverty in the city as incongruous with crafting a new image of Durban as an elite sports tourist destination. While fisherfolk who have been part of the beachfront landscape for generations were kept away during the World Cup, surfers were welcome and thus more easily enjoyed the fan park.

Despite their best efforts, however, the local municipality (along with FIFA and various policing agencies) could not completely control people and spaces during the World Cup. An example of the limits of the intersection of government and corporate power was the unexpected presence of an informal trader, prior to a match, near a security checkpoint for Moses Mabhida Stadium. This man was sitting among football fans, hands occupied with wire, next to a life-size beaded sculpture of two South African players (one of whom is clearly Siphiwe Tshabalala, the tournament's first scorer, as indicated by the dreadlocks and the number eight on his kit) lifting the World Cup. Informal bead workers are common in Durban, selling intricate sculptures, ornaments, and other goods while simultaneously creating new pieces. Clearly a utopian construction (South Africa's early exit was never much in doubt, despite some heart-stopping expectations), the presence of the bead worker and his sculpture raised a number of interesting questions. Despite the heavy police presence and harsh anti-ambush marketing regulations (we witnessed examples of individuals who were immediately confronted by security personnel), the man had somehow eluded controls and pushed his sculpture on a trolley to a spot within the greater stadium precinct. How had he managed to insert himself into a rolling sea of ticket-wielding fans? How long was he allowed to remain unmolested? Did someone purchase the sculpture? A mask was also tucked into the ropes steadying the piece and a vuvuzela attached—perhaps extra items for a quick tourist sale? Was special access feasible because of the ingenuity of the work itself, or was this perhaps a sanctioned activity? Did the man's bright yellow reflective vest indicate some official recognition? Was he simply a fan, accepted by all as such?

Whatever the reason, his presence within this World Cup space demonstrated how certain enterprising individuals challenged spatial controls put in place by the organizers. Despite tight restrictions, this bead worker innovatively made the stadium space less prescriptive and in this way exposed it to forms of commerce and consumption starkly different from FIFA's norms. To fans, his presence was unremarkable. Amid the crazy costumes, fanatical and fantastic get-ups, and general football mania, the trader was unconsciously assimilated into the fan space. Of course, such an isolated episode does not indicate a wholesale shift in attitudes toward the use of World Cup stadium spaces. But it is an example of possible economic and social integrations that may not have occurred without the inspiration of the World Cup revelry given the persistence of elements of social and economic segregation in post-apartheid South Africa.

It is easy to be cynical about such spaces close to the stadium and the beachfront and argue that the centralization of formal leisure activities reinforces privilege in historically advantaged areas of the city. However, the stadium and beach areas were not the city's only organized World Cup fan spaces. Viewing facilities were also offered in other areas of Durban—in the apartheid-created townships of Umlazi (south of central Durban) and KwaMashu (north). While the structure and layout of Durban—still influenced by the legacy of apartheid urban planning and social engineering—implies the continuation of race and class differences in these viewing spaces, at least the municipality made an effort to provide facilities for the working poor to experience the World Cup (at least televisually). We did not spend enough time in the township fan zones to make many comparative observations between them and the one on the beachfront (and our sole visit was not at peak attendance). Nevertheless, the attempt to offer facilities and recreational opportunities in different parts of the city and to people other than the affluent is an important part of the complex postapartheid endeavor.

In many ways, our experience of Durban's World Cup highlighted the complexities of postapartheid cities. The 2010 tournament provided new insight into Durban's potential as a city and in particular to the potential of Durban's public spaces as places where the urban identity of the city is made and remade through a diversity of individual and collective interactions. The 2010 World Cup certainly has left behind some infrastructure in the form of improved roads, the Moses Mabhida Stadium, and a redeveloped beachfront. Anecdotal evidence appears to show that even criminals were on their best behavior during the monthlong tournament, as crime rates dipped. There are, however, many competing agendas and ideas for Durban's future and how the city's public spaces should be used and by whom. At the risk of over-simplifying the situation, it seems that powerful and well-connected probusiness interests eager to accelerate the growth of leisure tourism are competing with social-development agendas focused on extending basic services to the majority of the population.

The ultimate success of the World Cup in ushering in permanent, new (refreshed) lived geographies in Durban is far from determined. The 2010 experience is now part of Durbanites' collective memories, the exceptional experiences of the tournament will undoubtedly affect future uses of the city. South Africa has come a long way, and no one can deny that the country (with Durban and other host cities playing a significant role) put on a magnificent global football carnival. However, now that the party has ended, life still goes on in South Africa.

Returning to the beachfront a month or so after the World Cup's final whistle brought home the question about which aspects of Durban's World Cup geographies will endure. Many of the tangible signs that Durban had been host of this megaevent were gone or fading; the flags that had adorned almost every car had largely been taken down, and those that remained were showing their wear. Even so, there was still a vibrancy in the way people were using these reconfigured and refreshed spaces that were part of the investment in being a host city. The beach-front seems to be more welcoming to those at play in the sand and sea and to others who exercise along the promenade, a meeting point for friends and families and a source of local pride. In some ways this is not new: The beachfront has always been a place where Durbanites flock for recreation, especially during the December holidays. Yet World Cup activities seem to have reacquainted many Durban residents with this space. Whether these men, women, and children will keep coming back remains to be seen.

What happened in Durban during the World Cup indicates a changed sense of the way in which residents experienced their city's leisure spaces and geography. At the same time, the competition was not necessarily a positive experience for all, as the example of the fish-erfolk illustrates. At best, then, World Cup geographies are dynamic spaces where some of the struggles over the different potential directions of how this postapartheid city may evolve played out. While not fully manufactured, residents' and visitors' engagements with Durban's public space also were not completely spontaneous. The use of the stadium precinct and the various fan zones and surrounding areas during the World Cup was constrained by specific legislated limits of what FIFA and local authorities deemed acceptable conduct. Consequently, Durban's World Cup spaces were concurrently spaces of contestation and exclusion. Given the fleeting nature of the event, how much the World Cup experience speaks to abiding fundamental changes in the public space of Durban is a little less clear. The success of the World Cup in Durban was largely the result of Durbanites choosing to engage in public spaces with diverse people and at unusual times of day.

It is too soon to know if this is a long-term change and what will become of these spaces as the memories of June–July 2010 fade. One of the most significant challenges of place-making initiatives centered on extraordinary planetary events is whether and how the positive uses and experiences of the events can be maintained and enhanced when the emotional and financial revenues stop flowing. This is the main challenge that Durban and other host cities now face. The answer will fundamentally shape the legacy of the World Cup.

NOTES

We appreciate the input of Gerhard Maré, Peter Alegi, and Chris Bolsmann, who read earlier versions of this essay.

   1. For more information, see Orli Bass, "Aiming for Africa: Durban, 2010, and Notions of African Urban Identity," in *Development and Dreams: The Urban Legacy of the 2010 Football World Cup*, ed. Udesh Pillay, Richard Tomlinson, and Orli Bass (Cape Town: HSRC Press, 2009), 246–65; David Roberts, "Durban's Future?: Re-Branding through the Production/Policing of Event-Specific Places at the 2010 World Cup," *Sport in Society* 13, 10 (2010): 1462–73.

   2. Peter Alegi, "'A Nation to Be Reckoned With': The Politics of World Cup Stadium Construction in Cape Town and Durban, South Africa," *African Studies* 67, 3 (2008): 397–422; Sam Sole, "Durban's Moses Mabhida Stadium: Arch of Hope or Yoke of Debt?," in *Player and Referee: Conflicting Interests and the 2010 FIFA World Cup*, ed. Collette Schulz-Herzenberg (Pretoria: Institute for Security Studies, 2010), 169–201.

   3. Thobani Ngqulunga, "Fan Park: Durban Has the Highest Attendance," *Witness*, June 22, 2010, http://www.witness.co.za/index.php?showcontent&global[_id]=42744, accessed January 26, 2011. For a discussion of fan parks' potential to have positive effects on spatial and social capital, see Christoph Haferburg, Theresa Golka, and Marie Selter, "Public Viewing Areas: Urban Interventions in the Con-

text of Mega-Events," in *Development and Dreams*, ed. Pillay, Tomlinson, and Bass, 174–99.

4. Glen Thompson, "Making Waves, Making Men: The Emergence of a Professional Surfing Masculinity in South Africa during the Late 1970s," in *Changing Men in Southern Africa*, ed. Robert Morrell (London: Zed; Pietermaritzburg: University of Natal Press, 2001), 91–104; Glen Thompson, "Reimagining Surf City: Surfing and the Making of the Post-Apartheid Beach in South Africa," *International Journal of the History of Sport* 28, 15 (2011): 2115–29.

5. Barry Bearak, "South Africa Braces for New Attacks on Immigrants," July 10, 2010, *New York Times*, http://www.nytimes.com/2010/07/10/world/africa/10safrica.html, accessed August 10, 2011.

6. eThekwini Municipality, "2010 FIFA World Cup South Africa By-Laws," http://ccs.ukzn.ac.za/files/Fifa%20ethekwini%20law.pdf, accessed September 23, 2012. For more on World Cup policing strategies in Durban, see Roberts, "Durban's Future?"

7. Patrick Bond, "FIFA Profits Beat Players, People, and Planet: South Africa's World Cup Boosts Local Spirits, at the Cost of Fattened Swiss Wallets," unpublished paper (2010); Patrick Bond, "When 'Phansi FIFA, Phansi' Is Forbidden Speech," *Pambazuka News*, July 8, 2010, http://pambazuka.org/en/category/features/65767, accessed July 9, 2010.

Cape Town, the City without and within the White Lines

KILLIAN DOHERTY

THE OPPORTUNITY TO IMMERSE MYSELF in human experiences at the confluence of urban spaces where vastly differing cultural influences meet and how these spaces physically and experientially can shape a city intrigues me as an architect. This professional curiosity heightened my sense of anticipation as I landed in Cape Town on my first journey to the African continent. I was also excited at the prospect of spending time in a host city for seven matches of the 2010 World Cup. In 2008, I had spent time in New Orleans working on reconstruction projects immediately after the catastrophe of Hurricane Katrina. Like Cape Town, New Orleans is a port city with a predominantly black population and a history marked by slavery, racism, poverty, and segregation.[1] New Orleans exemplified the convergence of tragedy, corruption, political neglect, and a vibrant popular culture created and sustained by tenacious people struggling to cope in the aftermath of a shocking disaster.

The cultural confluence I observed taking place more or less organically in the public spaces of New Orleans seemed stymied, altered, almost manufactured in the case of Cape Town. As the authors of *Cape Town in the Twentieth Century* have pointed out, "Existing geographical features combined with the 'modern' science of town planning and beliefs in 'racial' difference to produce the sometimes very different senses of place that exist among its three million citizens today."[2] Greater Cape Town is divided between the Cape Flats, dominated by proletarian African and coloured townships, and the city bowl (below

Table Mountain), the southern and northern suburbs—areas with many prosperous neighborhoods inhabited by white people and an increasingly racially diverse middle class.[3]

Exacerbating the legacy of apartheid social engineering and more recent gentrification trends, in 2010 FIFA commandeered Cape Town's rare and therefore crucial major public spaces, a process that reinforced economic segregation and presented a generic, pallid, and global tourist image. For example, the Grand Parade in the heart of the central city—where one hundred thousand people congregated to hear Nelson Mandela's first speech after his release from prison on February 11, 1990—was the site of the official World Cup Fan Fest. Despite well-meaning attempts by the local authorities to remake urban space in a way that transcended old and new social divisions, the 2010 World Cup inadvertently reproduced patterns of injustice and exclusion in Cape Town.

Like all other host cities, Cape Town adopted a new set of World Cup bylaws contained in the Special Measures Act passed by Parliament in 2006. As per FIFA mandate, certain key public spaces within the city were categorized as "controlled access sites" or "exclusion zones." The former definition applied to, among others, stadiums, Fan Fests, hotels used by World Cup teams and FIFA delegates, practice facilities, and public viewing areas. "Exclusion zones" were designated areas within one kilometer (0.6 mile) of the perimeter of a venue or stadium. Inside these FIFA "sites" and "zones," special rules regulated advertisements and signage, street trading and vending, beautification and acceptable decorum, and traffic controls and road closures. South African security forces rigorously policed these FIFA spaces, and the government set up a special court for the duration of the tournament to adjudicate violations and infringements of these and other laws.

Urban beautification initiatives were another revealing aspect of the privatization of public space and Cape Town's handling of FIFA's demands. In the buildup to the tournament, the number of poor people deported to municipal "Temporary Relocation Areas" increased significantly. For example, at Blikkiesdorp ("Tin can town" in Afrikaans), twenty miles (thirty-two kilometers) from downtown, 366 people claimed that they were relocated because of their close proximity to Athlone Stadium, an official World Cup training ground. With 15,000 people living in heavily policed, overcrowded conditions in tents and shacks, the Western Cape Anti-Eviction Campaign stated that Blikkies-dorp seemed like a concentration camp.[4]

This grim story stood in stark juxtaposition to the tangible upgrad-ing of "global" Cape Town's transport infrastructure for the benefit of affluent residents and World Cup tourists. The airport, the main train station, and the N2 highway were significantly revamped, an example of how the World Cup served as a catalyst for government-funded projects. In accordance with the temporary FIFA bylaws, these public spaces and transport links were saturated with World Cup advertis-ing, effectively creating an alternate experience for football tourists. This kind of urban development also exposed the primacy of FIFA's self-interest over the needs and wants of the majority of the city's population as well as South African authorities' willingness to play along with the governing body. This exclusionary, even discrimina-tory process decisively shaped Cape Town's World Cup experience and raised troubling questions about the effectiveness of the "Football for Hope" program, FIFA's premier corporate social responsibility initia-tive, launched in 2007.

In partnership with Grassroot Soccer, the Khayelitsha Develop-ment Forum, and other NGOs and sponsors, FIFA intended Football for Hope to "develop the game, touch the world and build a better fu-ture" in poor communities.[5] Football for Hope planned to build twenty centers across the African continent and use football for public health education and gender empowerment purposes. The first center opened in the neighborhood of Harare in the heart of Khayelitsha.[6] Located on the sand dunes of the Cape Flats nearly twenty miles from down-town Cape Town, Khayelitsha is one of South Africa's largest town-ships. Developed between 1983 and 1985 by the apartheid government as a ghetto for black Africans forcibly removed from neighborhoods and townships closer to town, Khayelitsha today is the nation's second-largest township, with an estimated 1.5 million residents, nearly half of whom are under the age of nineteen.[7]

The FIFA Football for Hope center in Khayelitsha consists of a small community building with changing rooms, office spaces, and a caretaker's flat that fronts onto a reduced size football pitch with an ar-tificial surface. Landscaped surroundings facilitate public spectatorship. Planned by ARG Design, a local firm, and built by Architecture for Humanity, an American NGO, the center does not opt for the South

African vernacular architecture of barricading itself in. There are no surrounding fences, and the caretaker flat allows for a degree of self-policing. Khayelitsha's Football for Hope center stands at one end of an open space, with a residential cul-de-sac at the other end. The layout allows a new pedestrian footpath to pick up where the cul-de-sac ends, linking the center to the opposite end of the site, where another community building erected by the Violence Prevention through Urban Upgrading stands. This formerly abandoned, poorly lit, and dangerous tract of land now physically reconnects spaces in this part of Harare.

Eschewing the typical urban planning and architectural practices of fragmentation, exclusion, and fortification typically found in South Africa, the center, despite its simplicity, asserted itself as a paradigm for inclusiveness, consolidating severed tracts of the community that could now fully engage. "This was more like a crime spot, but now it is more like an activity spot where people come to enjoy themselves," said Zamayedwa Sogayise, chair of the Khayelitsha Development Forum.[8]

I visited the center to take photographs for Architecture for Humanity. Children ran around the landscaped areas under the watchful eye of their parents, who sat in the shade of the pergola. Scheduled activities were also running at the center. When a football game kicked off on the plastic surface, it felt like the entire community congregated, with spectators standing on the sidelines, drumming their support directly on the boards around the perimeter of the pitch. It seemed like a contemporary expression of a long-established community tradition, too serendipitous to be impromptu, even though I was informed that I was watching the first game played at the center.

Under the World Cup bylaws the Football for Hope Center was designated as a "controlled access site" on the day of its official inauguration, which coincided with the festivities surrounding the World Cup final draw in December 2009. I attended this opening and was struck by the unusually visible police presence on the streets of Khayelitsha. The convivial, communal atmosphere that I experienced in my earlier visit was noticeably absent. A fifteen-foot-high perimeter fence now enveloped the center, and private security guards controlled access and checked tickets at the entrance. Temporary tiered seating and white VIP tents flanked either side of the center; from a presentation podium, FIFA president Sepp Blatter delivered his "Football for Hope" homily. These incongruous structural elements blocked out views of both the playing space and the gritty neighborhood around it. Local residents and police officers came together on the edges of the controlled area, finding a spot on the embankments to peer over the perimeter fence. The logos of FIFA's corporate partners adorned the advertising boards surrounding the pitch. These corporate logos would become a permanent feature of this center and of projected Football for Hope centers in Namibia, Lesotho, Kenya, Rwanda, Ghana, Mali, and other African nations.

The meeting of the FIFA and Khayelitsha worlds at the perimeter fence revealed some of the contradictions of World Cup development and the deeper motives behind this social responsibility program. This exclusive FIFA celebration was taking place in a tough place whose origins lay in residential segregation and racial oppression. This project embraced the tenets of inclusiveness in its urban design but rendered that design temporarily exclusive for a public relations exercise. Such processes of inclusion and exclusion at the Football for Hope Center in Khayelitsha can be compared with those observed at the FIFA Fan Fest at the Grand Parade in the city center during the World Cup.

The Grand Parade was the epicenter of Cape Town's World Cup celebrations. Surrounded on three sides by City Hall, the Castle of Good Hope, and the Cape Town railway station, the Grand Parade underwent extensive refurbishment for the World Cup that enabled the general public to watch the games on a huge TV screen. During the tournament, I walked by the entrance to the Fan Fest zone on my way to work in the morning as revelers congregated in multicolored regalia with the cacophony of vuvuzelas reverberating in the streets. Men and women of different racial and ethnic backgrounds stood in line at the entrance (the Fan Fest was surrounded by a temporary fence), slowly filing into the open space with tiered seating facing the large screen. The atmosphere at the Grand Parade was lively. The convergence of tourists and Capetonians in joint celebration within this space contrasted starkly with the stymied atmosphere experienced at the opening of the Football for Hope Center in Khayelitsha. But FIFA's stiff restrictions on conduct, use, and access also shaped people's experiences at the Fan Fest.

At the Grand Parade and near the Cape Town stadium at Green Point, fans were inundated by FIFA-approved products, including food catered by Headline Leisure, the company contracted to supply

FIFA spaces. Gone were Cape Town's market stalls and their aromatic haze. As a result of such exclusionary policies and procedures, some Cape Town vendors claimed to have lost 20,000 rand ($3,400) during the World Cup. Considering that South Africa's minimum subsistence level is $2,300 per year, that level of loss of personal revenue is significant.

The experience within and around FIFA-controlled spaces clearly resembled other standardized, global corporate events. The absence of local historical and cultural content produced a sense of placelessness, an artificial feeling of familiarity, a flatness, and a homogeneity that defines and symbolizes FIFA-style globalization. The influence of large transnational corporations and the strength of a country's economic attributes and resources are key factors in ranking a "world-class" city in a global hierarchy. Composed of both global and local components, a city is the synthetic outcome of these two seemingly contradictory forces.

Given that FIFA is staging the World Cup in Brazil in 2014, can Cape Town's experience provide some lessons for future host nations to counter this movement toward increasingly generic urban experiences? A starting point would be for FIFA to create a more flexible framework that adapts to the local context without the need for social exclusion and marginalization of workers and the poor. Berlin is not the same city as Cape Town (or Rio de Janeiro or Moscow), so FIFA's rules, guidelines, bylaws, and social responsibility programs should be tailored to suit local needs and conditions, and not the other way around.

FIFA must be less parasitic and more altruistic. In South Africa, for example, informal street traders should have been permitted to sell their wares within the FIFA exclusion zones. Perhaps a compromise could have allowed traders to buy and sell some FIFA-sanctioned goods. The Football for Hope Center in Khayelitsha was too narrowly focused on football despite the rhetoric about public health and education. Its long-term sustainability remains in doubt. Considering that scarce public funds built stadiums and infrastructure projects and that FIFA earned massive profits from the 2010 World Cup, it seems reasonable to expect that in the future, national governments can pressure FIFA to pay for more of the hosting costs. Since contemporary world cities' economic strategies and marketing campaigns often rely on hosting major sporting events, it is important to question hosting agreements and bylaws that empower multinational corporations to appropriate public space. By doing so, host cities and nations can take a critical step toward making megaevents more inclusive, equitable, and locally sustainable.

NOTES

1. See Christopher Saunders, "Cape Town and New Orleans," *Safundi* 1, 1 (2000): 1–6.

2. Vivian Bickford-Smith, Elizabeth van Heyningen, and Nigel Worden, *Cape Town in the Twentieth Century: An Illustrated Social History* (Claremont: Philip, 1999), 7.

3. Christoph Haferburg, Theresa Golka, and Marie Selter, "Public Viewing Areas: Urban Interventions in the Context of Mega-Events," in *Development and Dreams: The Urban Legacy of the 2010 Football World Cup*, ed. Udesh Pillay, Richard Tomlinson, and Orli Bass (Pretoria: HSRC Press, 2009), 174–99.

4. For more details, see Ashraf Cassiem, "Western Cape Anti-Eviction Campaign," speech at Rhodes University's teach-in on the 2010 World Cup, Grahamstown, September 2010, http://www.youtube.com/watch?v=Nf0SBMGJeQU, accessed August 5, 2011.

5. For further information, see Grassroot Soccer, "Football for Hope Center Opens Its Doors to Khayelitsha and the World," http://www.grassrootsoccer.org/2009/12/08/football-for-hope-center-opens-its-doors-to-khayelitsha-and-the-world/, accessed August 5, 2011; Architecture for Humanity, "Khayelitsha Football for Hope Center," n.d., http://architectureforhumanity.org/node/825, accessed August 5, 2011; FIFA.com, "Opening of First Football for Hope Center Heralds a New Dawn for Khayelitsha," December 5, 2009, http://www.fifa.com/aboutfifa/socialresponsibility/news/newsid=1144491/index.html, accessed August 5, 2011.

6. Another Football for Hope center will open later in Alexandra, in the northern suburbs of Johannesburg.

7. On the establishment of Khayelitsha, see Surplus People Project, *Khayelitsha: New Home, Old Story* (Cape Town: Surplus People Project, 1984). For a different perspective, see Steven Otter, *Khayelitsha: uMlungu in a Township* (Johannesburg: Penguin, 2007).

8. Quoted in "Football for Hope Center Opens Its Doors."

PART 2

World Cup Sounds, Visual Culture, and Aesthetics

World Cup Music and Football Noise

The Lion King, *Waka Waka, and the Vuvuzela*

JENNIFER DOYLE

WITH ESPN'S BROADCAST of the World Cup's opening match, my fellow tweeters began to crack jokes about the *Lion King*. We imagined Rafiki and Mufasa calling the matches and half expected the referees to lift up the Jabulani to announce the arrival of the New Ball. Some folks simply observed that there was a good reason for this resemblance. The score used by ESPN to frame its coverage was written by Lisle Moore. The Utah composer gave us muscular music for a sporting event, up-beat music for a media event organized around putting us all in the mood to buy a shirt, a ball, or a Coke. Layered over the orchestral swells are the oddly familiar sounds of African voices—or, I should say, African-sounding voices. Africa is scored here as a noble landscape, peopled by a unified chorus, singing together in a harmonic convergence of tribal cultures.

"With the exception of the African choir," reported the *Salt Lake Tribune* on June 10, 2010, "all of the music is performed by Utah musicians." The "African choir" lending this score a sense of location is actually made up of members of the *Lion King*'s Broadway cast. The choir from New York City was hired to sonically channel an idea of African authenticity keyed to the ears of ESPN's U.S. audience. The same of course holds true for all scores produced by the World Cup broadcasting networks, as they reach for music that their imagined audience will understand. Without a doubt, we are hearing not African music but, to invoke the Congolese philosopher Valentin Mudimbe, a musical "idea of Africa."[1]

Much can be gained by listening to the sound draped over the 2010 World Cup. This is nowhere more obvious than the "Official 2010 FIFA World Cup™ Song," "Waka Waka (This Time for Africa)," sung by Colombian pop star Shakira and Freshlyground, a South African Afro-fusion band. As numerous bloggers have pointed out, the global pop hit has a clear relationship to a Cameroonian military song, "Zangaléwa," popularized by the group Golden Sounds in 1986. "Waka Waka" does not just borrow from "Zangaléwa"—listening to the two reveals that the chorus to "Waka Waka" is a direct use of "Zangaléwa."

Dibussi Tande, a Cameroonian digital activist, places this appropriation within a longer history of intellectual theft in Africa. In a May 23, 2010, post on his blog *Scribbles from the Den*, Tande begins with Michael Jackson's use of a hit song by Cameroonian makossa master Mano Dibango.[2] The words and melody of "Soul Makossa" provide the distinctive sound of "Wanna Be Startin' Somethin'," the opening track on Jackson's *Thriller* album. Dibango sued Jackson and won. Dibango's song was actually the B side of "Movement Ewondo," a song composed for the 1972 African Nations Cup hosted by Cameroon and won by Congo-Brazzaville. It's a frenetic football score in which strings seems to scurry underneath Dibango's expressive and light-footed sax.

Jackson's theft of recognizable lyrics and melodies pales in comparison with what Shakira and Sony music pulled off with "Waka Waka." Given their use of a song known to a generation of fans of African pop, it's surprising that they thought they could get away with such plagiarism. But, of course, that is how entitlement works—you do not notice the theft of that which you feel is already yours.

Tande points out that the origins of the song were only acknowledged by FIFA, Shakira, and others in response to online activism by those who were horrified to see the song stolen. Under pressure from the Cameroonian musicians and their advocates, FIFA stated that "Waka Waka" is a "remix" of the Golden Sounds hit. This appropriation of African music into a musical idea of Africa is a never-ending story. "For decades, African artists have had their works plagiarized by the West with little or no compensation or acknowledgement," writes Tande. "The most memorable example of the theft of the intellectual rights of an African artist is that of Solomon Popoli Linda who in 1939 wrote the song 'Mbube' and received 10 shillings (less than $US 2) for his efforts. The song which later became the pop hit 'The Lion Sleeps Tonight' was reinterpreted by dozens of American artists without Linda or his family receiving a dime. In fact, he died penniless." In 1995, according to Tande, "the 'Lion Sleeps Tonight' earned an estimated $15 million dollars just for its use in the movie *Lion King*—a movie which has since grossed about 800 million USD worldwide. Linda's descendants sued Walt Disney for 1.5 million dollars with the full backing of the South African government. Disney settled for an undisclosed sum just as the trial was about to begin."[3] Disney is not eager for its consumers to know that behind that feel-good African sound is the noise of the gears of neocolonial exploitation, turning, turning.

Perhaps more interesting, in terms of the spin an artist can put on the same song, is K'naan's "Wavin' Flag," the ubiquitous official song for Coca-Cola's 2010 World Cup advertising campaign as well as the soundtrack for the Electronic Arts video game *2010 FIFA World Cup South Africa*. The song began as rousing melody tracking fantasies of precolonial glory and postcolonial resistance:

> So many wars, settling scores,
> Bringing us promises leaving us poor,
> I heard them say, love is the way,
> Love is the answer, that's what they say,
> But look how they treat us,
> Make us believers,
> We fight their battles, then they deceive us,
> Try to control us, they couldn't hold us
> Cause we just move forward like Buffalo Soldiers
>
> But we struggling, fighting to eat
> And we wondering, when we'll be free
> So we patiently wait for that faithful day
> It's not far away . . .

The song's chorus then repeats a wistful thought: "When I get older I will be stronger / They'll call me freedom just like a wavin' flag / And then it goes back, and then it goes back, and then it goes back." While supported by anthem-like muscle, the song is hardly the sort of tune one imagines selling Coca-Cola and video games. All of these lines were thus removed from the World Cup version. The refrain "And then it goes back, and then it goes back" remains, however, like a phantom limb. It's a strange chant for a football anthem, in which forward motion is the more usually celebrated run of play.

The words literally describe the movement of a flag, but without the context of the song's original words, the phrase has lost its sense. Within the original lyrics, the refrain describes the movement of nationalist impulses toward and away from freedom's horizon. Those words promise both "if we go forward, we also go back" and power "goes back" to the people from whom it was stolen.

In addition, we have K'naan's very dense reference to Buffalo Soldiers—all-black regiments of the U.S. Army established after the Civil War. These soldiers supported the federal government in the Indian Wars, and their story gestures to a very complicated knot in American history, in which the complexities of racial oppression are condensed into an emblem of the trauma of slavery, erasing the full interaction of race and empire in American nationalism. (The 1870 legislation naturalizing people of African descent as U.S. citizens, for example, also reinforced eighteenth-century legislation barring people of Asian and Hispanic descent from that citizenship.) This reference, perhaps accidentally, underscores the colonial twist embedded in that phrase "moving forward." Of course, I am probably overreading by seeing in K'Naan's lyrics a story about settler colonialism, but it does not seem like a stretch to say that in the story of his participation in its revision for (more) commercial use, we see something of the problem of the World Cup interface.

In "When I Get Older," a title that nods to "Wavin' Flag," Mumbai-based journalist and blogger Supriya Nair warns liberal American pundits to check their impulses to read in African national teams an allegory for Africa itself. "Where you see models of correlation between dictators and football victories," Nair argues, "others would see the run of play as the rest of the world knows it: of a history of possession dominated by those who wrote the rules, of enforced migrations and unwilling recruitments; of contests that we must always resist seeing as wars, because they are only fought—and won—on the field."[4]

We do well to listen to other music, not co-opted by FIFA and its corporate tentacles. Nomadic Wax produced "World Cup," a pulsating twelve-minute track in which sixteen emcees from Africa, Europe, and the Americas contribute sixteen bars of lyrics speaking to and about the event. The grimmest lines come from emcee Emile YX from the Grassy Park section of Cape Town, who sums up the neo-imperial relationship between FIFA and South Africa, as the latter subsidized the former's World Cup profits:

> The attention world gathers for the wrong reason
> It's the long cold-hearted capitalist season
> Where basic human freedoms violated for money
> In the land of gold, we chase a gold cup, that's funny
> Suddenly money changes "never & never again"
> Never say never, the same money's running everything
> Where Khoi & San bodies hung, impaled and battered
> Is where they built the stadium & 4 billion got Blattered
> But we'll foot the bill, just to foot their ball
> On the graces of our ancestors, how can we stand tall?
> Here Hegemony erases the memory of the San
> And lands send players to get played by the man
> This scams like "Yes we can tans [Obama]" distracting nations
> Subduing revolution with media mind occupation
> When FIFA's moneymaking machine moves on
> Has Africa finally the World's respect won?

Emile YX boils down a critique launched by activists and academics across South Africa. As emcees toggle between bragging about their skills on the pitch and on the mike, between love for their national team and critical reads like this one, "World Cup" distills both the desire and the danger of looking for redemption in FIFA's tournament. Like much critical hip-hop, "World Cup" is a portrait in ambivalence.

No team bore the burden of redemptive hope more than Ghana. Cheery anthems abound in its stands. Ghana is home of "hiplife," a hybrid movement that combines the sounds of up-tempo Ghanaian highlife, hip-hop, and pop. Ghanaian artists working in this genre regularly make use of Jama song (football chants). In his 2006 survey of hiplife and World Cup music, African music blogger Chale describes Jama as a form of "public music"—songs known, sung, and in essence owned by the Ghanaian public.[5] Jama is woven throughout much hiplife and feeds back into Jama as fans break into songs that have been recast by their favorite emcees and pop artists.

Ghanaian musicians regularly produce new anthems for their national squad, called the Black Stars. For the 2006 World Cup, the group G-Force produced a whole album celebrating the team (*Faith in the Black Star*). That year, an all-star lineup of hiplife musicians produced "Oseiye" as the Black Stars' official theme song in the lead-up to the 2008 African Nations Cup. In "Blackstar 2010," Trosky Blackman sings for the Ghanaian squad over a bouncy synthesizer backdrop, the song coalescing in the familiar soccer chant, "Olé, Olé, Olé, Olé, Olé, Olé." The genre migrates: English DJ and producer Richy Pitch crafted "Football Jama" after attending the 2008 African Nations Cup. The song remixes crowd noise, drumming, and the whistles of fans with Jama chants and rapid-fire football-centered lyrics from U.K. artists Sway and M3NSA who speak hypothetically as team captain and chief supporter. The song is not exactly Jama but a use of Jama—a musical essay on football noise. This kind of portrait of the sonic landscape of the sport is itself a subgenre of football music—the record "Pelé," by Bosco De Oliveira's samba band, Arakatuba, uses whistles, drums, and crowd noise from broadcasts to create a conversation with match experience. An excerpt from Pitch's track opens Rodney Quarcoo's "Obama We Are Sorry," a fantastic video showing ecstatic fans swarming, dancing, and singing in the streets celebrating the Black Stars' World Cup win over the United States. (People can be heard singing "Obama We Are Sorry," and one fan carries this apology on a sign.) That video closes with Wanlov the Kubolor's "Goal Again" (featuring Kwabena Jones). Wanlov the Kubalor's track is from a concept album, *Yellow Card—Stomach Direction*. The entire album is a musical conversation with football fandom. That it is the follow-up album to *Green Card* gives a sense of the album's bite. "Stomach direction" refers to a kick made in whatever direction the stomach faces: The term can mean not only shots sent wide but also a certain kind of thoughtless greed. "Goal Again" drifts from direct rapping (often in pidgin) about the Black Stars and football in Ghana to match calling, in which "Goooooal" becomes the song's refrain. (The album itself is full of hilarious and grounded dialogic interludes in which a fan rants, theorizes, and laments about the national side.) Most of these tracks are made available by artists as free downloads.

Kwabena Jones and the United States–based MC M.anifest produced "Vuvuzela Blackstars," yet another celebration of the cruelly eliminated squad, via an appreciation of the controversial plastic horn (see the essay by Solomon Waliaula in this collection). Much of this track sounds pushed through the program Autotune, giving the entire song's background a reedy texture evocative of the vuvuzela. Making the viral rounds in 2010 was a comic duet produced by a Turkish football fan site (90.turk.com), "African Vuvuzela vs. Turkish Zurna." Two stereotyped characters, one African and one Turkish, blow their respective horns. The zurna appears hopelessly quaint until a crowd of chanting Turkish football fans swarms around "Ali" with drums. The zurna wins.

Point taken, for by the end of the 2010 World Cup, the vuvuzela had been removed from the world of "public music," and fans who now plant their lips on it seem to have opted for the world plastic noise. And so unfolds the debate over the authenticity of the vuvuzela, as an African sound (as asserted by FIFA's Sepp Blatter). Like many football artifacts, these vuvuzelas were manufactured in China; the people in the stands of the South African World Cup did not represent South African football culture. And it is unfair to reduce the whole of any fan culture to what Elina Shatkin has aptly described as a "glorified kazoo."[6]

Although they were marketed as African artifacts by the media, vuvuzelas have been used in North American stands for years. Their strange, sad bleating had always struck me as depressing, perhaps because at the Los Angeles Galaxy and Chivas USA games I attend, they are blown by people sitting in their assigned seats, watching the dutiful play of American soccer. Whatever spirit they channel, in the smaller stadiums of Major League Soccer matches (for which twenty thousand is a good turnout), their noise is manageable. That human scale is true to South African league football, too.

But South Africa's stadiums were scaled up for the World Cup. A gathering of seventeen thousand people—some with drums, some with vuvuzelas, some with trumpets—makes one kind of aural experience, a cacophony, in which song and noise can wrestle playfully. Sounded by audiences of seventy thousand or more, however, the vuvuzela is a nightmare, a sonic hornet's nest, especially for networks broadcasting the tournament.

This quantity of vuvuzelas amplifies stadium affect itself—broadcasting anxiety, suspense, frustration, and happiness as simply volume. A team attacks at a tense moment in the match, and the volume goes up. The horns throb when it feels like something important might happen, when something needs to happen. Attention drifts and the noise fades. It communicates degrees of intensity—a sonically disorienting sense of hope and alarm.

Radio and television productions of World Cup matches rode these waves of sonic attack. Sound editors balanced the imperative that they communicate the audience's volume (the aural effect of a packed stadium) with the need to create a watchable, listenable broadcast. If your network did not edit out enough of the vuvuzela noise, you could download sound editing programs with vuvuzela-killing features. Online Media Technologies promised, "The Vuvuzela Remover feature contains 6 filters adjusted to reject frequencies typical of this African horn."[7]

The vuvuzela is the sound not exactly of resistance but of interference—the noise of a multitude that stands in the way of the desire to hear a pretty African song. The challenge of mixing the sound of the vuvuzela into live broadcasts of World Cup matches translated into noise the problem that the World Cup is a commercial event in which an enormously diverse and fluid cultural activity (football, as a sport one plays and watches) is converted into hard cash. Each match looks like a dollar bill, played on a bright green rectangle, even though in most parts of the world the game is played on uneven brown surfaces. It is played by a single sex—by men who appear to be straight, by men who work together within a team and subordinate politics to the desire to win. It is a global illusion, in which a whole world wants the same thing, sees the same thing, and listens to the same song, over and over again. "Sport goes on and on and on, you see," writes Lynne Truss in an essay confessing her lack of interest in who wins or loses and the ease with which she cut the sport out of her life after years of writing about it. Stepping back, she noticed that everything is the same—winners, losers. It is the same story, over and over again.[8]

For me, the vuvuzela provided the noise of the World Cup in the truest sense: the sound of all that the spectacle collects, organizes, and disciplines into a consumable form. It announced in a single, unrelenting note what FIFA does on a disciplinary level by organizing football into a single global event.

For the illusion of a "World Cup" to work, we need to believe that teams have equal resources, that they practice and play on the same surfaces, and that they grow up with the same kind of care and development. We need to believe that the best players are chosen by the best managers, that the best teams qualify for the tournament. We need the illusion of a level playing field—on which Ghana can beat the United States, for example—and fans can laugh and say, "Obama, we are sorry." We need a zone of suppressed contradiction in which we can rage at the unfairness of it all while celebrating the glory of La Furia Roja, in which we can laugh at the paradox of our passion for a process that is in reality foul, full of prejudice and corruption.

Corporations sell us their products with fantasies of poor boys who need only a ball to forget their troubles. Layered over those images are tracks from K'Naan, Shakira, Coca-Cola, and Disney, music that itself feeds on that which is outside of the entertainment complex but is always in the process of being absorbed into it. The favelas, ghettos, and townships in which those commercials are set are leveled to make room for the stadium green. The noise of such spaces is captured and repackaged as a catchy jingle. The vuvuzela, blown by tens of thousands of people at network microphones makes an entirely different kind of sound—something close to what Jacques Attali described as a sonic "liquidation of meaning."[9] The plastic trumpet heralds the conclusion of a process that has turned the joys of improvisation into so much programming.

NOTES

1. Valentin Y. Mudimbe, *The Idea of Africa* (Bloomington: Indiana University Press, 1994).

2. Dibussi Tande, "Undermining African Intellectual and Artistic Rights," *Scribbles from the Den*, May 23, 2010, http://www.dibussi.com/2010/05/undermin ing-african-intellectual-and-artistic-rights-.html, accessed September 22, 2011.

3. Ibid.

4. Roswitha, "When I Get Older," July 3, 2010, http://angrynun.blogspot .com/2010/07/when-i-get-older.html, accessed December 3, 2011.

5. Chale, "Jama—Osee, Osee, Black Starts Ei, Forward Ever!," *Museke: Home of the African Music Fan*, June 24, 2010, http://www.museke.com/en/node/349, ac-cessed November 18, 2011.

6. Conversation with the author, June 2000.

7. Press release from Online Media Technologies Ltd., "Vuvuzela Killer aka AVS Audio Editor 6.1: Enjoy True World Cup 2010 Videos," distributed by SourceWire News Distribution, http://www.sourcewire.com/news/57507/vuvu zela-killer-aka-avs-audio-editor-enjoy-true-world-cup, accessed November 12, 2012.

8. Lynne Truss, *Get Her Off the Pitch! How Sport Took Over My Life* (London: HarperCollins, 2010), 287.

9. Jacques Attali, *Noise: The Political Economy of Music* (Manchester: Manches-ter University Press, 1985).

The Vuvuzela as Paradox of Leisure and Noise

A Sociocultural Perspective

SOLOMON WALIAULA

THE CHARACTER AND CONSEQUENCE of stadium noise produced by long plastic horns known as vuvuzelas became the subject of sustained international debate during the 2009 Confederations Cup in South Africa, the dress rehearsal for the 2010 World Cup. The vuvuzela performances of fans in Johannesburg, Pretoria, Bloemfontein, and Rustenburg caught the attention of the world, and print, broadcast, and Internet media wondered whether the noisemaker would be welcome at the World Cup.

One of the most striking contributions to this debate came not from sports media but from the medical profession. Writing in scientific journals, some doctors argued that no one within a six-foot radius of a vuvuzela, including the person blowing it, should be exposed for more than one minute to a deafening noise that averages between 113 and 131 decibels.[1] Noting that an ordinary person should be exposed to less than fifteen minutes of 100-decibel noise per day, members of the medical community warned that exposure to vuvuzela sounds at World Cup stadiums might even lead to permanent hearing loss. A letter published in the esteemed *South African Medical Journal* after the tournament revealed another kind of vuvuzela-induced health problem: a thyroid cyst! According to W. A. Mann and K. Jungheim, "a 42-year-old man presented with acute painful swelling on the neck and difficulty in swallowing. An ultrasound scan confirmed the clinical suspicion of a

thyroid cyst with a volume of 2 ml. . . . [T]he cyst was successfully emptied by fine-needle aspiration . . . and the patient was immediately free
of complaints. On being asked whether he had raised heavy weights or
pressed strongly, he responded that he had blown a vuvuzela during a
recent World Cup soccer game."[2]

Despite such medical opinions and ongoing criticism of vuvuzelas,
FIFA chose to embrace them. "We should not try to Europeanize an
African World Cup," Sepp Blatter told the media; the vuvuzela "is what
African and South African football is all about: noise, excitement, dancing, shouting and enjoyment."[3] Even so, Blatter was probably unaware
of the cultural resonance of "noise" in African ritual contexts. Using
my anthropological fieldwork on the biennial Bukusu initiation ritual
in the Kenyan community where I grew up and then comparing it to a
similar performance across the border in Uganda, intriguing if speculative connections can be made between centuries-old agrarian rites
of passage and the twenty-first-century global cultural festival of the
World Cup.[4]

IT IS JUNE 22, 2010, and I am at the Auberge Lucienne Marie in Dakar, Senegal, for an academic conference hosted by Codesria, a prestigious West
African think-tank. The last two matches in Group A are under way:
South Africa versus France at Mangaung Stadium in Bloemfontein, and
Mexico versus Uruguay at Rustenburg Stadium. The hosts have the
good fortune of playing against a French side devastated by internecine
fighting and poor results on the pitch. Having lost to Mexico in their
previous match, Les Bleus have virtually no hope of progressing to the
next round. To avoid becoming the first host nation not to advance past
the group stages, South Africa has to beat France by a large margin.

The atmosphere in the hotel where I watch the match is tense. The
majority of the viewers, mainly Senegalese and Cameroonians, seem
torn between backing former colonial masters France and supporting
South Africa. The crowd in Dakar seems to know the clubs on which
the Frenchmen play, clearly feeling a sense of solidarity with a team
made up of so many black athletes with West African and Caribbean
ties. In contrast, the South African players—except for English Premier
League players Aaron Mokoena and Steven Pienaar—are unknown to
most viewers in the room. In fact, only a young woman from Swaziland
is fully committed to Bafana Bafana.

The sound of the vuvuzelas in the stadiums is so loud that it eludes the sophisticated control of the television production team, drowning out the voices of the two Francophone commentators. The television cameras occasionally pick out the agents of this din. Each of the performers seems so completely absorbed in noisemaking that it is unclear whether they are even following the game. How can they expend so much energy blowing vuvuzelas, mostly standing and moving around, and still have the capacity to concentrate on the game itself? Maybe they have their own strategies for tracking the game. Maybe they accommodate the game within the larger vuvuzela performance.

Watching in Dakar, I imagine that the energy of "doing vuvuzela" might have a cleansing effect on the performers. Do fans leave the stadium more emotionally balanced after two hours of trumpeting? Does the ear-bursting noise clear a clogged-up nervous system and anxiety regarding situations we cannot change such as the results of a soccer match? Can it temporarily silence fears of not accomplishing goals such as having our team reach the next round? Does the vuvuzela quiet down internal dialogue? Does it help keep the peace? Maybe blowing the vuvuzela turns the soccer match into a ritual that facilitates a confrontation between an individual and himself or herself, provoking a sort of catharsis. What if I take the vuvuzela experience out of football and bring it into a wider discussion of African cultural forms and the ways in which they mediate the relationship between individual and society? How does South African fans' horn blowing compare with noisemaking in ancient rites of passage in East African cultures?

KHUMINYA IS A MALE RITE of passage practiced among the Bukusu people of western Kenya; they are part of the broader Luhya ethnic community. The term *khuminya* comes from the Bukusu noun *omuminyi*, meaning deaf person. Within the ritual context, *khuminya* translates literally as "to make a lot of noise that could make someone deaf." Metaphorically, however, it means "to harden" a young person, to induce a deafening process that helps him cope with the physical pain of circumcision. The initiation process lasts about one week and comprises many activities performed in different parts of the community, involving kin, friends, neighbors, and the community. The ritual brings together everyone, regardless of age, gender, and socioeconomic class; each individual has a role. The ritual also incorporates Bukusu ancestors and therefore the spiritual realm of existence. Ancestors are invoked and accommodated in beer-drinking ceremonies, animal sacrifices, and special incantations led by the elders of the community.

Comparing *khuminya* in Kenya with vuvuzela in South Africa requires a consideration of the activities that take place between the time when the initiation candidates arrive from their maternal uncles' homes at dawn and when they are taken to the river, the penultimate stage of the ritual. Taking place at night, this is a kind of wake characterized by a mix of activities within the home and around the homestead. Under cover of darkness, the youth take center stage and engage in a bacchanal set of performances that are, on the surface, nothing more than a disorganized session of song, dance, chants, blowing of horns, whistles, and verbal art. A panoptic view of the entire performance might simply describe it as a noisy, disorganized frenzy.

However, closer examination reveals that there is always a soloist leading the song and dance revolving around the initiates. A concentric circle made up of close relatives, neighbors, and family friends sings songs overtly relevant to the occasion. At the same time, other concentric circles consisting of carefree and bacchanal performers develop around the nucleus of initiates. Tension exists between the orderly and musically harmonious group closest to the center and the chaotic, cacophonous, and noisy group(s) on the fringes. People on the margins are a sideshow to the main dance, but they also become alternative foci of the ritual as they retain contact with the main nucleus and follow a plot line framed between sundown and sunrise. The *khuminya* ritual culminates in circumcision in the early hours of the morning.

It is a highly gendered ritual. Unlike vuvuzela blowers in World Cup stadiums, all of the horn blowers in *khuminya* are men. The old-fashioned Bukusu horn is carved from animal horns and is designed in such a way as to require perceived male skill and energy to produce the proper sound. (These days, Bukusu horns are made out of plastic.) The sound of the horn can echo across hills and ridges. At night, far from city noises of factories and motor vehicles and the general ambience of electrified nightlife, the stillness of dark and relatively quiet rural nights is shredded by the most "visible" footnote of the Bukusu circumcision ritual: *khulanga* (calling out, inviting, invoking). The volume of the noise tends to turn away people who may wish to join in. However, the cacophony of horns and voices excites *khuminya* participants.

Across the border from Kenya, in northern Uganda, I found another interesting East African parallel with vuvuzelas in South Africa. Horn playing in the *orak*, a chaotic love dance of the Acoli people, is rich in sexual connotations. As a study by Kenyan scholar Okot p'Bitek points out, the ritual essentially is about people blowing horns.[5] The participants, most of whom are young, blow their horns and sing the praises of their lovers (or sometimes mock girls playing hard to get). There are as many soloists as there are participants. No one directs the performance; it somehow regulates itself. Brawls and fights between young men are not uncommon, but they too are somehow controlled. Most interesting for the purpose of this essay are the function and form of the horn blowing. Like *khuminya* and other rites of passage, *orak* is performed at night, thereby providing security and privacy and infusing the event with greater spiritual force.

The horn blowing draws attention to the blower, but paradoxically, in a context where everyone is making such noise, the cacophony that ensues does not allow a particular horn or set of horns to be heard. Rather, it produces a free-flowing sound accompanied by singing and a dominant soloist whose role is to call a tune in the midst of the "noise," thereby holding the center of this dance and preventing it from spiraling into chaos. "There is much competition among soloists, each one desiring to sing his lover's praise," Okot p'Bitek writes. "One leaps in the air and yells his love, while playing on the half-gourd. He is disrupted by others who beat unrhythmic noises, on their half gourds. [It is not] possible to hear and appreciate two, three, five, ten, many different poems at the same time. . . . [S]ome are humming, some blowing their horns, some making ululations. . . . [T]here is no audience, that is, some rascals merely watching the dance from a distance."[6]

As with the *khuminya*, men dominate the *orak* dance. Northern Ugandan culture perceives only men as having the physical strength to blow the horns loudly enough to be heard over the cacophonous din. While men are dominant, however, they are not all-powerful. The silent but strong presence of women is inescapable, as they are courted and fought over, praised for their beauty and offers of love, and occasionally vilified for rejecting their suitors.

The inclusiveness of the *orak* dance is crucial. People are engaged and enjoying the event. The ritual thus absorbs everyone, committing them to the reigning contest of tunes. The same holds true for the *khuminya* dance—it involves everyone in one way or another. This total immersion in the dances facilitates the accommodation to and reconstruction of apparent chaos into an enjoyable individual and communal experience. As with the stadium noise of vuvuzelas, outside observers tend to find these rituals far less pleasurable than insiders do, and many outsiders overlook the cultural rootedness and meaning of such loud performances.

These nighttime performances are intended to keep expressions of youthful passion and energy private, if not anonymous. Extremely loud noise provides an additional layer of privacy in the sense that many deep-seated anxieties, attitudes, and aspirations are expressed in conditions that cushion individuals from being held accountable for what they say or sing. Crucially, *khuminya* and *orak* entail the construction of sacred spaces in which tensions and conflicts associated with manhood are allowed to play out in socially and culturally sanctioned circumstances. These two dances, therefore, can be understood as socially constructed leisure activities performed and culturally legitimated in the framework of a ritual. In this sense, vuvuzela performances at South African stadiums can also be read as serving fans' leisure needs. "Doing vuvuzela" may well constitute a homegrown expression of individual and collective freedom, a creative and enjoyable form of audience participation that eludes the control of FIFA, its corporate sponsors, and its media partners.

Vuvuzela performances also recall the carnivalesque structure and texture of *khuminya* and *orak* dances. In the case of the latter, large groups of men upset behavioral norms; they take advantage of the cloak of darkness and temporary release from social control to engage in excessive noisemaking, blowing of horns and half calabashes, and other forms of self-expression ordinarily frowned upon. In the case of vuvuzelas, fans also take advantage of the special stadium atmosphere to engage in noisemaking usually not tolerated in ordinary life. Though these actions fall short of turning the FIFA world upside down, vuvuzela in football shares with Mikhail Bakhtin's conceptualization of the carnival an emphasis on the equality of participants, frank communication, and freedom of action that is largely absent from everyday life.[7]

Finally, a sort of conspiracy of selfishness runs through the two East African dances and doing vuvuzela. Bukusu and Akoli people engage in individual quests that are accommodated within group performances and collective objectives. *Khuminya* participants often compose self-serving songs and engage in verbal art; *orak* dancers rejoice in praise of themselves and their lovers. Similarly, the vuvuzela blower is also a kind of *imbongi* ("praise singer," in Zulu and Xhosa), basically concerned about himself or herself within the socioculturally sanctioned frame of a football stadium. Context is crucial, because horn blowing in some African societies can be laden with historical and locally specific qualities, functions, and meanings.

NOTES

1. De Wet Swanepoel, James W. Hall, and Dirk Koekemoer, "Vuvuzela—Good for Your Team, Bad for Your Ears," *South African Medical Journal* 100, 2 (2010): 99. See also De Wet Swanepoel and James W. Hall, "Football Match Spectator Sound Exposure and Effect on Hearing: A Pretest–Post-Test Study," *South African Medical Journal* 100, 4 (2010): 239–42.

2. W. A. Mann and K. Jungheim, "World Cup 2010 and Acute Pain in the Neck," *South African Medical Journal* 100, 10 (2010): 10. The letter noted that "no data on vuvuzela-induced thyroid cysts could be found in the literature."

3. Blatter quoted in J. du T Zaaijman, "Vuvuzelas: *Ex Africa Semper Aliquid Novis*—Again?" *South African Medical Journal* 100, 9 (2010): 546.

4. The Bukusu initiation rite of passage involves the circumcision of boys of between twelve and sixteen years. The rituals follow a strict calendar; they are held in August (and sometimes December) of every even year.

5. Okot p'Bitek, *Artist the Ruler: Essays on Art, Culture, and Values* (Nairobi: East African Education, 1986).

6. Ibid., 33.

7. Mikhail Bakhtin, *Rabelais and His World*, trans. Helen Iswolsky (Cambridge: MIT Press, 1968).

South African women in the stands, South Africa versus United States,
Cape Town Stadium, November 17, 2010. (Photograph by Peter Alegi.)

Camps Bay Primary School shows its support for the national team ahead of the 2010 World Cup, Cape Town, May 23, 2010. (Photograph by Peter Alegi.)

South African fans at a pub in Cape Town before the Nelson Mandela Challenge versus the United States, November 17, 2010. (Photograph by Peter Alegi.)

The iconic arch of Moses Mabhida Stadium, Durban, June 25, 2010.
(Photograph by Peter Alegi.)

Local vendors outside the exclusion zone around Mabhida Stadium, Durban, June 2010. (Photograph by David Roberts.)

Moses Mabhida Stadium sand sculpture, Durban beachfront, July 9, 2010. (Photograph by Chris Bolsmann.)

South African Muslim fans pray before the opening game, South Africa versus Mexico, Soccer City, June 11, 2010. (Photograph courtesy of Wiki Commons.)

Fans at a public viewing area in Soweto watch South Africa versus Mexico, June 11, 2010. (Photograph courtesy of Wiki Commons.)

"Exclusion and inclusion": ticket booth at Soccer City, June 23, 2010. (Photograph by Chris Bolsmann.)

South African fan blowing his vuvuzela at South Africa versus France, Free State Stadium, Bloemfontein, June 22, 2010. (Photograph by Chris Bolsmann.)

The World Cup brought many white South Africans, such as this female fan, closer to the game of the black majority. (Photograph by Chris Bolsmann.)

Halakasha! The Time Has Come!

Exhibiting the Art of Football Fandom

FIONA RANKIN-SMITH

THE 2010 WORLD CUP provided a momentous occasion for South Africans from across the social spectrum to celebrate this once-in-a-lifetime event. As the contributors to this book have noted, it was a month of spectacular excitement both on and off the pitch. The upbeat nature of the events permeated all aspects of life. Shopping malls, taverns and restaurants, public spaces and private homes—the entire country seemed to be draped in flags and banners. This popular enthusiasm for the World Cup had first exploded when South Africa was awarded the right to host the World Cup. "To some extent this outburst of euphoria surpassed" what the country experienced when it transitioned to democracy in 1994, wrote Ahmed Kathrada, who spent twenty-six years in apartheid prisons with his comrade, Nelson Mandela; "The scenes of jubilation, the spontaneous outpouring of celebration following FIFA's decision, the solidarity of pride and unity evoked by a sporting event should serve as a shining example to black and white alike" (see the essay by Daniel Herwitz in this volume).[1] Some of the most vivid moments of South Africa's celebration of nationhood were connected to sporting achievements on home soil: the Springboks' 1995 Rugby World Cup triumph and Bafana Bafana's victory in the 1996 African Nations Cup.

In 2009, the Standard Bank Gallery in Johannesburg appointed me to mount an exhibition that would run in June and July 2010, concurrently with the World Cup. My primary goal was to present an exhibition that would celebrate the African game, not simply the South

African game, and expose fans' passion to a world audience. The broad-ranging exhibition, *Halakasha!*, was framed mainly around the theme of local and African football supporters, imaging the politics and nationalist sentiment associated with football during and after the apartheid era. In addition, the exhibition made room for interpretations by young artists of the subject of football and traced the motif of magical power in the work of several artists. During this period, a series of international football-related documentaries and films were screened, and many other cultural institutions mounted exhibitions and events aimed at the influx of visitors. Steven Dubin, a visiting academic from New York, described how Johannesburg experienced an "unprecedented cultural effervescence in every imaginable venue at every level of production."[2] The constant throng of overseas visitors, together with South Africans and Africans from other countries, exuded a palpable sense of goodwill.

More than eight hundred people attended the exhibition opening on June 1. Instead of the usual individual opening speaker, organizers chose to stage the event like a panel discussion of television football commentators, with the speakers seated on a stage against a huge backdrop of Soccer City at night. Speakers included Nigerian football star Jay Jay Okocha, ex-Bafana goalkeeper Andre Arendse, Cameroonian public intellectual and football fan Achille Mbembe, and television host Neil Andrews. Aimed at the international sports-loving audience as well as local football fans, the exhibition sought to foster an appreciation of football not only as a sport but as a social and cultural phenomenon. "Halakasha is packed with art's stories of the love of football," wrote journalist Janet Smith.[3] in the June 19, 2010, issue of the *Saturday Star.* Indeed, to paraphrase Trinidadian intellectual C. L. R. James, football "is an art, not a bastard or a poor relation, but a full member of the community."[4]

According to the Standard Bank Gallery's records, a total of 3,316 people visited the exhibition. Although not a large figure compared to the numbers who attend blockbuster art exhibitions in Europe or North America, South Africans are much more inclined to support sporting events than museum and gallery exhibits and other forms of popular arts. It is difficult to gauge the audience's response to the exhibition, but comments written in the visitors' book were largely positive. The pupils from Johannesburg's Northcliff High School, for example, wrote, "SA pride firmly installed and reinforced, thank you Halakasha!!" For

Zibuyile Cerisa, also from Johannesburg, "A true African world cup [was] reflected." The reaction of overseas visitors was similarly encouraging: "Excellent—Out of this world—Unbelievable!" (Manesh from Kolkata, India); "What a superb exhibition!" (Dr. Michael Schaaf, Germany); "Love the hats, brilliant photos" (Ian, Oxfordshire, England); "Most astonishing designs and display" (Brian Moflofi, Brazil); "Wonderful exhibition, Powerful, reflects the beauty of the game" (Ambassador Rob De Vos, Netherlands).

Media responses to *Halakasha!* echoed the positive reactions of many visitors. The Johannesburg *Sunday Times* voted *Halakasha!* "Best Visual Art Experience" in 2010 and noted that the exhibition "proved that art can be accessible, thought provoking and fun."[5] For the *Mail and Guardian's* Jeremy Kuper, "This landmark exhibition is . . . an essential part of the football festivity taking place. And it provides an ideal way to explore the ways football has seeped into the popular consciousness."[6] A review of the exhibition in *Art South Africa* described it as "clearly devoted to the 'beautiful game' and a riotous jol [party] of a show."[7]

The exhibit emphasized spectators' self-branding in the colors and insignia of their favorite teams, a crucial part of the popular spectacle of football matches everywhere, including Africa. Local supporters also engage in performance in the form of face painting in the colors of their chosen teams. The *makarapa* helmet, a revamped plastic safety helmet, has become a ubiquitous accessory for South African supporters. These helmets are transformed into ritual headdresses by cutting them open and heat modeling them into insignia and branding associated football clubs.

A large installation of hundreds of garish *makarapas*, grouped into a circular raked formation mimicking a stadium, greeted visitors to the exhibition in the central atrium space in a visually loud but literally silent equivalent of a match experience. (The Standard Bank Gallery is divided into two downstairs rooms with a central space for projections and a large upper floor that is approached via left and right staircases. The upper level consists of a high-volume central circular atrium punctured with four sections that extend to the outer rectangular walls.)

The vuvuzela is a fairly recent addition to contemporary South African soccer matches. The sound of thousands of plastic horns being blown at once in a stadium is like a deafening swarm of bees, attesting to the massive support and enthusiasm of the games' ardent supporters. A site-specific installation featuring the vuvuzela was commissioned from two young artists, Rodan Kane Hart and Murray Kruger. Their work presented a number of vuvuzelas cast from cement using soil gathered from each of the new stadiums around the country, creating a variety of textures. A single solid cement vuvuzela was mounted inside a glass display cabinet alongside broken fragments displayed as if they were fossils excavated from a distant past and labeled "Silence" (the wish of many weary spectators by the end of the tournament).

Halakasha! also featured a selection of Nigerian Andrew Dosunmu's photographs of fans in a range of ingenious disguises—religious prophets, drummers and musicians, magicians, cross-dressers, tribal chiefs, and military characters. The exhibition represented Dosunmu's work documenting supporters of African soccer over the preceding eight years, including fans at the 2010 African Nations Cup in Luanda, Angola. The exhibition juxtaposed some of the traditional costumes and instruments that appeared in Dosunmu's works with similar objects in the Standard Bank permanent collections of African art housed at the Wits University Art Museum. Such items included drums from Angola and Ghana, woven fiber costumes, and masks. Installations also included items from Zulu women's traditional dress, including an *isidwaba* (married woman's skirt made from cowhide) and an *isicholo* (married woman's headdress) from the Wits and Standard Bank collections of African art. The hat and skirt were displayed in a glass case next to a life-sized photograph by Pieter Hugo of a Zulu male supporter of a hugely popular Johannesburg team, the Orlando Pirates, founded in 1937. The man was dressed as a Zulu woman, bare-chested with the exception of a black brassiere and wearing an *isidwaba* and *isicholo* wrapped in a black-and-white Pirates scarf.

One of the downstairs gallery spaces showed a wall of twelve striking life-sized black-and-white portraits of gay female footballers by gay activist photographer Zanele Muholi. Her controversial photographs of lesbians offended former arts and culture minister Lulu Xingwana, who deemed them "pornographic" and walked out of the exhibit.[8] Elsewhere in the exhibit, Kenyan photojournalist Antony Kaminju documented the elaborate costumes of Orlando Pirates and Kaizer Chiefs supporters. The performances and disguises assumed by supporters in the matches often take on a religious or mystical air. Temporarily transformed into priests, *sangomas* (diviners), wizards, and other mystical beings, fans cheer, dance, divine, and perform elaborate rituals in an attempt to improve their teams' fate.

In the center of the *makarapa* stadium at the heart of the exhibit was a raised altar-like circular platform covered in fake green turf on which six large freestanding woodcarvings were displayed. The carvings included Jackson Hlungwani's imposing *Hand of God*, which alludes to an often-entertained rumor of divine intervention in football. The match in question was the epic June 22, 1986, World Cup quarterfinal between Argentina and England: Diego Maradona scored using his hand, but astoundingly, the goal was allowed to stand. A few minutes later, Maradona added a mesmerizing second goal, subsequently voted "Goal of the Century," and Argentina went on to win the match, 2–1. At the postmatch press conference, Maradona attributed the fortuitous leniency of the referee on his first goal to "God's hand."

The altar included two other works from Hlungwani's *Christ Playing Football* series, a large block-like figure by that name from the Iziko Museum collection in Cape Town, and a smaller figure, *Christ Putting His Right Foot Forward*, as well as three carved wooden sculptures of football players by Nelson Mukhuba, a Venda-speaking artist who died in 1987. Other important sculptures included in the exhibition were Johannes Segogela's *Nkosi Sikelele*, depicting the Bafana Bafana team, its management, and a towering central figure of Nelson Mandela (wearing a Bafana jersey), with all the figures depicted lined up with their right arms patriotically covering their hearts while singing the South African national anthem. Other sculptures included a pair of Kevin Brand's large bronze replicas of *Füssball Players*, modeled from the figures of the universally known game of table soccer, placed centrally against a backdrop of vertical stripes in a pattern of colors taken from the flags of the qualifying African teams.

Paintings ranged from Gerhard Bhengu's 1926 watercolors of British colonial soldiers in striped kits playing football from the Killie Campbell Collections (perhaps the oldest football paintings by an African artist) and Durant Sihlali's watercolor of footballers on a street in Kliptown, near Soweto, to Mary Wafer's brooding oil painting of a floodlit football pitch at night. Joachim Schönfeldt's contemporary township scenes of the newly revamped Soccer City Stadium and the reconstructed Orlando Stadium in Soweto are painted on panels carved from old wooden doors and hand-embossed to resemble an interlacing wooden band, or ribbon. This band forms one continuous, infinite line that knots, crosses, and intersects itself to form an intricate arrangement of five convex circular shields on which the landscape is painted in oil. Each of these landscape paintings was completed over several days, working in situ.

Popular street art was represented by painted barber signs by O. A. Heavy from Teshie, a coastal town in Ghana, and Bruno N. Bihiza from the Democratic Republic of Congo. These signs seemed to say, "With a Samuel Eto'o crop or a Didier Drogba Afro-mullet or a Cristiano Ronaldo cut, you, too, can be just like them."[9] A selection of posters from the official FIFA collection of specifically commissioned prints by world-renowned artists was also exhibited, including William Kentridge's overhead kick and Kay Hassan's *Swanker Ball*.

A projected installation conceived by photographer Sally Gaule involved setting up a website inviting public intervention in the form of looped still images taken from cellphones. The photos were uploaded weekly and projected onto a screen on the floor bordered by green Astroturf outlined by white lines like those of a football field. Simon Gush's video installation *In the Company Of* featured a thirty-seven-minute video shot in Belgium of football players from various countries and speaking various languages as they attempted to play a match while negotiating railway tracks.

Halakasha! also displayed the role of spirituality and religion in local football. This distinctive element of the African game, as historian Peter Alegi shows, blurred the boundaries between the worlds of the rural and the urban, the traditional and the modern, Africa and the West.[10] In Durban in the earlier part of the twentieth century, for example, purificatory traditional Zulu practices previously performed by nineteenth-century *amabutho* (age regiments) before military encounters became part of the prematch rituals. The teams would camp together the night before a match around a fire and sleep naked together while being given *umuthi* (traditional medicine) by an *inyanga* (traditional healer). The morning before the match, players would drink a strong mixture followed by a vomiting (cleansing) ritual similar to those practiced by Zulu soldiers before going into battle. The symbolic reenactment of prebattle ritual had an important function in the construction of team spirit and confidence. *Isangoma* (diviners) and other specialists from different language groups across South Africa would use traditional medicine and ritual practices to ensure that their favored teams would win and to protect them from the magic of rival religious specialists. Prematch rituals could involve the throwing of bones to predict the outcome. Healers would strengthen the players by preparing *umuthi* to be rubbed on their legs.

Halakasha! featured examples of items associated with divination practices, including Tsonga beadwork worn by a traditional healer and a divination bowl with a full set of divining objects, a gourd with Zulu medicines for winning a match, and a Xhosa diviner's hat and fly whisk used in divining rituals. Pieter Hugo photographed an Orlando Pirates fan, Petrus Pamko, holding the leg bone from a large animal and a fly whisk; smaller bones dangle from his ears as he imitates a *sangoma*, illustrating the manner in which fans become bricoleurs, freely borrowing from their cultures' spiritual treasuries. A 1959 *Drum* photo captured the slaughtering of a sheep the night before a match for good luck; the caption explained, "Many footballers used to spend the night in the open in cemeteries." Photographs of fans in all sorts of "ecclesiastical trappings, such as mitres, crosses and Bibles—even a mock telephone so modern-day self-appointed prophets may 'call the gods'" brought home the central role of spirituality and religion in football cultures across Africa.[11] Upstairs, an image by Andrew Dosunmu caught Nigerian fans holding a chicken with its wings outstretched; the creature had been drenched in green paint. The same fans were denied access to the Nigeria-Argentina World Cup match at Ellis Park Stadium in Johannesburg after they were caught trying to smuggle in their "lucky" chicken.

The exhibition included a number of other images carefully selected from *Drum* magazine, which was probably the most widely circulated periodical aimed at black South Africans and a very influential outlet for black writing and photography during the apartheid era.[12] White rule in South Africa banished black people geographically to townships (impoverished urban ghettoes) and bantustans (rural "tribal" reserves). The best recreation facilities and soccer grounds in the country were off-limits to black people. Reflecting on the conditions for black Africans in the 1950s, famous *Drum* writer Lewis Nkosi remarked, "The lives that blacks were living were pretty appalling. One could not wait for the revolution to come along and rescue one from this kind of impoverished life. So anything that came along to provide the fantasy was welcome."[13] Football and the prospect of weekend excitement offered respite from the gloomy conditions. Endless debates regarding football offered a welcome distraction from life's general hardships. Sporting arenas provided a platform in which blacks could fight various forms of oppression; on the playing fields and in the role of supporters and fans, many black South Africans could express their abilities and creativity.

Although the effects of apartheid often devastated black South Africans, moments of inspiration still occurred in urban and social life. Not many people can claim to have captured the dichotomies of daily existence better than photographs from *Drum*, which are now owned by the Bailey History Archives. As the film producer Desiree Markgraff aptly notes, "The South Africa that the world has come to love—the South Africa that is loudmouthed, fast-talking and free-spirited had its gestation between the 1940s and 1980s in spaces hidden from the world."[14] Even in a place as brutal as Robben Island prison, football was taken very seriously. Political prisoners fought and won the right to play the game, which provided a rare opportunity for enjoyment and created a sense of unity and structure.[15] The exhibition displayed a selection of documents from the prisoners' football association as well as handmade football badges, which are permanently housed at Robben Island Museum/Mayibuye Archive at the University of the Western Cape. Through these invaluable historical photographs, the exhibition and its accompanying catalog not only celebrated the country's hosting of the 2010 World Cup but also honored the achievement of a nonracial, democratic South Africa.

As Karin Preller noted in a review of *Halakasha!*, the visual spectacle in the exhibition was both critically and intellectually challenging. Admitting that she had been apprehensive about such a large-scale exhibition dedicated solely to football, Preller, a lecturer at the University of Johannesburg, found that "the exhibition exceeded expectations and circumvented pitfalls that could easily have resulted in forced and literal connections between the works on display."[16] She also found that the show was thoughtfully curated, resulting in a compelling visual manifestation of the history and rituals associated with football in South Africa and the continent as a whole. For Preller, "The exhibition succeeded in situating contemporary African art and visual culture in a global context."[17]

Artist Anthea Moys directed a special performance at the Standard

Bank Gallery during one of the most cathartic moments of the 2010 World Cup. Decked out in their full regalia, fans of Chiefs and Pirates, the country's two most popular clubs in the country, staged a mock battle around the central sculptures on the altar in the circular atrium. About a week before the event was to take place, we realized that we had made a terrible mistake—the performance was to be staged at exactly the same time as the crucial match between South Africa and France in Bloemfontein! To avoid scuttling the performance, we decided to show the match live in the exhibition space so that our guests could enjoy both spectacles. After watching South Africa beat France 2–1 but nevertheless fail to advance to the next round, the excited crowd was in the appropriate mood for the rowdy confrontation. During the chaotic procession around the gallery, Chiefs and Pirates fans' paraphernalia slowly began to unravel, leaving a trail of debris similar to the aftermath of a marquee match. It was a fitting celebration of what the exhibition set out to achieve.

NOTES

1. Ahmed Kathrada, *Memoirs* (Cape Town: Zebra, 2008), 371, quoted in Peter Alegi, "'A Nation to Be Reckoned With': The Politics of World Cup Stadium Construction in Cape Town and Durban, South Africa," *African Studies* 67, 3 (2008): 397.

2. Steven Dubin, "Final Whistle," *Art South Africa* 9, 1 (2010): 72–76.

3. Janet Smith, "Football through the Artists' Eyes," *Saturday Star*, June 19, 2010.

4. James quoted in Chris Thurman, "Poor Relations?," in *Sport versus Art: A South African Contest*, ed. Chris Thurman (Johannesburg: Wits University Press, 2010), 8.

5. *Sunday Times*, December 26, 2010.

6. Jeremy Kuper, "Laduuuuuuuuuuuuuuuma!," *Mail and Guardian Online*, July 6, 2010, http://mg.co.za/article/2010-7-6-laduuuuuuuuuuuuuuuma, accessed August 10, 2011.

7. Dubin, "Final Whistle."

8. Samples of Muholi's work can be viewed on her website: http://www.zanel emuholi.com/photography.htm, accessed July 22, 2011. See also John Turnbull, "From Johannesburg, Lesbian Footballers Chosen to Play, Choosing to Live," June 14, 2010, http://www.theglobalgame.com/blog/2010/06/from-johannesburg-lesbian-footballers-chosen-to-play-choosing-to-live/, accessed August 12, 2011.

9. Kuper, "Laduuuuuuuuuuuuuuuma!"

10. Peter Alegi, *Laduma!: Soccer, Politics and Society in South Africa* (Pietermaritzburg: University of KwaZulu-Natal Press, 2004).

11. Dubin, "Final Whistle," 73.

12. Michael Chapman, ed., *The Drum Decade: Stories from the 1950s* (Pieter-maritzburg: University of Natal Press, 2001).

13. Alegi, *Laduma!*, 87. See also Lewis Nkosi, *Home and Exile* (London: Long-mans, 1965); Lindy Stiebel and Liz Gunner, eds., *Still Beating the Drum: Critical Perspectives on Lewis Nkosi* (Johannesburg: Wits University Press, 2006).

14. Desiree Markgraff, unpublished proposal for a television series (Bomb Shelter Production Company, 2009).

15. For more on the Makana Football Association on Robben Island, see Chuck Korr and Marvin Close, *More Than Just a Game: Football v. Apartheid* (London: Collins, 2008).

16. Karin Preller, "Review," *de Arte* 82 (2010): 66–71.

17. Ibid.

Soccer Bleu

The View from Paris

JOHN SAMUEL HARPHAM

ON A QUIET CORRIDOR of a street, perched at the top of a hill sixty-three meters above the city of Paris, there is a bar named Le Village. Like the surrounding neighborhood, which is tucked in between the high-rises and boulevards of the southeast part of the city, the bar is modest. The food is edible, and after slight renovations recently, the sign out front is neon. The bar has a small dark back room, and off it is a place for betting on horses. But the main action goes on in the rectangular front room, which opens onto the street through three full-length windows. Le Village is not in the Michelin guide. But precisely because of its ordinariness, the bar can be a kind of portal into the complexities of France, soccer, and the ways in which the two throw light on each other.

Appropriately enough, I cannot recall the first time I stooped under the bar's low entrance and walked inside. But at some point in the summer of 2008, while a student in Paris, I began spending long afternoons at the bar, and I found I could not stay away. My compulsion to go there every day puzzled my friends, my professors, and most of all the bar's regulars, who still look at me like a stranger. But these were the days of the European Championship soccer tournament, and I became transfixed by the soccer talk in the bar. When my studies ended, I returned home, but on the eve of the World Cup in June 2010, I boarded a plane for Paris to settle back in at Le Village.

With this intention, on a gray Thursday evening in the middle of June, I took the orange metro line to where it dead-ends at a traffic circle in the Thirteenth Arrondissement, walked a block past travel agents and wine stores, negotiated a six-way stoplight, and walked two more blocks on Rue de la Butte aux Cailles until the familiar sight of Le Village, a squat and hollow structure, came up on my left. It was 7:30 p.m., and I was early.

In an hour, the French national team would meet Mexico in Les Bleus' second game of the World Cup, but now the bar was almost empty. Sound muted, a game show played on the televisions, and the paper soccer balls strung up on the walls were flapping in the breeze. Six days earlier, in their first match of the World Cup, Les Bleus had played Uruguay to a scoreless draw.[1] Despite its talent, the team was struggling and would have to collect itself tonight to advance.

This was, in other words, not a game to come early for; skepticism was the appropriate position. But considering that in the weeks to come this tournament would become known in France simply as Le Désastre, this was a prelapsarian moment in the history of French soccer. Considering, moreover, that tonight's events would open up that abyss, this was *the* moment before the fall. I read *Le Monde* and sipped a beer, and Le Village continued to feel like the inside of a Dali painting.

The game began almost unnoticed, catching off guard what had become just moments before a humming, huddling, gathering crowd; the field shuddered to life in a frenzy. Ribéry was knocked down at midfield; Mexico hit the post, but the play was offside; a combination of passes sprung Evra, the French captain, streaking for goal. He was brought down with a foul—a chance!—but Anelka, an imposing French forward of uncertain commitment, sent the free kick flying over the Mexican net. A soft backward pass for France was cleared just in time, a breakaway shot for Mexico missed high, Ribéry stole a pass and rushed down the left side before running himself into a corner. A set of clever, quick passes freed Ribéry to drive a cross spinning in front of the Mexican goal, but no one was there to meet it. Mexico gathered the ball, recovered, and attacked on a high pass deep into the French side. Twenty-five minutes in, the field was a flurry of little dramas and no score.

As the first half churned on in this way, the bar fell into a kind of rapture. The old man across from me, whose hair and beard almost met up near the middle of his face, dug into a plate of steak frites between long gazes at the television. Across the room, a stranger with graying, gelled hair tried to kiss a younger woman. The owner of the bar, Daniel

Bouldoyré, who speaks in a chuckling Auvergne accent understood by only a handful of regulars, approached two men to my left, and great amusement followed concerning a "beer" and a "championship." Most of the patrons in the bar stared at the game in silence, arms crossed, chins up, reacting to every shift of momentum. This first half—with the rhythmic expansion and contraction of the field, the evenness of the struggle—was for these men the height of pleasure and the point of the game.

Not many of the men in Le Village had played soccer with distinction, but almost all had grown up playing the game—in parks, at school, in the army, and in neighborhood clubs. Playing soccer had been for them a metronome to mark off the stages of life. And when they watched it now, they saw the game with a player's sensibility. Soccer was for them neither art nor war; it was almost nothing at all other than a complex of internal tensions. Back and forth, tac-tac-tac, pass, pass, defenders bearing down, escape, pass, run on to it, and so on—the idea being to put oneself in the position of the man on the field and imagine. The name they had for the highest form of soccer was the *beau jeu*, or beautiful game, and it signified to them the style of play that was most immersed in the inner importance of the contest. The *beau jeu* was about the honesty of total commitment, the difficulty of fatigue, the courage of coming back, and the way in which individuals come together around a common aim. Artistry was nice; winning was good, even very good. But the men in the bar most valued surrender to the act of the game. I had been in the bar for many mediocre matches. Tonight was the first time I saw the *beau jeu*.

The ethic of the *beau jeu* runs throughout the culture of French soccer like rebar, guiding it in a hundred hidden ways and finally helping to explain one of the most striking aspects of soccer in France today—the resentment of 1998. That year, Les Bleus, playing at home, won their first World Cup. In the aftermath of the triumph, according to historian Laurent Dubois, the ethnically diverse French side was "immediately tied to a powerful, even utopian sense that the victory represented and promised a profound social and political transformation, one that would release France from inequality and racism and allow a new society to flourish."[2] *Black-blanc-beur*, a phrase describing the team's black, white, and North African composition, became the slogan of the day and the model for a new France.

Today, 1998 seems far off. With each passing World Cup, it becomes clearer that no "new society" will flourish. Yet for the men in the bar, the important lesson of that moment, as they call it, is not that French society will never change but that soccer must not be enlisted to change it—it is nothing more than an independent act, a beautiful game. The most knowledgeable fans in the bar refused even to speak about the cultural impact of that World Cup. In the bar, soccer at its best is not significant, only perfect; the events of 1998 have dissolved into short-hand for a time when culture threatened craft.

We found ourselves sunk in the appreciation of this craft, when, with the half nearing on the still scoreless game, both teams were visibly tiring. The ball was puttering around in the midfield. Ribéry extracted himself from a defender and sprinted down the sideline, but with no result. It was halftime.

The people in the bar emptied onto the street to smoke in the chilly evening. All around, exhausted men from other bars were spilling out onto the sidewalk to do the same, as if the buildings themselves were breathing them out in a deep exhalation. Halftime was my favorite part of the game, because the men were willing to talk. But tonight I was too worn out for conversation, and so I walked up and down the cobble-stone Rue de la Butte aux Cailles past the crowds of the Taverne de la Butte, the Dandelion, and the Mocking Blackbird.

Until the mid-nineteenth century, the neighborhood of the Butte aux Cailles, which includes the street and the surrounding hill, was a semirural tangle of shacks on the banks of a stream, La Bièvre. Most residents of the hill were preindustrial laborers of various sorts and traveling merchants known as *chiffoniers*, who scavenged and resold scraps of cloth. In 1860, the Butte was incorporated into the city, along with the rest of the Thirteenth Arrondissement. Under the direction of Baron Haussmann, the architect of modern Paris, reform soon followed. Much of the arrondissement was cut through with boulevards and metro lines, and the river was canalized and built over, the pace of modernization resulting in part from the city's desire to control the Thirteenth, whose leading roles in the 1848 revolutions and 1871 Paris Commune had earned it a reputation as an independent working-class area. During this period, the Thirteenth acquired the crowded squalor of the industrializing city but little of its charm.

Today, much of the Thirteenth has the ahistorical look of many North American big cities: loud commercial boulevards, tall white apartment buildings, and a large population of recent immigrants. But the Butte aux Cailles is more or less the same. It is wealthier than before, and the *chiffoniers* have disappeared. But the streets still run like veins over the hill, many unchanged from before the annexation. Most of the residents are artists, merchants, and workers. The Butte, they say with pride, is *populaire*, or of the people. On summer evenings, festivals take place in the streets, and the hill again seems like a hamlet on the outskirts of a city.

This was one of those evocative nights. The hum along the street was an echo of that old Butte aux Cailles, resting in the shade of the stream. Le Village, too, was a distillery of that past. The clientele came from all walks of life, and I generally could not tell a man's occupation from his appearance, but the regulars were older and more solidly middle class than at the surrounding bars. They were almost all male—a little ripple of excitement went through the men in the bar whenever a woman walked in. There was no music, and no one spoke English. Le Village was a place for casually employed journalists, construction workers, philosophy professors, architects, and retired accountants to come for a drink and a sandwich, see the old crowd, shake hands. As I made my way back to the bar, halftime was ending, and the smoke-filled street was emptying back inside.

Play had resumed by the time I returned to my seat in a corner of the front room. The game was again swinging wildly from end to end, until, out of a characterless exchange in the midfield, a breakthrough. A French midfielder, Malouda, brought the ball over to the left side and passed it to Evra, who flicked it behind him to Ribéry, who laid it back for Malouda, who had kept running toward the goal, and who, with one preparatory dribble, clobbered the Jabulani ball on goal. The Mexican goalkeeper tipped it over the crossbar. But here was the *beau jeu* in its purest form!

And at this moment, a man I had never seen before stumbled into the bar. Taking note of the play, he loudly chanted, "Allez la France! Allez la France!" and waved his arms, exhorting the bar to join in. The men looked away. A few approached the drunk soothingly and asked him to stop. He did, and the men guided him into a seat. In the back room another fan rang a cowbell and called out "Allez les Bleus!" He, too, was chided and calmed down. Now, at the point of peak excitement in the game, the bar sat in silence.

The men had been put off by the drunkard's indiscretion, but a more fundamental taboo also hung over the quiet bar, a taboo that cuts to the heart of what makes French soccer culture distinctive. The only other time the bar dropped into that discomforting quiet during a match was just before it began, when La Marseillaise was played. From my first game in the bar, I had been struck by the men's indifference to the national anthem. When it came on just before the kickoff of each game, their focus would go slack. Almost no one watched, and no one sang. When I asked the men about this moment, almost every one of them answered with the same universalizing response, "On n'est pas patriot en France" (One is not patriotic in France), delivered without condescension, just as a fact. Their distrust of patriotism was also the key to this midgame silence. The drunkard's real offense had been what he had said rather than the way he had said it.

So with order restored, the game continued, and conversations resumed. The French produced nothing from a corner kick they had earned. And then, in the sixty-fourth minute, without even the courtesy of a warning, a short pass up the middle of the field found Mexican forward Javier "Chicharito" Hernández all alone thirty yards from the French goal. He gathered the ball, slid past the French keeper, Lloris, and knocked it home for a goal. 1–0.

The air went out of the bar. The man across from me looked up from his steak and, seeing the goal, slumped down in his chair until he was almost under the table. Claude and Manuel, two old friends who watched every game together, went slack-jawed, their chins almost dipping into their round mugs of beer. For a time, the team seemed awoken by the goal, and for a time, we got behind them—parties to the resistance. ("2–1 pour la France," said a fat man in the opposite corner of the bar, to general satisfaction.) Yet within minutes of the goal, without any decisive or singular event, it became clear that the game had fallen out of reach with quiet finality.

Soccer is a game of impressions, a back-and-forth flow in which many of the essential events and qualities cannot be measured and the one definite measure, the score, is a crude summary grafted onto a far more intricate phenomenon. By looking at a box score, you can re-create a baseball game. But understanding a soccer match is hardly statistical. It is a matter of constructing, from the chaos of a thousand little gestures, a sense of what is happening. And after those few promising minutes following the goal, without knowing exactly where it had come from, there came a growing sense that something had been unhinged on the French side. The effort that had seemed in the first half like initiative now seemed like selfishness; what had seemed like patience now seemed like a crippling inability to strike. Ribéry was dancing over the ball, shoulders hunched, apparently with no idea where the goal was. The men in the bar later told me that they, too, had seen everything collapse during these minutes; it was "the descent into the Underworld," one mathematics professor said.

It struck us as no surprise, then, when, in the seventy-eighth minute, Eric Abidal brought down Pablo Barrera in the French box and thirty-seven-year-old Cuauhtémoc Blanco converted the penalty. After the goal, conversation erupted in the bar about the French coach, Domenech; Anelka; and the French Football Federation, the salaries of all these people, the weather, the most recent political scandal, and how all these things were, in their own little ways, crummy as hell. With the game an afterthought, the bar became a roiling din. The beer, it became clear, had won a championship, and a trophy was brought out. People peering through the windows from the street saw the score, recoiled, and polemicized. The bartender went out to smoke. The bartender's wife went out to smoke. Everyone went out to smoke. The young man next to me with a missing front tooth threw up his hands melodramatically: "Bye, bye, la France."

Whenever I talked to the bar patrons about soccer, I would begin by asking them if they were *supporteurs*, or fans, of the team.[3] They almost never were—at most they were *supporteurs* "sometimes," "slightly," or "not right now." They might talk passionately, even compulsively, about the team, but not being a *supporteur*—not wearing costumes to games, not weeping ridiculously over losses, not feeling as if their abject selves were in play in every match—was a point of honor with them. Their interest was analytical. In wins, they seemed to admire without celebration; in losses, they disengaged without remorse. (Five days later, when France's World Cup ended in a loss to South Africa, the small crowd in the bar abandoned Les Bleus and cheered on its opponents—satisfied, in some abstract sense, to see weakness punished.) To observe, to critique, to turn the team over in all its dimensions—this was the ideal in the bar. The *supporteur's* loyalty was a sign of ignorance. The clear vision of faults, especially when the faults were so clear, was delicious.

The men in the bar spent the final minutes of the game in a daze. The French players fouled the Mexicans viciously and several times booted the ball high into the stands, disgusted with the rules, the boundaries, and the entire situation. But by this time, almost no one in the bar was watching.

When the game ended, the patrons stared straight ahead for a while, and no one said a word. Then they stood up, gathered their coats, and prepared to leave. "There is no happiness," the man across from me muttered, his steak frites finished. Two men sitting at the bar whom I'd arranged to meet after the game said they just could not talk with me right now, so sorry about this, and waved me off. Outside it was night-time, and I leaned against a car and watched the men leave in groups of two and three. In France, the acidity directed at the national team draws equally from ironic detachment and real emotional investment. More of the latter, and no one would criticize; more of the former, no one would care.

The men were walking away from the game now, but in a larger sense they were also leaving soccer. In the United States, soccer is a favored sport of the affluent and the intellectual. Less brutal than football, more graceful than basketball, global in its scope, soccer is taken to be the purest and most cosmopolitan of all the sports we know.[4] But in Le Village, soccer carries none of this charm. The 2010 team's disgrace only confirmed the men's sense that soccer has become a study in contemporary decadence. It is the artless game, played by uneducated and overpaid prima donnas and surrounded by a creeping *footbusiness*. We see soccer as the most European sport, but they see it as the most American, a mass spectacle with a degraded celebrity culture. And in a culture where it is impossible to overstate the distaste for money and all that money brings, the hyperprofessionalized state of soccer today is grating.

There is also one less-principled factor behind the bar's distaste for soccer. In recent years, more and more of the best French players have been black. In many forms, in many ways, race and racism were a fact of life in discussions at Le Village and France as a whole about what was wrong with the team.[5] Many in France blamed the team's disintegration on the "bad boy" culture of the black and Arab housing projects that produced many of France's soccer stars. As sociology professor and Village regular Yves Lichtenberger explained to me, "The multicultural mix [*métissage*] that appeared in 1998 as richness now appears as rottenness."

The men in the bar do not jeer. They are never violent. Most are like Xavier Touzé, a middle-aged father I got to know while we watched many games together. Touzé's first memory of Les Bleus is of the free-scoring (white) midfielder Michel Platini, who played in the late 1970s and 1980s. Touzé spoke in clipped phrases, and with each sentence it seemed he would stop. "I am not such a fan of the team these days," he said. "The team is very colored. Do you know what I mean? It is black. I am not racist, I am French—you are writing this down, correct? But I just cannot identify with this team."

The bar was soon empty. In the cool June night, I started to walk down Rue de la Butte aux Cailles back toward the metro. Along the way, orange light from the street lamps shimmered on the cobblestone. The patrons from the other bars were still milling about and talking. But the hum from before the game was gone. Les Bleus were not yet out of the tournament, but there was a finality in this defeat that would be hard to overcome. Turning off the street, I was alone now. For better or worse, it felt like an ordinary summer night in Paris.

NOTES

1. For more on French football, see Geoff Hare, *Football in France: A Cultural History* (Oxford: Berg, 2003).

2. Laurent Dubois, *Soccer Empire: The World Cup and the Future of France* (Berkley, University of California Press, 2010), 157.

3. On the distinction between fans and supporters, see Richard Giulianotti, "Supporters, Followers, Fans, and Flaneurs: A Taxonomy of Spectator Identities in Football," *Journal of Sport and Social Issues* 26, 1 (2002): 25–46.

4. Cf. Franklin Foer, *How Soccer Explains the World: An Unlikely Theory of Globalization* (New York: HarperCollins, 2004), esp. 235–48.

5. John Hoberman, "France's Soccer Debacle Lifts Lid on Racial Tensions," *Foreign Policy*, July 2010, http://www.foreignpolicy.com/articles/2010/07/01/le_scandal, accessed July 29, 2011; Paul Silverstein, "The Tragedy and Farce of French Football Politics," *Social Text*, 2010, http://www.socialtextjournal.org/periscope/2010/07/the-tragedy-and-farce-of-french-football-politics.php, accessed August 24, 2011.

PART 3

Spectatorship, Patriotism, Nationalism, and Pan-Africanism

Ghana's Black Stars

A Fifty-Year Journey to the
World Cup Quarterfinals

CRAIG WAITE

IT'S THE 120TH MINUTE—the last gasp of extra time—of the World Cup quarterfinal between Ghana and Uruguay at Soccer City. The game is tied 1–1 as Asamoah Gyan steps up to take the most important shot in African soccer history. I could not believe that Ghana's Black Stars were about to become the first African team to reach the World Cup semifinals. After surprising Serbia 1–0 in their opening match and deservedly beating the United States 2–1 in the round of sixteen, a victory over Uruguay in the quarterfinals would cement Ghana's place as sentimental favorites. I was sitting in my living room in Bloomington, Indiana, half a world away from the events on the screen. Having spent several years researching and writing a doctoral dissertation on Ghana's football history, I wished I were back in Accra's Independence Square to witness the upcoming victory celebration—dancing, singing, and the euphoric Ghanaian brand of public revelry on an unprecedented scale. In that instant, I thought of how what was about to happen was not simply the culmination of a four-year rebuilding project or a lucky tournament run for the national team. It was much, much more important than that.

Gyan's penalty was a moment embedded in a century-long historical process of Africa's adoption and adaptation of a European game. A Ghanaian victory held the potential to constitute and represent African equality and achievement on a global stage. But Gyan missed! His penalty struck the top of the crossbar and went over the goal. Oh no! The encroaching ecstasy of victory was replaced by a sickening feeling that a penalty shoot-out defeat was cruelly approaching. For Ghanaians and Africans who had embraced the Black Stars as the flag-bearers for the continent—South Africans had taken to calling the side BaGhana BaGhana—the anticlimactic shoot-out quickly confirmed those fears, leaving us pondering what might have been. I sought solace in the knowledge that Gyan and his teammates owed their brush with history in 2010 to Ghana's national football teams from fifty years earlier. Just like the 2010 team, the accomplishments of the first Black Star sides had showcased the possibilities of African independence and the game's capacity to generate national pride in Ghana as well as unity across the entire continent. For Ghana and, to some extent, Africa as well, the larger implications of the 2010 World Cup spectacle had roots in events that took place in the first decade of independence.

GHANA, FORMERLY KNOWN AS the Gold Coast, achieved independence from Britain in 1957, the first African nation south of the Sahara to do so. Within the next decade, most other African colonies freed themselves from the shackles of European rule. Today, most members of Ghana's national team play professionally for European clubs, but in the 1950s, none of them played overseas. In fact, none of them played professionally at all. Although British sailors had introduced football to the Gold Coast at the turn of the twentieth century, players and fans did not begin looking for new football opportunities overseas for a long time. Beginning in the 1930s, regular matches with representative teams from Nigeria served as the pinnacle of football competitions for much of the colonial period.[1] The Gold Coast touring team to Britain in 1951 marked the beginning of Ghana's integration into global soccer and perhaps an early expression of a growing nationalism at home.[2] In Britain, the Gold Coast squad lost nine of its ten matches. But that encounter with Europe became a turning point in the country's football history. It illuminated the broad possibilities that this hugely popular pastime could offer to a new nation struggling to create a cohesive national identity and acquire international recognition and to a ruling party, the Convention People's Party (CPP), eager to acquire greater political legitimacy.

Kwame Nkrumah, Ghana's first president and founder of the CPP, saw the distinct political and social advantages of promoting football.[3] In 1957, to improve football in independent Ghana, Nkrumah appointed Ohene Djan as the minister of the central organization of sports. Nkrumah also tasked Djan with enhancing the Ghanaian national team's international profile. Charles Kumi Gyamfi, a legendary player and coach, described in a 2008 interview with me in Accra how Nkrumah had hosted a formal dinner for the Black Stars before an international tournament. "At the end of it, the last word that he will give us was, 'Go and come, not with the shield, but on the shield!' It is a proverb. He was telling us . . . 'Go and die. Die and get the victory and I will like to see you come back carried on the shield.'"

Football in independent Ghana was both imported and exported, as international teams came to play in Ghana and the Black Stars traveled abroad. Throughout his presidency, Nkrumah invited clubs from Europe's best leagues were invited to play in Ghana. Djan and the Sports Council spent a lot of money hosting international teams and projecting an image of African football ascendency. For example, Sir Stanley Matthews toured Ghana with Blackpool in May 1957 and played alongside some of Ghana's best players in exhibition matches. Over the next decade the squads that toured Ghana included Real Madrid (five-time European champions between 1956–60), Moscow Dynamo, Fortuna Düsseldorf, West Ham United, and Vasco de Gama from Rio de Janeiro. At the same time, many African national teams as well as East Germany and an Italian select team of Serie C semiprofessionals played in Ghana.

The Black Stars were the first sub-Saharan African team to qualify for the Olympic Games, competing in Tokyo in 1964 and finishing a very respectable seventh in a field of sixteen teams. As other African colonies achieved nationhood in the 1960s, Ghana also hosted major football tournaments and used these competitions as a way of promoting newfound freedoms. Independence celebrations in Uganda, Kenya, and other African countries featured football tournaments that included Ghana. The Black Stars were invited to these celebrations not only because they were a terrific soccer team but also because Nkrumah's Ghana symbolized African freedom and pan-African unity. In the late 1950s and early 1960s, the Black Stars established themselves as models of African achievement and international success.

Hosting international football tournaments raised Ghana's global profile even more. Long before a World Cup was played in Africa, Ghana's political leaders began laying the foundation for precisely that possibility. In 1963, the African Nations Cup took place in Accra and Kumasi. This competition had been launched in 1957 in Sudan and pitted the best African national teams against one another. Ghanaians took great pride in hosting the fourth edition of the contest, the first time that West African teams participated. Ghana's victory at home helped legitimize CPP rule and sparked massive street celebrations not seen since 1957.

Nkrumah and other CPP politicians hoped that football triumphs would help assert Ghana's political leadership in postcolonial Africa. For this reason, Nkrumah employed Djan in his cabinet from 1958 to 1966 as director of the Central Organisation of Sport. Djan was also a member of several pioneering African sports institutions that worked to establish and legitimize pan-African sports competitions rivaling those found in Europe and elsewhere. In this capacity, Djan worked with sports representatives from other African countries to promote social and political awareness throughout the continent. As a member of FIFA's executive board in the 1960s, Djan played a key role in the group's decision to suspend the all-white Football Association of South Africa in 1964 as a consequence of the country's apartheid policy.[4]

Despite the efforts of many African players and officials in the 1960s, the World Cup continued to exclude African teams. Until 1970, FIFA refused to guarantee an African nation a berth in the final tournament. Qualification could only come through a playoff system weighted heavily against African teams. This demeaning treatment of newly independent and assertive African countries outraged Djan and other African football executives, who organized a boycott of the 1966 World Cup in England. The boycott paid dividends as FIFA finally guaranteed Africa a place in the finals for the first time at Mexico 1970.

On the domestic front, Nkrumah instructed Djan in 1960 to form the Real Republikans Football Club. The name was borrowed from Real Madrid, the best club team in the world at the time, but it had an added political connotation. Another name for the Republikans was Osagyefo's Own Club, and the letters *OOC* were stitched onto the front of players' uniforms. *Osagyefo* means "redeemer" in Twi, the most widely spoken Ghanaian language. Nkrumah was thus claiming the best players as his own and the national team as a symbol of his political strength. Real Republikans filled its ranks by poaching the two best players from other top Ghanaian sides, a decision that elicited mixed reactions from Hearts of Oak, Asante Kotoko, and other clubs. This all-star team of sorts competed in Ghana's top league in the early 1960s and gave the players, who came from different geographic regions, time and resources to gel as a team. These men forged friendships on and off the field that strengthened the quality of play of both Real Republikans and the Black Stars.

Since members of Real Republikans and the Black Stars were seen as Ghanaian ambassadors to the world, they were often employed by government agencies. Most members of the national team worked for the Farmers Council, Builders Brigade, or Sports Council. Employers frequently gave the footballers time off work to train. During difficult times, families of the Black Stars were financially supported. For example, when Edward Acquah's father died during the buildup to an important Black Stars match, Ghana's Sports Council took care of all funeral expenses.

Overseas tours both showcased Ghanaian football talent and lubricated friendly diplomatic relationships. In 1961, for example, the Black Stars became the first sub-Saharan African national team to tour Eastern Europe. Facing teams from the Soviet Union, West and East Germany, and Czechoslovakia as well as fellow West African travelers Nigeria and Mali, Ghana won twelve matches, lost four, and tied five. "The tour on the whole has helped dissipate some of the ignorant fallacies existing in Europe about Africa and Africans and, no doubt, the Black Stars," Djan recalled. "These uncontroversial sports ambassadors of Ghana, have put a case across in Europe for Africa."[5]

By the mid-1960s, Ghana's Black Stars had more than lived up to their grand expectations: They had won the 1963 African Nations Cup in Ghana and successfully defended their title in Tunisia two years later. The Black Stars had earned international respect and become the undeniable kings of African football.

So how do the Black Stars of the first decade of independence compare with the 2010 World Cup team? One obvious difference is that twenty-one of the twenty-three players on the 2010 World Cup squad were based overseas.[6] In the 1960s, every member of the Black Stars was based in Ghana. However, one important similarity is the race and nationality of the head coach. During the World Cup in South Africa, it was not hard to pick out the team's Serbian coach, Milovan Rajevac—a lone middle-aged white, European man surrounded by a dozen young black players on the bench. But the real story of interest is not why Ghana's 2010 coach was still a white European, just as had been the case fifty years earlier. The more fascinating question is why the decisions of Ghana's sports administrators involving coach selection today hark back to the ideologies of the 1950s. To better understand this philosophical return, we must consider the evolution of the Black Stars' coaching position.

During the historic 1951 tour of Britain, Ghana did not have a full-time coach, in keeping with common practice throughout the country: Prominent players (often captains) did most of the coaching. The 1951 touring team was presided over by football officials and administrators who focused on logistical work. But that tour became an integral step in the future development of African football coaching. Firsthand experience against quality European sides taught the Gold Coast players that they needed better training regimens and specialized equipment to compete on an international level.

Independence from Britain encouraged more independent thinking in terms of football styles and tactics. So that Ghana could become more competitive, Emmanuel F. K. Epton, who worked in London's Office of the High Commissioner for Ghana, was tasked in 1957 with selecting a permanent coach for the new Ghanaian national team. After a few months' work, George Ainsley became Ghana's first European coach. Ainsley, a former Sunderland, Bolton, and Leeds player with ties to the English Football Association, generated great enthusiasm and interest for "scientific football" among Ghanaian clubs and footballers. Ainsley preached a philosophy of ball control and short passing that ran contrary to the long-ball tactics employed by most Ghanaian players. In ten months, he increased nationwide interest in new scientific coaching methods.[7]

Ainsley was the first of three Europeans to coach the Black Stars between 1957 and 1961, a contingent that included Andreas Sjoberg of Sweden and Joseff Ember of Hungary. The general idea was that the Ghanaians would in the short run learn from the best European coaches available. But having foreigners coach the team proved counterproductive to Nkrumah's prominent philosophy that Africans were just as capable as Europeans. In 1958, a few months after Ainsley was hired as national team coach, two retiring members of the Black Stars, E. C. Briandt and James Adjaye, were sent to West Germany to study coaching at the Sports Academy of Cologne. This was the first step in a critical philosophical shift among sport officials and political leaders, who now sought to Africanize, or indigenize, the game in Ghana but to do so in dialogue with the wider football world. In the process, Ghana would create an African model for other newly independent countries to emulate. Nkrumah advocated African individualism and strength as well as the possibility of a United States of Africa. He envisioned sports as an extension of nationalism that "could mobilize the youth of the nation around a common identity . . . and create pride and self-respect in the people of Africa"[8] Nkrumah believed it was vital to show the rest of the world that if Europeans could do something, so could Africans.

After returning from West Germany in 1959, Adjaye and Briandt were deployed into regions of Ghana where football was woefully underdeveloped. Adjaye helped establish the game in the Northern and Brong-Ahafo regions, but Briandt, who had been coerced into going to Germany, was unhappy as a coach and soon resigned his position. In the wake of Adjaye and Briandt's experience, the Ghana Amateur Football Association sent a dozen more footballers to study coaching in West Germany and Czechoslovakia over the next few years. One of these men, Charles Kumi (C. K.) Gyamfi, embarked on a coaching course with Fortuna Düsseldorf in West Germany in 1961. He was asked to return to Ghana in 1962 as an assistant to Joseff Ember. Gyamfi then became the first Ghanaian head coach of the Black Stars when the team went to Uganda later that year to play for the Uhuru (Freedom) Cup.

Employing a local coach was highly unusual in Africa, both constituting and symbolizing Nkrumah's ideologies of Africanization and populism. European coaches initially were perceived as experts with greater experience than Ghanaian coaches, who had grown up playing the game but lacked professional training and cosmopolitan credentials. Overseas coaches had often studied the game, and many had attended formal coaching schools. But Gyamfi temporarily ended the trend of hiring Europeans.

During his tenure as Black Stars' head coach, Gyamfi took coaching courses abroad and invited foreign coaches to Ghana to share their ideas and expertise. For example, the *Daily Graphic*, Accra's main daily newspaper, reported on June 6, 1962, that Gyamfi had spent four weeks in the training camp of Brazil's national team to study its training methods and tactics. This choice made sense for two reasons. First, Brazil had won the World Cup in 1958 and 1962. Second, Ghana was preparing to host the 1963 African Nations Cup, a major political project. Gyamfi would be the only African head coach at the tournament, and when his Black Stars took the African title, the victory seemed to validate Nkrumah's vision and approach and to provide a model for other African nations. Gyamfi stayed on as coach of the Black Stars until the military coup of 1966, when he was summarily sacked because the new leadership associated Gyamfi with the old Nkrumah regime. Gyamfi ultimately spent the majority of his coaching career outside Ghana, including stints in Somalia, Kenya, and the Seychelles.

Throughout the 1960s, the helm of the Black Stars was manned by local coaches, yet in 2010, Europeans were again patrolling the sidelines in the form of Rajevac. The nationality of the Ghanaian national squad's coach is the subject of constant public and private debate within the country.[9] Former players as well as nonplayers often see the Black Stars' employment of a non-Ghanaian head coach as a reversal of philosophy and worry about how the team and the country are showcased to the world. During my research in Ghana, the country hosted the 2008 African Nations Cup, and many Ghanaians claimed that Egypt won the tournament because its team had an Egyptian head coach and most players came from Egyptian club teams. In other words, the popular view in Ghana is that success will be fleeting until the Ghana Football Association returns to the Nkrumahist football coaching philosophy. Yet people are also divided about the overwhelmingly overseas-based nature of the 2010 World Cup squad. Locals often publicly criticize these players for leaving Ghana for more lucrative contracts elsewhere, claiming that athletes are interested only in making as much money as possible. But critics also take obvious pride in watching their fellow countrymen compete for the world's best clubs against the world's best players.

Nkrumah's overthrow just two months after Ghana won its second consecutive African title changed the country's political landscape. Football heroes during Nkrumah's time were among the constituents swept aside by the new military rulers. The Real Republikans were disbanded. Some players were jailed. Gyamfi lost his job. Perceived as popular symbols of the ousted regime, many Black Stars players were dropped from the team. Generous government funding and political support for football also dried up. The Black Stars struggled for a while, although they won the Nations Cup in 1978 and 1982. At the youth level, Ghana won the under-seventeen World Cup in 1991 and 1995 and the under-twenty World Cup in 2009.

Today, walking down the streets of Accra or Kumasi or Sekondi, one can see many more Ghanaians wearing the jerseys of Chelsea, Manchester United, and Inter Milan than sporting the colors of the Ghanaian national team. This reality is more the result of player migration, the popularity of European satellite television, and expanding Internet access than the notion that Ghanaians are no longer very good footballers or are newcomers to the game. Nothing could be further from the truth. Such past greats as C. K. Gyamfi, Baba Yara, James Adjaye, Chris Briandt, Osei Kofi, and many others paved the way long before the fame and wealth earned by European-based Ghanaian stars Michael Essien, Asamoah Gyan, Sulley Muntari, and others. When Ghana came within a penalty kick of becoming the first African team to reach the World Cup semifinals in 2010, that success was born of the historical legacy of generations of Black Stars inspired by Nkrumah's nationalist and pan-Africanist call: "Go and die on the shield, and bring glory to Ghana!"

NOTES

1. For more details on African football history, culture, and politics, see Peter Alegi, *African Soccerscapes: How a Continent Changed the World's Game* (London: Hurst; Athens: Ohio University Press, 2010); Paul Darby, *Africa Football and FIFA: Politics, Colonialism, and Resistance* (London: Cass, 2002); Paul Dietschy and D. C. Kemo-Keimbou, *Africa and the Football World* (Paris: EPA, 2008).

2. Phil Vasili, *The First Black Footballer, Arthur Wharton, 1865–1930: An Absence of Memory* (London: Cass, 1998).

3. David Birmingham, *Kwame Nkrumah: The Father of African Nationalism* (Athens: Ohio University Press, 1998); Richard Rathbone, *Nkrumah and the Chiefs: The Politics of Chieftaincy in Ghana, 1951–60* (Accra: Reimmer; Athens: Ohio University Press; Oxford: Currey, 2000).

4. Peter Alegi, *Laduma!: Soccer Politics and Society in South Africa, from Its Origins to 2010* (Scottsville: University of KwaZulu-Natal Press, 2010); Paul Darby, "Africa and the World Cup: Politics, Eurocentrism, and Resistance," *International Journal of the History of Sport* 22, 5 (2005): 883–905.

5. Ohene Djan, *A Short History of Soccer in Ghana and the Rise of the Black Star Eleven* (Accra: n.p., 1964), 32.

6. Paul Darby, "'Go Outside': The History, Economics, and Geography of Ghanaian Football Labour Migration," *African Historical Review* 42, 1 (2010): 19–41.

7. On changing modes of play, see Jonathan Wilson, *Inverting the Pyramid: The History of Football Tactics* (London: Orion, 2008).

8. Darby, *Africa Football and FIFA*, 36.

9. The employment of European coaches, often of dubious quality, by African national teams has also been criticized elsewhere on the continent. For example, see Bea Vidacs, *Visions of a Better World: Football in the Cameroonian Social Imagination* (Berlin: LIT, 2010), 137–44.

To Sing or Not to Sing?

National Anthems, Football Obsessions, and Bafana Bafana's World Cup

CHRIS BOLSMANN

IN THE SPIRIT OF RECONCILIATION of a free South Africa, the new national anthem combined "Nkosi Sikelel' iAfrika" (God Bless Africa), a religious hymn turned liberation song originally composed by Enoch Sontonga in 1897, with two stanzas from "Die Stem," the national anthem used under apartheid. In 1988, as a student at Pretoria Boys High School, a whites-only institution except for the Malawian ambassador's son, I refused to sing "Die Stem." Four years later, I also refused to sing the parts of the anthem that included "Die Stem" when I first watched Bafana Bafana play against Cameroon, shortly after the country's re-admission into international football. I continued to refrain from singing that part of our national anthem at every one of the nearly fifty games I watched Bafana play over the next two decades.

But on June 11, 2010, I sang the full South African anthem at the opening match of the World Cup between South Africa and Mexico. High up in block 507, row Y, with a lump in my throat I had to pinch myself as I was witnessing the start of a World Cup in my country with my national team taking center stage. I was part of a football World Cup, the globe's biggest sporting event. I was "home," enjoying the game of the majority of South Africans. Boyhood dreams and obsessions were unfolding in front of me.

I was introduced to football as a six-year-old in Pretoria, apartheid South Africa's administrative capital and a bastion of Afrikaner nation-

109

alism. In sporting terms in the late 1970s and 1980s, Pretoria was synonymous with rugby, Loftus Versveld stadium, Northern Transvaal,
and the legendary number 10 fly-half, Naas Botha. Hatfield Primary
School, less than three kilometers from Loftus Versveld, was a typical
lower-middle-class school for English-speakers. Like the students at
every other whites-only English-speaking primary school in South Africa, we played football. I was not a keen runner, and Christopher, who
lived across the road and was five years older than me, was a goalkeeper.
So I became a goalkeeper and hardly ever played anywhere else.

In May 1979, Christopher and I watched the South African Broadcasting Corporation's live television broadcast of the English FA Cup
final between Arsenal and Manchester United. (National television
was still in its infancy in South Africa, having been introduced only in
1976.) A red team played against a yellow team, just like our table football game of Subbuteo played a few hours earlier (Arsenal won 3–2).
Like Arsenal's Pat Jennings and United's Gary Bailey, I wore a drab ol-
ive green goalkeeper jersey, as did Christopher—that was the standard
for goalkeepers at the time. I had a connection with United's Bailey, an
English-born South African who played for England twice in the mid-
1980s, but Christopher supported Arsenal. Since I did not like their
yellow shirts and I refused to be associated with the losing team and
goalkeeper, I did not have a team to support. (Christopher would never
let me live that one down.)

CHANGING SCHOOLS CAN BE TRAUMATIC, and leaving Hatfield for Pretoria
Boys High School was tough for me. Christopher had graduated in
1984, the year before I started, and most of my friends went to either
Clapham or Pretoria Technical High School. Worse still, Boys High
did not play football! "We" played rugby instead and did so quite well
and for a long time—more than one hundred years.[1] So as a new boy
at school, I had to choose between hockey and rugby. Hockey seemed
odd; rugby vaguely interesting. I was tall for my age group and was
shoved into the scrum—lock, to be precise—and I hated it. I was not
allowed to kick the ball or pass it; I was expected to push and push and
push.

Saturday meant playing rugby for Boys High (under-thirteen B or
C teams) in the morning and football for Club International in the
afternoon. I stopped playing rugby after a year and became an outcast

at school as a result of my love of football. Many years later, a Boys High headmaster explained to me in an interview that it was a matter of tradition and class that Boys High played rugby and would always do so. This proud institutional bias has endured despite the fact that several outstanding footballers have attended the school over the years, including Steve and Roy Wegerle and more recently Mark Fish and Phil Evans.

Club International was a neighborhood football club near my parents' house on Prospect Street. It had been established in the 1970s and leased its ground, known as "the Pound," from the city council. Despite a name with cosmopolitan ambitions and the occasional English, German, or Portuguese player, there was nothing particularly international about Club Inter; all of us were white South Africans. Black players were not permitted to play for white amateur teams, especially not in Pretoria's white suburbs.

Club International fielded a couple of junior teams and several senior teams. As I got older, I began to train and then play for the senior sides with players ten years older than me. It seemed that every football conversation revolved around English teams, usually Liverpool and Manchester United. I still recall two young players arriving for training at the Pound wearing Southampton and Aston Villa shirts, proclaiming their allegiance to these English clubs neither could tell me much about. I never quite understood this South African obsession with English teams, particularly since many of these supporters had never been to England and had no English family connections.[2] Since my father is German, my football allegiance drifted toward Germany. This heritage also meant that Harald "Toni" Schumacher, Cologne and West Germany's brilliant but brutal goalkeeper in the 1980s, became my hero.

Club Inter regularly struggled to field full teams, and in the mid-1980s, a time of revolutionary militancy and martial law in South Africa, black footballers were allowed to join our teams. Aubrey was one such player. He used to hang around the park near the Pound, and we would include him in our pickup games. He brought along his younger brother and a friend, and they joined our team. They were also much more skillful than any of our players and played with the juniors on Saturday mornings and the seniors in the afternoons. Aubrey introduced me to the Mamelodi Sundowns and the "other" Pretoria. Established in the early 1960s, the Sundowns became one of the country's most popular and successful professional football teams. The Sundowns were based in Aubrey's township of Mamelodi, adjacent to Pretoria, and my first visit to a black township was to watch the Sundowns at the H. M. Pitje Stadium in the mid-1980s. My initiation into the Sundowns gave me the privilege of seeing the extravagant (and white) Mark Anderson playing goal for the Brazilians, as the Sundowns were affectionately known because of their yellow shirts and blue shorts and crowd-pleasing playing style.

At around the same time, I joined a local restaurant and kitchen staff team run by Peter, a waiter at a Hatfield steakhouse. The Hatfield All Stars were a black team that practiced every afternoon or when Club Inter officials were not guarding the Pound's grass pitch against "illegal" games. The Hatfield All Stars played challenge matches in various black townships, where my expensive Uhlsport goalkeeper gloves were introduced to magic (*umuthi* in Zulu) and alternative ways of influencing the outcome of a match. Thanks to football and in spite of apartheid, I got to know many black players, fans, coaches, and supporters at a time when the only other black people I encountered were domestic workers, gardeners, and trash collectors. Interactions on the field of play made me much more aware of and sensitive to racial segregation and injustice.

Pretoria clubs and Transvaal teams have a long tradition of traveling to Durban, on the coast, in July to play against local teams and spend a weekend enjoying the beach and its attractions. On one such tour with Northern Transvaal, we were on the beach kicking a ball around. At this stage there was only one black player in our team, and one of the Durban lifeguards informed us that our black teammate was not permitted on this whites-only beach. Our team refused to tolerate this insult, and we all marched off the beach together. Football had become much more than a game to me; it was an obsession that shaped me socially and politically.

In the early 1990s, as the African National Congress and the National Party formally negotiated a transition from apartheid to democracy, Pretoria's hallowed rugby stadium, Loftus Versveld, started hosting matches of the racially integrated (and black-run) National Soccer League.[3] Welcoming professional football made good economic sense, despite vehement opposition from local whites. Sundowns played at Loftus against touring European opposition several times and increasingly played their league and cup fixtures there. These transformations were bound up with the growing economic purchase of South African football and of course the rise of black political power.

Much has been made of Nelson Mandela's appearance at the 1995 rugby World Cup final in a Springbok jersey at Ellis Park in Johannesburg.[4] Less acknowledged and more important for me is that on the day of his inauguration a year earlier, Mandela appeared at halftime of the South Africa–Zambia match also played at Ellis Park. My football obsession meant I chose to attend that match instead of joining the crowd at the inauguration ceremony on the lawns of the Union Buildings in Pretoria. An extended halftime break allowed the new president of South Africa to be formally introduced to the teams. After the restart, Bafana scored two quick goals to beat the Zambians.

Another crucial moment was South Africa's hosting of the 1996 African Nations Cup. Bafana Bafana lifted the trophy in front of more than one hundred thousand delirious fans, including me. Mandela, flanked by fellow Nobel Peace laureate F. W. de Klerk and other dignitaries, wore the gold-colored shirt of Bafana and handed over the trophy to the (white) South African captain, Neil Tovey. Watching the 1996 final in the stadium was a special experience, and I intended to celebrate this victory by partying in Pretoria's Sunnyside neighborhood, as I had done the year before after the rugby triumph, joining a mixed crowd celebrating the all-white Springbok team (Chester Williams excepted) in Esselen Street, Sunnyside's main thoroughfare, lined with bars and restaurants. The 1996 Bafana Bafana championship side was genuinely representative of South Africa's "Rainbow Nation." It featured African, coloured, and white players as well as Clive Barker, the white coach who had a long history of working with black clubs. But this time it seemed as if white Pretoria did not want to embrace South Africa's triumphant footballers: Esselen Street was dead.

I REMEMBER LISTENING to the 1982 World Cup on shortwave radio; four years later, I watched delayed highlights from Mexico on South African television. Finally, South Africans could enjoy live television broadcasts of the World Cup from Italy in 1990 and from the United States in 1994. (Between World Cups, my insatiable appetite for world football was satiated by reading overseas magazines such as *World Soccer, Kicker, Fussball, Shoot,* and *Match.*)

When Bafana Bafana qualified for the World Cup in 1998 and 2002, I watched again on television as "our" team failed to qualify for the second round in both tournaments. In June 1998, around thirty friends crammed into my Pretoria apartment to watch France beat South Africa 3–0 in "our" first-ever game at the World Cup finals. As payback, a number of us (fueled by beer) marched across the road at the end of the game and duly made our marks at the gates of the French embassy.

After failing to qualify for the 2006 World Cup, South Africa automatically qualified as hosts in 2010. I was in Mexico City in May 2004 when FIFA announced that South Africa was to host the tournament. Mexican friends were quick to congratulate me but asked whether the country could pull it off. I was not worried about South Africa's ability to host the World Cup, but I was quite concerned about how Bafana would perform on the field. Ever since the euphoric heights of the 1996–98 period, Bafana's performances were on the wane: between the mid-1990s and 2010, South Africa had plunged from a top-twenty team to eighty-third in the FIFA rankings!

In the seven months or so between the draw and the opening game, I found myself reverting to schoolboy activities such as collecting adhesive football stickers produced by Panini, a venerable Italian company that since the 1960s has sold World Cup sticker albums and packs. With more disposable income than I had the last time I collected Panini stickers in 1982, I soon filled most of my sticker book and accumulated hundreds of doubles. As a patriotic South African, I refused to trade my Bafana doubles. Not sure how to swap my stacks of other doubles, and not willing to hang around primary school playgrounds near our North London home, I went online and found similar middle-aged men enacting such youthful obsessions. But there was more. I bought Electronic Arts Sports' FIFA 2010 video game, and South Africa won the World Cup in my living room many times. (I had no such luck when I played against online opposition.) My obsession led me to purchase the home and away Bafana shirts, although I was annoyed that neither had the Protea logo stitched onto them. I rectified this problem at a store at Johannesburg's O. R. Tambo Airport in early June. As I walked out into the terminal's new arrival hall, an enormous football suspended from the roof greeted me.

Next stop: Soccer City. Also known as FNB Stadium, Soccer City opened in 1989 with an official capacity of seventy-six thousand, which made it the largest football ground in South Africa. The National Soccer League commissioned the facility's construction between Johannesburg and Soweto on mining land obtained with funds from First National Bank (FNB)[5] and South African Breweries, among others, and with the permission of the reform-minded apartheid government. Entering the stadium on June 11, 2010, I was struck by the incredible transformation of this historic venue. The original stadium had left spectators unprotected from the sun, but now most seats were covered, and the place had been converted into a calabash-like cauldron. After passing through the security perimeter, we were greeted with corporate stands selling overpriced hot dogs and Budweiser beer rather than by the informal traders who are a hallmark of South African football stadiums. Stewards directed us to our seats high up in the stadium, a striking departure from the South African tradition of taking the nearest available seat.

This was not the typical local football crowd. Since the 1970s, South African professional football crowds have been overwhelmingly black, but at World Cup matches, fans were remarkably racially and ethnically diverse. Annoyingly, some spectators were dressed in the green jerseys of South Africa's rugby team, the Springboks. These novices obviously did not know Mexico would be wearing green. The typical South African football fan was priced out of the tournament. Exacerbating the problem, initial ticket sales were conducted online, thereby excluding fans without credit cards, computers, or Internet access. Even when tickets were sold over the counter in April 2010, the special 20 dollar Category 4 tickets for South Africans remained beyond the reach of many working people.

Despite the unusual crowd, the opening game's atmosphere was electric. Siphiwe Tshabalala's stunning goal against Mexico in the fifty-fifth minute gave us hope. But with ten minutes left, Mexico equalized. In the end, South Africa gained a credible draw. On our way home we stopped for a *boerewors* (sausage) roll and a beer in Johannesburg's city center. A South African fan approached my Mexican wife, dressed in her green top and Bafana scarf, and asked her whether she was "confused": We all laughed together. I laughed even louder the following day when I read the *Pretoria News* headline, "Don't forget the 'Boks,'" referring to the national rugby team, which was set to play France at Newlands Stadium in Cape Town that day. I could not understand why an international rugby match had been scheduled on the second day of the football World Cup. I didn't know whether to laugh or cry when I drove past Hoërskool Menlopark, a prestigious, primarily white, Afrikaans-language high school. In 1987, it had hosted a national high school track-and-field meet and refused to allow Nkululeko Skweyiya, a black athlete from Durban, to compete. Now the school billboard proclaimed, "Menlo lief Bafana Bafana!" (Menlo loves Bafana Bafana). I don't think football is played at the school.

After the draw with Mexico, I was eager with anticipation that we would qualify for the second round. This dream was shattered a few days later when Uruguay beat South Africa 3–0 in Pretoria. I never enjoy watching football at Loftus Versveld because the connotations with rugby, racism, and conservative Pretoria remain vivid. Loftus Versveld was freezing on the night of the Uruguay match. I was tense and worried, since Uruguay had earned a draw against France in Cape Town and was a relatively unknown quantity. After twenty-four minutes, Uruguay took the lead on a thunderous shot by Diego Forlán that caught Bafana goalkeeper Itumeleng Khune flat-footed. (Could my boyhood hero Mark Anderson have done better?)

Maybe it was the number of traditional rugby supporters at Loftus Versveld that made for a flat and unenthusiastic crowd. I was infuriated when South African fans started leaving with twenty minutes to go. These folks were not real football fans; the real ones who support the team no matter what had been priced out of the tournament. Those white folks who stayed seemed more content to blow vuvuzelas (very poorly) than to support the national team. A night to forget was about to get worse. Khune was again at fault in the eightieth minute when he gave away a penalty and was red-carded. Forlán converted to make it 2–0 Uruguay. The South Americans scored another goal in added time, resulting in a 3–0 debacle that virtually assured Bafana Bafana's elimination with one game left.

Bafana's last game was against France at the Free State Rugby Stadium in Bloemfontein, home of the Free State Cheetahs rugby team. Another rugby stadium: an ominous sign. Bloemfontein is a fascinating city in the geographic center of the country; it is cold in winter and hot in summer. It has long been associated with Afrikaners and Afrikaner nationalism, although this does not tell the whole story. For example, the African National Congress (ANC), the main liberation movement and today's ruling party, was formed in the city in 1912. Bloemfontein has also been the site of sports milestones: The first South African football team to tour Europe was a black team from Bloemfontein that played dozens of matches in Britain in 1899.[6] The city is also home to Bloemfontein Celtic, a club renowned for its fanatically loyal and passionate fans.

The daytime drive from Pretoria to Bloemfontein along the N1 highway resembled a pilgrimage. At the toll gates, thousands of fans blew vuvuzelas and exchanged smiles. After a few hours, we approached the Free State Rugby Stadium in the heart of the city, adjacent to the Loch Logan Waterfront complex, a typical South African middle-class shopping mall with fast-food chain restaurants, clothing stores, cinemas, and other amenities that "offer welcome respite from the threatening realities of racialized poverty, homelessness, and over-crowding in the teeming streets of the dangerous city."[7] The mall was packed with South African fans and a few French supporters still licking their wounds after an embarrassing defeat against Mexico five days earlier in Polokwane. The police appeared keen to remove small groups of street children hanging around the entrance that connects the mall to the stadium. This was not *their* World Cup.

Inside the stadium, I was seated in the late afternoon sun. The atmosphere was quite different from Pretoria. It was warmer, and fans were singing and blowing their vuvuzelas (properly). The French started poorly, and Bafana went ahead 2–0. I was in football dreamland. Suddenly, the impossible seemed possible. With two more goals, we could qualify for the second round on goal differential, edging out either the Uruguayans or Mexicans, depending on the outcome of their game, which was going on simultaneously in Rustenburg (see the essays by Sergio Varela Hernández and David Patrick Lane in this volume). However, Steven Pienaar seemed to want to showboat and play backward rather than attack the French defense, penetrate, and shoot. A group of young Afrikaners sitting behind me remarked that football seemed like a difficult game to play and praised the skill of World Cup players.

Despite having played with a man advantage for an hour after a French player was sent off, we failed to capitalize and let the French back into the game. South Africa's 2–1 victory was not enough to advance to the second round, yet the inspired Bloemfontein crowd danced and sang and celebrated the victory in carnivalesque fashion. I was distraught; we had been knocked out of our own World Cup, what was there to celebrate? While I did root for Ghana against Uruguay in that heart-wrenching quarterfinal match, my World Cup had really ended on June 22 in Bloemfontein.

Less than six months after the end of the 2010 World Cup, I was at Twickenham in Southwest London to watch the Springboks play against the Barbarians, a rugby all-star team of sorts. Much to the annoyance of some of my rugby-supporting friends, I had nicknamed the Springboks the "All-Whites" during the 1990s, summing up my ambivalence and indifference to the side. I had never seen the team play live and, persuaded by my wife, I agreed to purchase tickets for the game. Under my heavy winter coat I proudly wore my yellow Bafana Bafana shirt. We watched the Springboks lose at the end of an indifferent series of matches in Britain. I refrained from singing the "Die Stem" parts of our national anthem. Old habits die hard.

NOTES

1. For more details, see Paul Dobson, *Rugby in South Africa: A History, 1861–1988* (Cape Town: South African Rugby Board, 1989); David R. Black and John Nauright, *Rugby and the South African Nation* (Manchester: Manchester University Press, 1998).

2. For an intriguing perspective on this phenomenon, see Sean Jacobs, "'It Wasn't That I Did Not Like South African Football': Media, History, and Biography," in *South Africa and the Global Game: Football, Apartheid, and Beyond,* ed. Peter Alegi and Chris Bolsmann (London: Routledge, 2010), 95–104.

3. On the National Soccer League, see Peter Alegi and Chris Bolsmann, "From Apartheid to Unity: White Capital and Black Power in the Racial Integration of South African Football, 1976–1992," *African Historical Review* 42, 1 (2010): 2–18.

4. See, for example, see John Carlin, *Playing the Enemy: Nelson Mandela and the Game That Made a Nation* (London: Atlantic, 2008), which provided the basis for the film *Invictus*, directed by Clint Eastwood (Warner Bros., 2009).

5. Formed after the British sanctions-busting Barclays Bank was compelled to sell its South African stake, FNB was an official national partner of FIFA for the 2010 World Cup.

6. For more details of the 1899 tour, see Chris Bolsmann, "The 1899 Orange Free State Football Team of Europe: 'Race,' Imperial Loyalty, and Sports Spectacle," *International Journal of the History of Sport* 28, 1 (2011): 81–97.

7. Martin J. Murray, "Building the 'New South Africa': Urban Space, Architectural Design, and the Disruption of Historical Memory," in *History Making and Present Day Politics: The Meaning of Collective Memory in South Africa*, ed. Hans Erik Stolten (Uppsala: Nordiska Afrikainstitutet, 2007), 234.

An Aficionado's Perspectives on the Complexity and Contradictions of Rooting for a Team in the 2010 World Cup

SIMON ADETONA AKINDES

I WAS BORN AND GREW UP in Benin, West Africa. I have played and been an aficionado of the "beautiful game" for as long as I can remember. My love affair with the World Cup was lived through French magazines such as *Le Miroir du Football, France Football, L'Equipe, Afrique Football,* and *Onze* and occasionally through television. Although the desire to watch a live World Cup game in Europe or Latin America was burning, it remained pure imagination, a kind of fairy tale. At the time, it was financially too onerous for my dream to be realized. In 1994, I was studying at Ohio University when the United States hosted the World Cup. I was so close to the grandiose commercial mass ritual with which the world had grown infatuated, but despite my lifelong passion for football, I did not seriously think of attending any of the games. As a graduate student and teaching assistant, I had limited financial means, and perhaps oddly, I avoided catching the World Cup fever. Even after I started working as a full-time academic in the United States, I did not feel the urge to travel to the World Cup tournaments in France in 1998, South Korea and Japan in 2002, or Germany in 2006.

Then came South Africa 2010. Experiencing it became a personal act of devotion and a historic obligation. This time around, I was not going to miss it. Travel from the United States would be expensive, but the occasion was monumental. South Africa, the former pariah state, had the privilege of hosting the World Cup and of representing Africa as a whole. In my consciousness and political landscape, South Africa represented many symbols, often contradictory ones. It was not a vacation destination like Cancún in Mexico, Copacabana in Brazil, or Varadero in Cuba. My link to South Africa was organic, almost umbilical. As an African, I grew up following intimately the struggle against apartheid. I read Dennis Brutus, Alex La Guma, André Brink, J. M. Coetzee, Nadine Gordimer, Mtutuzeli Matshoba, Breyten Breytenbach, Sipho Sepamla, and many other great South African writers. I listened to musical giants like Abdullah Ibrahim, Hugh Masekela, Miriam Makeba, Mzwakhe Mbuli, Bayete, Vusi Mahlasela, and Johnny Clegg.

Apartheid was a crime against humanity. It harshly affected black South Africans, of course, but it was also an insult and a traumatic assault on the psyche of all Africans. South African religious customs and beliefs, "traditional" political structures, and a shared past of colonial racism and exploitation meant that the struggle in South Africa echoed throughout Africa, the diaspora, and indeed much of the world.[1] In short, for political and cultural reasons, although a native of Benin, I considered South Africa home. As the preparations for the 2010 tournament got under way, I cherished the hope that a home team would win the cup on liberated South African soil. Any victory by Cameroon, Nigeria, Ivory Coast, Ghana, Algeria, or South Africa would also be mine. The way I saw it, it was time to add an African country to the list of past World Cup winners, which featured only European and South American nations: Brazil (five times), Italy (four), Germany (three), Argentina and Uruguay (two), and England and France (one).

South Africa 2010 meant conflicted pride. It inspired hope for a new dawn, an "African Renaissance," to use the phrase of former South African president Thabo Mbeki.[2] South Africa offered the possibility and hope of imagining an alternative path of development, different from the one-dimensional, free-market-oriented dogma that has taken hold of the continent. A successful World Cup in South Africa could flatter and reawaken my Africanness. Yet my satisfaction with black South Africans wielding political power was partially countered by the knowledge that much of the country's land and wealth still belonged to the white minority. As Nelson Mandela explained in his autobiography, *Long Walk to Freedom*, "The truth is that we are not yet free; we

have merely achieved the freedom to be free, the right not to be op-
pressed. . . . We have not taken the final step of our journey, but the first
step on a longer and even more difficult road."[3]

Beyond such political and cultural considerations, the 2010 World
Cup had the potential to enrich my relationship with my teenage son,
Tunji, born in Ohio. He shares my love of football, but having grown
up in the United States, Tunji has even more complex identity issues
than I do. Every day, he interacts with people from four or more "racial" backgrounds (his mother is Japanese American) and receives conflicting messages despite being fully immersed in the Age of Obama, as
some analysts have quickly and controversially termed allegedly post-
racial America.[4]

In addition to reinforcing our shared love for the game and strength-
ening our father-son bond, the 2010 World Cup was an opportunity for
my son to experience a different part of Africa, a richly diverse continent of nearly one billion people living in more than fifty nations and
speaking more than two thousand languages. The tournament would
also allow me to visit South African friends with whom I had studied
in the United States, some of whom knew very little of Africa north of
their border or had distorted views of "Africans" they had been spoon-
fed in Bantu Education schools under apartheid's separate and unequal
schooling system. Going to South Africa also entailed a degree of com-
plicity with the view that South Africa was an emerging nation leaping
into global modernity and a powerful African nation ready to assume
the mantle of the continent's political, economic, and military leadership.

Above all, as a deterritorialized football aficionado at the World
Cup, I was to grapple directly with the complicated relationship between territory and rooting for a team. Given the rational and irrational dimensions of place and the overt and covert contradictions of
football loyalties in the Internet and satellite television age, technology,
globalization, and migration have physically disconnected many of us
from the players, clubs, and nations we are almost obliged to support.
In my case, my most indelible memories, my food tastes, my accent,
my word choices, my figures of speech, and the sounds that flood my
head were passed on to me in Benin. They are intrinsically part of me
(though not mine alone), but since I left Benin, much has been added
and transformed.

I now live and work in Wisconsin, in the midwestern part of the United States, yet I unconditionally support Arsenal, the North London club in the English Premier League.[5] I follow the careers of some prominent African stars in European leagues, but I am more and more ignorant of football on the African continent. I am unable to identify with a local club in Benin or Africa, though I refuse to surrender to the nationalist folly and bastardized patriotism generated by national teams. I claim Benin—as in the people, the culture, the land that shaped my life—but I do not fetishize the flag or the national anthem.

My football loyalty is to a (foreign) club, not a nation. My awkward position is similar to that articulated by expatriate South African academic Grant Farred: "South Africa is where I was born, but it is only partly who I am. America is where I live and work, but it does not even begin to define me. National identity is not ontology," he writes. "Besides, as somebody who is not a lover of the nation—not the one of my birth, the one I live in or any other—I never support a country during the World Cup. I only root for Liverpool players representing their country."[6] Unlike Farred, however, I do not root for players, because teams make players, not vice versa. I root for the collective quality of the game or spirit. The attacking football that I played in Benin and came to love was introduced to me in the years of WM (3-2-2-3) and 4-2-4 tactical formations. Since I stopped playing competitively, "I have learned to accept myself for who I am: a beggar for good soccer," in the words of Uruguayan author Eduardo Galeano. "And when good soccer happens, I give thanks for the miracle and I don't give a damn which team or country performs it."[7]

JOHANNESBURG: JUNE 23, 2010. Tunji and I are at Soccer City for the evening match between Ghana and Germany. Like most people inside the massive calabash-shaped arena, I wanted Ghana to win. Over the years, I have developed an emotional attachment to Ghanaian football. I grew up in the 1970s, when Ghana produced some of the most exquisite football I had ever seen. Since then, local players such as Osei Kofi, Mfum, John Owusu, Kofi Pare, Robert Mensah, Charles Odametey, Adolf Armah, Karim Abdul Razak, Ibrahim Sunday, Opoku Nti Afriye, and Abedi Pelé delighted crowds all over the continent. The Black Stars deployed a highly technical style that combined exceptional individual skills with a strong sense of collective movement; no wonder they were known as the Brazilians of Africa. Ghana's 2010 team does not measure up to the great teams of the past, but moments of brilliance by Kwadwo Asamoah or André Ayew (son of three-time African Player of the Year Abedi Pelé) filled me with joy and served as a reminder that the recent decline in creativity, improvisation, and flair does not mean all is lost for African football. Or maybe I am simply nostalgic for something that never existed. As I took my seat with Tunji and eighty thousand other supporters, I thought of Ghana's reputation and results and believed the Black Stars deserved a glorious run in this World Cup. That Ghana is not far from Benin strengthened my solidarity and support for the Black Stars, but my intensity differed from Tunji's. Africa for him does not have the same meaning as it does for me despite his blood connections.

My support for Ghana stemmed mainly from these geographic and affective considerations, but German football has never fascinated me. Generally speaking, the German squad tends to prioritize discipline and organization over inspiration and improvisation. Of course, World Cup football is serious business, but it should not be *so* serious. It is a game; it is choreography and must remain so. As a spectator, I seek to experience aesthetic pleasure of the highest quality. That is one of the reasons why I watch games these days—not for the flag; not to establish the illusion of some form of ethnic, racial, national, or continental superiority; not to assert the superiority of organizational skills or efficiency; not to sustain any type of exceptionalism, but to reenact the beauty and unpredictability of life in its totality. Football does not merely resemble life; it *is* life.

Leading up to the Ghana match, the Germans had shown some impressive qualities, thrashing Australia 4–0 before losing to Serbia 1–0 after playing most of the match with only ten men after striker Miroslav Klose was sent off. The youthfulness and enthusiasm of players such as Schweinsteiger, Khedira, Özil, and Müller elicited my admiration. This new spirit of spontaneity and panache was nurtured by coach Joachim Löw, the former assistant to Jürgen Klinsmann, the coach who had instilled this new approach during the 2006 World Cup. The German team also included many players of different national origins. Right of blood (*jus sanguinis*) had given way to right of soil (*jus soli*), as Germany was no longer exclusively Teutonic, white, or even European, for that matter, with the inclusion of Middle Easterners, Afro-Europeans, and Turkish-born players. Eleven of its twenty-three players were either children of immigrants or were born abroad: Sami Khedira (Tunisia); Jérôme Boateng (Ghana); Dennis Aogo (Nigeria); Mesut Özil and Serdar Tasci (Turkey); Miroslav Klose, Lukas Podolski, and Piotr Trochowski (Poland); Mario Gómez (Spain); Cacau (Brazil); and Marko Marin (Serbia).

Intriguingly, brothers Kevin-Prince Boateng and Jérôme Boateng, born in Germany to a German mother and Ghanaian father, played against each other at Soccer City, the former for Ghana, the latter for Germany. The Boateng brothers' experience in the Ghana-Germany match revealed both the importance and the futility of nationalism. The contradiction of two black brothers playing against each other at Soccer City undermined rigid understandings and conceptualizations of family, national unity, and identity. A delightful Özil strike from outside the box gave Jérôme Boateng's Germany a 1–0 victory and ticket to the next round, but Ghana also went through thanks to Australia's victory over Serbia.

Tunji and I next attended the South Korea–Uruguay match on June 26 in Port Elizabeth in the Eastern Cape Province. By this point, Tunji could not watch a game without his vuvuzela. Before the World Cup, I heard the vuvuzela blowing at a friendly game in Chicago between Senegal and Mexico. As other authors in this volume note, the vuvuzela became a symbol of a clash of (football) civilizations at the World Cup. Subsequently, it has been banned in Europe by UEFA and by several English Premier League clubs (including my beloved Arsenal) as well as at several stadiums in the United States, New Zealand, Australia, and China. The vuvuzela controversy inspired columnist Fred Khumalo of the Johannesburg *Sunday Times* to compose a praise poem in honor of the horn:

> They said you sounded like a goat at the slaughterhouse
> Ah, the shallowness of their minds, the bloody cows!
> A swarm of angry bees, they called you
> as I blew you, and blew you.
> Parreira [South Africa's coach] was right,
> Vuvuzela, you are a hero.

> A thing for small minds they called you
> A weapon of war I shall call you
> not unlike [ANC politician] Malema's tjatjarag observations,
> and hallucinations.
> Parreira was right, Vuvuzela, you are a hero.

Inside the gleaming new forty-two-thousand-seat Nelson Mandela Bay/Port Elizabeth Stadium, I realized the limits of being a football aficionado at the World Cup, especially one coming from the United States. I could not name a single Korean player. How global is the game? In the United States, Fox Soccer and ESPN show mostly European matches. Aficionados hungry for Latin American, African, and Asian matches must pay additional fees for special satellite packages in Spanish or Arabic. Despite hosting the 2002 World Cup (with Japan), South Korea is better known for its huge industrial corporations—Hyundai (a FIFA sponsor), LG, and Samsung—than for its football prowess. Korean and Uruguayan supporters in the stadium spiked the atmosphere with their banners, flags, singing, and chanting.

I am rooting for South Korea. The Red Devils display one of the best styles of the World Cup. It is a kind of East Asian interpretation of the Barcelona way of playing, a web of simple, short passes, quick players, and well-spread positioning across the field. One major weakness: the Koreans lack a good finisher. I have not watched any of their previous games, but they seduce me. Another reason for supporting South Korea had to do with my wish to expand the "club" of World Cup winners beyond Europe and South America. Uruguay had already been world champions twice (1930 and 1950).

Rooting for a team depends on a string of mixed, discordant considerations and feelings and on who the opponents are. Why do I support a team when no one is asking me to do so? Does it really affect the quality of the game or its outcome? Has rooting for a team become mostly commercial or political, so a few owners or leaders can benefit from it? How important is my support when I am not directly implicated in the game through betting, owning shares, or buying merchandise? Situational support reveals various aspects of one's individual identity and sense of collective belonging but not their messy totality. Luis Suárez scores twice and Uruguay, tricky and calculating, wins 2–1 in extra time. Together with his teammate, Diego Forlán, Suárez's excellent World Cup performances overshadowed heavily marketed yet underachieving world stars such as Rooney, Kaká, and Ronaldo.

Three days later, my son and I watched Spain versus Portugal at the Fan Fest in Port Elizabeth. It was packed mostly with white spectators (locals and foreigners), some of whom were from Spain and Portugal. Young black teens (mostly coloured, with some Africans), dressed in cool Western clothes inside the official FIFA viewing area were more interested in playing football and hanging out with their girlfriends than watching the game. My son, who had wanted to watch the game, suddenly became a local teenager. They shared English, the passion of playing, and fashion style. The teenagers socialized and drank the omnipresent and unavoidable Coke. FIFA regulations stipulate that only products from its official commercial partners are allowed in the immediate vicinity of all World Cup sites. Anyone else interested in doing business in the "FIFA Kingdom" had to apply to the host city's municipal office for an "events permit."

The South African authorities policed FIFA's ownership claims over the phrase *World Cup*. The use of the following terms was prohibited: *2010 FIFA World Cup South Africa, World Cup 2010, RSA 2010, Football World Cup, FIFA World Cup, South Africa 2010, SA 2010/ ZA 2010, 2010 FIFA World Cup, Soccer World Cup, World Cup, South Africa World Cup*, all names of all South African venue cities with the figure "2010" behind them, *Twenty Ten/2010*, and *World Cup South Africa* as well as the Fifa. com logo, the official emblem, and the official poster. The organizers did not tolerate even an indirect allusion to the World Cup. For example, they forced low-cost airline Kulula to remove a humorous advertisement in which the carrier claimed to be "the unofficial carrier of you-know-what."

We stayed on in Port Elizabeth, and on July 2, all eyes were on the glamorous quarterfinal between Brazil and the Netherlands. Brazil has won the most world titles, produced the greatest player in history—Pelé—and consistently exports a huge number of talented footballers around the world. Like most Africans and people from the global south, I am enamored with Brazil because of the team's unbridled, improvised, and spontaneously elegant style of play. I like the idea that Brazilian football seems inspired by samba music and capoeira dance. I support Brazil because of its Africanness, a cultural legacy clearly evident in Brazilian music, literature, arts, cuisine, and religion. I do not feel guilty for my bias. Africans generally identify with the Brazilian team; 40 percent of African slaves who survived the Middle Passage landed in Brazil, so the connection is historically grounded in the transatlantic connections of a brutal past.

However, as the West African saying goes, "No condition is permanent." When Brazil embraced the risk-avoiding, conservative tactics preferred by European sides, my support for the Selecão started to wane. It did not completely dissipate, though, as I still admire the likes of Neymar, Dani Alves, and Pato. Maybe I supported Brazil for sentimental reasons only, or possibly because I grew up in the times of Pelé, the first black global star in a constellation of white soccer players.

When I joined hundreds of local supporters outside Brazil's hotel in Port Elizabeth, I was extremely disappointed that the team bus was parked very close to the hotel entrance and blocked our view of Brazilian players, including the revered Kaká, Robinho, Maicon, and Alves as they boarded on the way to practice. At that moment, I was reminded of how the "beautiful game" has been taken away from us, the people. In the eyes of the World Cup organizers and sponsors, our role seemed to be limited to worshiping players as if they were earthly gods and to consuming a commodity called football.

STARTING WITH THE QUARTERFINALS, Tunji and I watched every game with a lot of interest and passion, but only on television. Ghana-Uruguay was probably the most important game for Africa and Africans, along with the opener between South Africa and Mexico. In that game, South Africa's Siphiwe Tshabalala scored a beautiful goal that stood until Bafana captain Aaron Mokoena lingered too long on the backline and kept three Mexican players onside, including Rafael Marquez, who made no mistake and hammered home the equalizer from close range. After losing badly to Uruguay, it was clear that only a miracle would propel South Africa into the second round. Fortunately, Ghana rose to the forefront, ready to carry the continent on its broad shoulders.

Nineteen of Ghana's twenty-three squad members were based in Europe. According to statistics compiled by the *Football Is Coming Home* blog, more than 80 percent of Africans taking part in the 2010 World Cup played for European clubs, mainly in England, Spain, Italy, Germany, and France.[8] In Nigeria's case, the entire twenty-three-man squad played overseas (in nine European countries). All but one of Ivory Coast and Cameroon's team members played in Europe, and only three members of Algeria's team played in the local league. South Africa was a partial exception to the overall trend, with only seven players based overseas because of the country's commercially successful domestic league. A thorough examination of African player migration is beyond the scope of this essay, but a major cause of this exodus to Europe is linked to the reality that African countries generally rank among the world's poorest in terms of per capita income, educational levels, industrialization, and life expectancy. "It's Africa's time," the 2010 World Cup slogan said, but in reality only thirty-six thousand of the more than three million tickets sold were purchased by Africans from outside South Africa. The limited "African" character of the World Cup was further captured by Colombian pop star Shakira's performance of "Waka Waka," the official song of the World Cup (with backing from Freshlyground, a South African group). Rubbing salt in the wound, as Jennifer Doyle's essay in this volume reveals, the song was plagiarized from a Cameroonian artist's song of the 1980s.

For the all-European final, my son and I chose to support Spain instead of the Netherlands. Tunji had been rooting for Spain since the beginning of the tournament and bought a Fernando Torres number 9 jersey before we arrived in South Africa. At the Johannesburg airport, someone asked him why an African American boy with an African father was supporting Spain. Tunji simply replied that he "liked their game." I, too, enjoyed watching Spain playing a fluid game based on collective movement and a web of short, accurate passes. Had Germany defeated Spain in the semifinals to face the Netherlands in the final, I would have had to think twice about my choice. I have never been able to shake the memory of the German genocide against the Herero people in Namibia in the first decade of the twentieth century. Or maybe I was simply looking for a rationalization for rooting for Spain. I also could not overlook the fact that Afrikaner nationalists—the architects of apartheid—were proud descendants of the Dutch (to the chagrin of many Dutch supporters). The logic of my partiality does not necessarily make sense, especially because I knew that many Dutch people and organizations had supported the liberation struggles of African people.

Every time I have to choose a nation or club to root for (when Arsenal is not involved), the personal, the political, the historical, the aesthetic, and the emotional merge to inform my choice. But really, aside from the potential pleasure that comes from picking a winning side, what difference does my support make as I sit in front of a television or in a crowd of fans at a stadium. The reality is that such a choice does not dramatically affect my life. But it is a barometer, albeit an unscientific one, of how I experience, understand, and position myself vis-à-vis the town, country, region, or continent involved.

After Spain defeated the Netherlands 1–0 in that dreary final, I was pleased that the 2010 World Cup had indeed anointed a new winner, a winner whose philosophy of the game is close to mine, not one of those pragmatic winners for whom killing the game to win is a priority. After all, the World Cup must have different winners. As we know, the tournament was a triumph for South Africa, which delivered a first-class event with a passion and spirit that Brazil, Russia, and Qatar will struggle to match over the next twelve years.

White South Africans warmed up to football, a sport upon which many whites had previously looked down as a "black" game. Whites' allegiance to football, whether ephemeral or not, was also somewhat ambivalent. "A lot of whites have two flags on their cars, a South African flag and a European one," noted Zola Maseko in a *Mail and Guardian* op-ed piece, "their head sensibly in Africa, where they enjoy a first-world lifestyle at cut-rate third-world prices, and their hearts in the land of their ancestors: Greece, Spain, England, Portugal, France, Germany and the like." Black South Africans, Maseko continued, were not immune from exhibiting multiple loyalties, even if for different reasons. "It's likely we [South Africa] won't reach the second-round knockout stage, so we need another horse to sustain our interest in the remainder of the spectacle." Maseko then went on to explain that prior to the first democratic elections, "we didn't have a country to support and many of us supported other countries, usually Brazil (simply because they were the best), and still harbor tender feelings for our previous love."[9]

As soon as the World Cup ended, the South African government announced that Durban would bid to host the Olympics. Are megaevents becoming the drugs that South Africa, like other "darker nations" of the world, needs to satisfy itself and to unite around a proud postapartheid identity?[10]

Government corruption and mishandling of public funds in South Africa tempered the festive, feel-good atmosphere of the World Cup. I was struck by the numerous reports of mismanagement, bribery, and crass accumulation by members of the African National Congress leadership and by the news that five government agencies spent more than fourteen million dollars to buy World Cup tickets for their employees. "'It's the most selfish way of spending money and it is recklessness of the worst kind,' Zwelinzima Vavi, general secretary of South Africa's biggest trade union federation, COSATU," told the Johannesburg *Sunday Times*.[11] Critics of such wasteful expenditure noted that this money could have run 205 public schools in Gauteng Province for one year. I also worried about the eviction of poor people from downtown areas in various cities and their deportation to tent cities thirty miles away, as in the case of the Blikkiesdorp "temporary relocation area" on the outskirts of Cape Town. I was deeply concerned about rumors of planned violent attacks against African immigrants after the World Cup. Such negative news served as a reminder that, despite hosting a successful World Cup, South Africa still has a lot to do before it earns the leadership role to which it aspires on the continent. There is no question that the country marketed or branded itself capably with the 2010 World Cup, but its image would be enhanced even more if it narrowed the gaping divide between rich and poor, vastly improved public education, and expanded basic health care services to all its citizens, particularly in the countryside.

NOTES

1. There is a rich and growing literature on the international dimensions of the struggle against apartheid, including South African Democracy Education Trust, *The Road to Democracy in South Africa*, vol. 3, *International Solidarity* (Pretoria: University of South Africa Press, 2008); Francis Njubi Nesbitt, *Race for Sanctions: African Americans against Apartheid, 1946–1994* (Bloomington: Indiana University Press, 2004); Nordic Africa Institute, *Liberation in Southern Africa: The Role of the Nordic Countries* (Uppsala: Nordic Africa Institute, 2002), http://www.liberation africa.se/publications/, accessed December 1, 2011.

2. Elias K. Bongmba, "Reflections on Thabo Mbeki's African Renaissance," *Journal of Southern African Studies* 30, 2 (2004): 291–316; Malegapuru William Makgoba, ed., *The African Renaissance: the New Struggle* (Johannesburg: Mafube and Tafelberg, 1999).

3. Nelson Mandela, *Long Walk to Freedom* (Boston: Back Bay, 1995), 624.

4. Cf. Horace Campbell, *Barack Obama and 21st Century Politics: A Revolutionary Moment in the USA* (London: Pluto, 2010); Paul Tiyambe Zeleza, *Barack Obama and African Diasporas: Dialogues and Dissensions* (Banbury, UK: Ayebia Clarke; Athens: Ohio University Press, 2009).

5. On Arsenal fandom, see Nick Hornby, *Fever Pitch* (London: Penguin, 2000); Richard Vokes, "Arsenal in Bugamba: The Rise of English Premier League Football in Uganda," *Anthropology Today* 26, 3 (2010): 10–15.

6. Grant Farred, *Long Distance Love: A Passion for Football* (Philadelphia: Temple University Press, 2008), 6.

7. Eduardo Galeano, *Soccer in Sun and Shadow* (New York: Verso, 1998), 1.

8. Peter Alegi, "African World Cup Squads Reveal Euro Domination," June 4, 2010, http://www.footballiscominghome.info/the-players/african-world-cup-squads-reveal-euro-domination/, accessed August 11, 2011.

9. Zola Maseko, "Rainbow-Nation Patriotism, Pah!" *Mail and Guardian On-line*, June 21, 2010, http://mg.co.za/article/2010-6-21-rainbownation-patriotism -pah, accessed June 22, 2010.

10. Cf. Vijay Prashad, *The Darker Nations: A People's History of the Third World* (New York: New Press, 2007). On emerging nations' growing appetite for hosting global megaevents, see David R. Black and Janis van der Westhuizen, "The Allure of Global Games for 'Semi-Peripheral' Polities and Spaces: A Research Agenda," *Third World Quarterly* 25, 7 (2004): 1195–1214.

11. "Paper: South African Government Agencies Overspent on World Cup," *USA Today*, July 4, 2010, http://www.usatoday.com/sports/soccer/worldcup/2010 -07-04-south-africa-government-spending_N.htm, accessed September 27, 2012.

Chronicling the Uruguayan World Cup Experience across South Africa

DAVID PATRICK LANE

THE FOOTBALL PRESS IMPOSES certain stories on us, and the one about Uruguay went like this: Uruguay, which back in 1930 staged and won the first ever World Cup, has for decades engaged in brutal and mean-spirited tactics that have made the team a disgrace to the "beautiful game." Uruguay was the last nation to qualify for the 2010 World Cup in South Africa, barely beating Costa Rica in a playoff. Uruguay may have its history and passion, but modern football has moved on, and the country is now a quaint relic, better surveyed in a museum than on the pitch. A small republic of 3.5 million people with few sponsors or stars cannot be taken seriously in the global game. So what was expected of Uruguay in South Africa? It was easy to predict that they would kick, punch, and spit their way to an ignominious early bath; there were "temperamental" issues, proclaimed the previews. The notion that the Uruguayan team could challenge such stereotypes and elevate its football above cynicism was scarcely contemplated. Football fans were prepared for the worst, while related football industries preferred to concentrate on more lucrative commodities. Few could conceive of how a poorly packaged product such as Uruguay could make such an enormous contribution to the World Cup in South Africa. But it did. And this is how I saw the Uruguayans do it.

THE REPUBLIC TO THE EAST of the Uruguay River is a mongrel nation, neighbor to the two big dogs of South America, Argentina and Brazil.

But this is not your classic underdog story. On the contrary, Uruguay, despite doing what underdogs do, became the stray of the tournament, ugly, unloved, and unwanted. The reason for such widespread ill feeling was that Uruguay had knocked out Ghana—Africa's last hope for victory—in an epic quarterfinal match that will long be remembered for a controversial hand ball. But before Black Star fans were bitten, Uruguay's pedigree had to be reassessed by pundits and punters alike.

How was it possible to succeed in South Africa without being a neatly packaged, globally recognized football brand? That was the question commentators began to ask of Uruguay as La Celeste stood up against the prevailing consensus that football accomplishments were positively correlated to a nation's size and wealth. Uruguay's success in South Africa was rather more about team *simpatico*, straightforward coaching, and the structuring of a low-key home away from home in the host country. The Uruguayans were skillful as individuals, but it was this *simpatico*, a rare quality one cannot create or impose—compatible, pleasant and good to be around—that would serve them best. They liked each other. They believed in each other.

Uruguay chose to set up camp in Kimberley—home of De Beers, the apartheid regime's house arrest location for Pan Africanist Congress founder Robert Sobukwe, a nonsubversive sort of place. No World Cup games were scheduled here in the Northern Cape Province. The action and distractions were elsewhere, on the coasts or within the sphere of Johannesburg's influence. Kimberley was important once, but these days it clings to the crevices of its famed Big Hole. A sparkling rock discovered in 1866 on the land of the Griqua people (descendants of pastoralist Khoikhoi and mixed-race South Africans) led to a stampede of diamond prospectors. Thousands of individuals bought claims in the De Beers mine and, assisted by African male migrants, shovel by shovel dismantled a *kopje* (small hill) to create what was at the time the world's largest diamond mine. (You can now mark out about twenty-five football pitches across the surface area of the Big Hole.) By the early 1870s, Kimberley was the second-largest city in South Africa, trailing only Cape Town. Less than two decades later, Kimberley diamonds had made Cecil Rhodes rich and famous, as he bought out competitors and created De Beers Consolidated Mines, which to this day maintains an almost complete monopoly over the world's diamond market.[1] Once known around the world as "the city of limitless opportunity," Kimberley was deemed unfit by FIFA to be a 2010 World Cup host city. The consolation prize was entertaining Uruguay.

Landing digs in Kimberley, however, was part of a grander Uruguayan strategy. Cartographers, gerrymanderers, real estate agents, and historians know all too well the importance of location. Kimberley's position just inside the border of the Northern Cape was a classic piece of British mapsmanship. But football coaches also know a thing or two about offensive and defensive positioning. Kimberley was a supremely strategic choice for Uruguay, and not just because the city was equidistant between Cape Town and Pretoria, the cities set to host La Celeste's opening battles against France and South Africa, but, more important, because Kimberley was an understated place similar to just about anywhere in provincial Uruguay. Uruguay was at home even in South Africa.

The locals responded with greetings and salutations for their Latin guests. A big billboard hung over the N12 highway on the city limits. "Hola Uruguay Hola. Welcome to Kimberley," it said, with the smiling faces of the town's elders and dignitaries decked out in their best Bafana strips, giving the welcome a personal touch—Ke Nako! The sky-blue bunting that adorned the highways and byways of Kimberley was fairly basic stuff, but it was the thought that counted.

Training was opened to local schoolkids. I watched children first mesmerized by players' passes and moves and later trying to emulate them. Little Afrikaner nippers once destined for an egg-chasing playtime (i.e., rugby) were adopting the round ball code. And they all wanted to be like Diego Forlán. An older man looked across at a loose ball like he wanted to latch on to it and score. He was Alcides Ghiggia.

Ghiggia is the last surviving link to Uruguay's 1950 World Cup victory in Brazil. The 1950 Uruguayan side had done more than just win a football match, more than even win a World Cup. By beating the Brazilians in their home country in the final game of the tournament, Ghiggia and his *muchachos* had disturbed the collective psyche of the Brazilian people. This game played in front of nearly two hundred thousand spectators at the Estádio do Maracanã in Rio de Janeiro became known as the Maracanaço (shock). Nelson Rodrigues (1912–80), a famed Brazilian playwright, once said of the match, "Everywhere has its irremediable national catastrophe, something like a Hiroshima. Our catastrophe, our Hiroshima, was the defeat by Uruguay in 1950."[2]

Roberto Muylaert, biographer of Barbosa, the Brazilian goalkeeper beaten at the near post by Ghiggia in the Maracanaço, once famously compared the grainy reel of Ghiggia's goal with Abraham Zapruder's footage of John F. Kennedy's assassination in Dallas. The goal and the gunshot had "the same dramatic pattern . . . the same movement . . . the same precision of an unstoppable trajectory."[3] Football writer Alex Bellos added, "They even share clouds of dust—one from a gun [in Dallas], and one from Ghiggia's left foot [in Rio de Janeiro]."[4] As Ghiggia waved good-bye from a white minivan, stirring up even more dust, I did my best to describe the Maracanaço to the kids, but they all still wanted to be like Diego Forlán.

Hoffe Park, home of the Griquas professional rugby team, served as Uruguay's training headquarters. This rusty rugby stadium did not feel very FIFA. Outside were no mesh fences or glossy Visa ads proclaiming "Go Fans," just tumbleweeds and a lad selling oranges—"10 Rand" per bag read the scrawl on a piece of cardboard. Inside, every blade of grass was getting a pedicure. About a mile away, the Uruguayan players were being pampered in a garden-variety four-star hotel with a stunning view of the world's largest mining sinkhole. This was not the country club base into which most other finalists had been beamed. Every day the players would lace up their boots, climb aboard their bus, and sing their way to the stadium. Whenever I saw the team vehicle, it was rocking to a football song. Diego Godin, Uruguay's central defender, acted as lead percussionist, drumming on the roof of the bus to the *candombe* beat. The players were being supporters. Understand that, and you understand Uruguayan football. Uruguay was not on safari.

Hendrik, a local man charged with guarding the team bus, was effusive with praise. The morning after beating Bafana 3–0 in Pretoria, the Uruguayans were back in Kimberley, he noted, training harder than ever. Hendrik believed his boys had not quite grasped this concept. Beatrice, the gatekeeper, was learning a new Spanish word every day, with the Uruguayan boys taking her tutoring just as seriously as they took training. Townsfolk often talked about their friendly exchanges with players or officials.

In short, the Uruguayans were being human beings, not hyped-up, overpaid football stars. The team never managed a night out at Pack's Tavern, Galeshewe Township's finest spot for drinking, dining, and dancing on the tables, but if they had, patrons assured me, bottles of

Castle Milk Stout and Savannah Dry would have been raised in their honor. According to these South Africans, Uruguay was performing like they wanted their boys to have performed. Bafana's beatdown in Pretoria had been a good lesson learned, they told me. "Our boys are interested only in themselves; they have no team spirit," was an oft-heard refrain in Kimberley.

Kimberley folk may not possess the football connoisseurship one finds in bunches in other football-mad South African cities, but they knew enough to know that the Uruguayans were applying themselves to a high standard of teamwork and football scholarship. Having a *tranquilo* place to train was only part of the story. Crucially, Uruguay relied on Oscar Tabárez to be their master of cones and chalkboards. The former teacher, known by his hardly original nom de guerre, El Maestro, was a stickler for discipline. In that, he was fortunate to delegate his authority to his two head boys, defender and captain Diego Lugano and the top striker in Europe in 2008–9, Diego Forlán.

Forlán's contribution in particular cannot be overstated. The blond thirty-one-year-old forward came from a famous football family, but he was far from a typical South American footballer. Forlán was the first Uruguayan international to have been educated in a private school and to have given serious consideration to a tennis rather than football career. But he was not the aloof or arrogant sort; instead, I found him to be approachable and humble—an oxymoronic modern footballer. Speaking with me in Mancunian-accented English, a legacy of a three-year stint with Manchester United, he offered a most cautionary and diplomatic assessment of Uruguay's prospects of winning the World Cup, yet I could see in his eyes that he believed victory was possible.

The importance of leadership, both on and off the field, was underlined when Uruguay faced France in the two teams' opening game on June 11 in Cape Town. French players were focused on *nombrilisme* (navel gazing), while coach Raymond Domench turned to astrology for lineup and tactical guidance. Tabárez announced his lineup for the France fixture three days in advance, a classic opening gambit designed to take advantage of French neuroses. The French did not seem to know what they were doing in South Africa. El Maestro signaled that the Uruguayans did. "The system we have chosen can adapt to the different things we could face against France," he said casually.[5] Surprisingly, there were places for defender Mauricio Victorino, who turns out for the Universidad de Chile, and midfielder Egidio Arévalo Ríos, who enforces the midfield for Peñarol of Montevideo. They were solid squad players but not the European-based performers pundits would have predicted. The message: Uruguay does not need stars.

The inclusion of such a pivotal player as Arévalo Ríos, though a welcome surprise, emphasized the paucity of representation from the Uruguayan league. The same was true for many of the other smaller nations in the tournament, with often only reserve goalkeepers stuck in the mud of their home leagues. Uruguay had once been a destination for professional footballers. Back in the day, black Brazilians snubbed at home could make it in Montevideo. Uruguay entered the twentieth century flourishing thanks to its livestock industry, a sector that had greatly benefited from improvements in canning, refrigeration, and shipping and that had most notably sustained, with Bully Beef, the British Army in World War I. This industry fostered immigration. It acted as a dynamo for economic transformation and coincided with seminal social legislation, such as education, health, unemployment, and pension provisions, the first of their kind anywhere in South America. Such significant developments also propelled local football and led to Montevideo's hosting of the first World Cup. Despite the saying "Como el Uruguay no hay" (There's no place like Uruguay) and the lazy label "the Switzerland of South America," Uruguay soon lost its comparative advantage with beef and, much like Kimberley, faced a decline in prosperity, relevance, and status. Uruguayan footballers ultimately replaced tins of Anglo and Fray Bentos (corned beef) as Uruguay's most famous export.

The children of Uruguayan émigrés were first to congregate in Cape Town ahead of Uruguay's World Cup fixture against France. Approximately 10 percent of Uruguay's population emigrated during the military dictatorship (1973–85), many of them departing for Australia. (Amnesty International reported that in 1976 Uruguay had more political prisoners per capita than any nation on earth. While Steve Biko and thousands of South Africans were being tortured, so were thousands of Uruguayans.)[6] During the World Cup, Australian Uruguayans proved particularly clannish and best at consuming copious amounts of Castle Lager. They may have grown up with cricket but their obsession with La Celeste was proving genetic. (Their beer-drinking proficiency must have been a learned trait.)

South Africans found the Uruguayan squad something of a mystery. Their colors were regularly confused with Argentina and the name mistaken for Paraguay. Given that this was Africa's first World Cup, I thought it important to highlight Uruguay's African connections whenever possible. Uruguay is not the most well known of diaspora destinations for Africans, but Afro-Uruguayans have made remarkable contributions to their nation. In between the bluster of football banter, I imparted a few Afro-Uruguayan vignettes, rather like commercial breaks or public service announcements. They were limited and embellished but found a receptive audience. A custodian at a lodge outside Kimberley was fascinated to hear that the father of Uruguay's independence, General José Gervasio Artigas, owed his life to a loyal detachment of 250 black Uruguayan lancers, the Artiguas-Cué, who protected him while he was in exile in the Paraguayan jungle. At the Falling Leaves Jazz spot in Gugulethu, an impoverished black township on the outskirts of Cape Town, I joined some ladies for their Sunday afternoon knees up. There followed an impromptu *candombe* session with tables substituting for *tamboriles* (barrel-shaped drums). A captivated crowd listened as I explained how Uruguayan football chants could be traced back to the *candombe* beats African slaves used to communicate on the sugar plantations.

On the road from Pretoria to Rustenburg, a hushed *kombi* (microbus) crowd heard me describe how Isabelino Gradín was Uruguay's first black player and how he was top scorer in the first South American championship, the Copa America, in 1916, which Uruguay won. I told the story of how José Andrade, whose first job was as a carnival musician, was the first black football player in the Olympics and was instrumental in helping Uruguay win Olympic gold in 1924 and 1928 as well as the inaugural World Cup in 1930. Most everyone had seen footage of Pelé, but no one in my audience knew of these two black Uruguayan trailblazers. A lady from Midrand dutifully scratched their names down on a piece of paper. This was information her son could use.

Uruguay arrived in Rustenburg for its final first-round match against Mexico leading the group (with four points) but still underdogs. I arrived in Rustenburg feeling like the *kombi* had brought me to a different country. However, the mobile signal suggested otherwise. A cacophony of text-message beeps from the Uruguayan contingent helped me to zero in on sleeping and drinking arrangements. I saw no sign of the Mexicans, but intelligence suggested that perhaps twenty thousand of them were expected at the match (see the essay by Sergio Varela Hernández in this volume). The intelligence proved correct, though sources failed to predict how many of them would be accompanied by leggy escorts from Sandton.

Uruguayan supporters were working out ways to smuggle whiskey into the stadium. A character dressed up in a Donald Duck costume in honor of Luis Suarez (known as "Pato" because some fans believed he looked like a duck, a moniker the striker did not appreciate) had a mini-bar built into his beak. A Scotsman following Uruguay kept his Johnny Walker in a place where only an American airport security guard would find it. It mattered little. Officials at the Royal Bafokeng Stadium were chill. The sun was warm. Everyone seemed to agree that this was the way the World Cup should be, regardless of FIFA's diktats.

When sections of the stadium began wildly celebrating, we knew South Africa had scored against France in Bloemfontein. South African schools had closed for the entire World Cup, but here a bloc of uniformed kids sang and swayed. This plaid maroon-and-custard crew added a delicious flavor to proceedings. Although the local children had been marginalized by the Mexicans, there were still more South African boys and girls at the Royal Bafokeng Stadium than at any other ground I attended during the tournament. Ticket prices had made attending the World Cup practically impossible for most South Africans, a regrettable legacy. I assume that these kids had received complimentary tickets courtesy of the Royal Bafokeng Nation or Platinum Stars, the local professional team. The match they were watching was secondary to the text messages being received from Bloemfontein. "It's 2–0 to South Africa," said the man gawking at his smartphone. (Oh, how I miss crackling transistor radios glued to the ears of football anoraks! Then I would have also known that the French were down to ten men.) Up popped Pato! Goal! It was our turn to celebrate. The Mexican masses were not amused, and a hail of plastic Budweiser bottles began raining down.

Having beaten Mexico 1–0 and won Group C, Uruguay traveled to Port Elizabeth for a round-of-sixteen match against South Korea. It was pouring in Port Elizabeth when five minutes in, the South Korean number 10 hit the post. I turned away in disbelief. Behind me was Jorge. "The Luck of the Champions," he said confidently. Jorge Christy was a giant bumblebee of a man. His ancestors were Irish, Welsh, and Scottish. They worked on the railroads in Uruguay, so it was no accident that he supported the yellow and black of Peñarol, which was founded in 1891 as the Central Uruguay Railway Cricket Club. Jorge was a mastermind of Uruguayan football and apparently had gained some notoriety as a child winner of a Uruguayan quiz show on the subject. He had been holding a grudge against FIFA since 1970, when he believed that a last-minute switch of Uruguay's World Cup semifinal venue had been concocted to Brazil's advantage. We had met in a Hatfield Square bar in Pretoria hours before Uruguay beat South Africa. Jorge was busy plotting trajectories than would ensure that Uruguay would get the opportunity to abominate Brazil in a Cape Town semifinal.

The subsequent trip from Port Elizabeth to Johannesburg was memorable for the wonderful South African hospitality. One of the disadvantages of following your team at a World Cup is you tend to catch only fragments of other games. It was frustrating to listen to Afrikaans radio commentary of the Germany-England match. There was high drama, but what was the score? A fast-food Wimpy Bar appeared on the horizon just in time for us to watch the second half. We were just outside Colesberg, near the birthplace of Paul Kruger. Why was there was no triple-decker burger named in honor of the Boer leader? As in the first stages of the South African (Anglo-Boer) War, the English were being humiliated. The locals of Teutonic extraction, with large girths and loose trousers, were enjoying the show.

One would not have predicted that this fast-food chain would soon host a Uruguayan Fan Fest, but anything is possible during a World Cup. Enter a convoy (two carloads) of members of Kimberley's African National Congress Youth League, conspicuous in their Celeste-blue long-sleeved T-shirts. They were from the "Base Camp That Sparkles" and were returning from Port Elizabeth, where they had been cheering on La Celeste. Uruguayan flags were unfurled, and a chorus of "Soy Celeste" followed. I interviewed the crew but later deleted the recording: One of the lads hadn't told his girlfriend he had gone to Port Elizabeth for the football.

How to avoid the vanquished English hordes while bedding down en route to Johannesburg? A motel on the outskirts of Bloemfontein provided sanctuary. A low-key place with locals gathered around an open fire watching the football. *Perfecto!* Uruguay was no longer a known unknown, and our hosts wanted to talk about the Uruguay–South Africa match in Pretoria. But first must come the drinking. "We raise a toast of our mighty Jägermeister for our guests from Uruguay," proclaimed Amos. For some reason, Jägermeister was viewed like a magic potion in this part of Africa. I sipped slowly. If that match had been played in Bloemfontein, they all agreed, the crowd would have lifted Bafana to a famous victory!

It was time for our intrepid Uruguayan crew to get a South African football education. "Here we can sing the ball into the goal," insisted a man in oily overalls. Amos cleared his throat and began to sing a Bloemfontein Celtic football song. I was a believer. I added fuel to the fire, recalling our small knot of Charrúas celebrating Uruguay's second goal at the Loftus Versfeld against Bafana. That was the moment to support *your* team, I said, to *sing* for *your* team. They passionately agreed. Preach, preacher, preach! We could have been filming a Castle Lager World Cup commercial. But reality was different.

There were ten minutes to go, a proverbial lifetime in football, when thousands of South Africans trundled away from the Highveld stadium, dragging their impotent vuvuzelas behind them. I risked getting bonked on my noggin with a vuvuzela when I shouted, "Stay and support your team" in the direction of the fleeing day-trippers. Those who remained loyal laughed when I followed up with a painful rhetorical football question: "Don't you know Uruguay are notorious at giving up two-goal leads with less than five minutes to go?" But it was not to be. Álvaro "Palito" Pereira was about to nod in Uruguay's third goal and effectively end South Africa's World Cup.

Among the regulars by the fire was a well-dressed man with presence. He was the mayor of Bloemfontein, the wonderfully named Playfair Morule. We talked football and politics. At the end of the evening, the mayor clinked his glass and gathered his constituents around. I had mentioned to the mayor the little things I had done as a teenage anti-apartheid campaigner. Morule had done a stretch on Robben Island and wanted to express his thanks for the solidarity of millions like me who supported the struggle. It was a moving moment. The mayor would be cheering for Ghana but nonetheless wished Uruguay luck.

It was hard to gauge support for Ghana, Africa's remaining hope in South Africa. Thoroughly unscientific surveys I conducted in KwaZulu-Natal and in the Eastern Cape pointed to local support switching to

Brazil. Earlier, in the Western Cape, second teams were proving as popular as the home team, with many folks hedged on Brazil, England, the Netherlands, Germany, Spain, Cameroon, and Ivory Coast. Without injured Michael Essien, the Black Stars had no stars. That was the problem. The Black Satellites had just won the under-twenty World Cup, but Ghana, despite its rich history (see Craig Waite's essay in this volume) and prodigious youth side, had been somewhat of an afterthought in South Africa.

The Uruguayan players said their good-byes to Kimberley—FIFA now mandated that the team move to the Sunnyside Park Hotel in Johannesburg. But a lasting friendship between folk in the Northern Cape and those to the east of the Uruguay River had been forged, and the Uruguayan Football Federation subsequently announced a reciprocal coaching arrangement with Kimberley. Supporters were waiting when the Uruguayan squad arrived at their new hotel. It was like an ambush. The hotel grounds had been infiltrated, and banners hung from every terrace and tree. The names of people and places from all over Uruguay were on display. There were slogans and slang, poems and predictions, but no trademarks. This was as organic as international football got. There was no money in merchandising Uruguay in South Africa, so almost no one did. Puma was the new provider of the team shirt, but few related products were produced, packaged, and sold.

As the players alit from the team bus, the biggest cheer was reserved for Diego "El Ruso" Pérez. Forlán and Suárez may have scored the most goals, but many fans believed that Pérez best exhibited *garra Charrúa*, or "Charrúan claws." The Charrúa were the indigenous people of Uruguay, and the term *garra Charrúa* is invoked when Uruguayans find themselves competing against invaders or, in the modern context, in sporting competition. In essence, it means victory in the face of certain defeat. I experienced it personally at the Nelson Mandela Bay Stadium in Port Elizabeth. While celebrating with supporters, Diego Lugano threw his training top into the crowd. I caught it. There was no question. I had the whole garment in my grasp. At least I thought I did. The next day I called my friend, Cecilia, in Montevideo. She laughed hard and told me, "Now you know what *garra Charrúa* is!"

The late, great Obdulio Varela most famously displayed *garra Charrúa* in the 1950 World Cup final. Uruguay went a goal down to hosts Brazil, but Obdulio, the captain, was having none of it and galvanized his team to victory. I am reminded of a story Eduardo Galeano told of Varela in his magical book, *Soccer in Sun and Shadow*. Varela refused to play in the new Peñarol shirt because he took umbrage at the then novel concept of corporate shirt sponsorship. He preferred to play in his old kit. Varela explained, "They used to drag us blacks around by rings in our noses. Those days are gone."[7] El Ruso roused the Uruguayan midfield in a manner reminiscent of Varela, yet despite his doggedness, some will always see him as a poor man's Obdulio. El Ruso now promotes fizzy drinks in Uruguay.

Uruguayans will always prefer maté, a sort of green tea sipped through a metal straw, to fizzy drinks. Much maté was being drunk in the hotel bar as tickets for the quarterfinal against Ghana were being dished out. Pablo (who had joined me on the road from Rustenberg to Port Elizabeth via Durban and Mthatha and back to Gauteng) had rearranged his flight. He did not want to miss Soccer City. But the quarterfinal would be his last match. He was philosophical. The place for the party is now Montevideo. Several charter planes of Uruguayans took a different view. A new class of supporters were arriving in Johannesburg. Pablo knew it, and he didn't like it. But the Uruguayan Federation was operating a most egalitarian ticket-distribution system. All the tickets were in Fabiana's handbag. Fabiana was the secretary to the president of the Uruguayan Football Federation, and she ran the show. There would be no ticket gouging, and genuine supporters would get tickets.

It may seem unfair or detached to define Luis Suárez's deliberate goal-saving hand ball simply as *garra Charrúa*—unfair, perhaps, to all the Uruguayans who have ever fought back or beat the odds, unfair to the memory of Obdulio Varela. Some observers saw something unsavory about refusing to lose in such a manner. For most fans, at least in South Africa, Suárez cheated. But there is no escaping the fact that the claw was there, and it was there because Suárez was there, tenaciously defending Charrúan territory. Suárez specialized in scoring goals, not saving goals, but in managing to pull off the greatest "save" of the 2010 World Cup, he showed Soccer City something about sacrifice. The world had turned to South Africa to see football stars, yet too many were shown wrapped up in their exaggerated sense of self to make a significant jot of difference. Suárez epitomized selflessness, surrendering himself for his team.

A Uruguayan press photographer playing musical chairs with the

Soccer City stewards sat on my lap. She couldn't look. But before Asamoah Gyan cracked his penalty against the crossbar, Jorge made a preemptive announcement, "The Luck of the Champions!" We never doubted that Gyan would miss.

But it wasn't all luck, Pablo insisted. Pablo had techie friends back in Montevideo. La Celeste was using proprietary software designed in Uruguay that mapped match dynamics and statistics—knowledge—to El Maestro. Uruguayans were proud of this innovation. Football was no longer just about their history. It was Uruguay's luck that Gyan could not convert the penalty. Such is football.

I imagine that it was difficult to defend Suárez or support Uruguay in South Africa or anywhere else outside Uruguay after the Black Stars were eliminated. Uruguay's contribution to the tournament had been seismic. An unexpected semifinalist after eliminating Ghana on penalties, this small nation was again a football force. The team had garnered this achievement with spirit, structure, and great skill. The players had been gracious guests, admired by their hosts in Kimberley. Such accomplishments and contributions were ignored or perhaps never understood as Uruguay quickly became the toxic scapegoat for the failings and inadequacies of other football associations, enterprises, and systems.

A pantomime of pan-Africanism clattered into the Suárez hand ball debate. Suárez's unbridled joy at Uruguay remaining in the game infuriated most people even more than the offense itself. Emotional commentary from self-appointed pundits seeking low-hanging fruit and affirmation proclaimed what they perceived as obvious injury and insult to Africa. Many and perhaps most locals agreed, including World Cup neofanatics and other Johnny-Come-Latelies, purveyors of rugby righteousness who had recently jumped on the Black Stars bandwagon. Uruguay had suddenly become not an underdog but rather a stray dog, best chased or kicked away.

I returned to Cape Town Stadium on July 6 to find it full of folk crowing for the Netherlands. Colonialism originated on the peninsula when the Dutch East India Company established a supply station for ships rounding the Cape of Good Hope in 1652. It was no surprise that Afrikaners would feel an allegiance to their kith and kin. What I found unsettling was the strident support the Netherlands received from those with more tangled connections to their former colonial rulers. Questions of local color and consciousness are complex and run deep, and although I admit myself not fully qualified to tackle the colonizer/colonized nuances of the Western Cape, I was rather bemused as I looked into the kaleidoscope of fans inside the stadium and saw an almost blanket endorsement of the brutal inheritors of "total football" that was the dour Dutch team of 2010.

I understood that some of the spectators were hanging onto the dreadlocks of such recent great Dutch players as Suriname-born Ruud Gullit, who had dedicated his 1987 European Player of the Year award to the imprisoned Nelson Mandela. Moreover, the Dutch were perhaps the most racially and ethically diverse team remaining in the tournament. Yet only a few weeks earlier, I interviewed local families purchasing tickets for the Cameroon-Netherlands first-round fixture, and they all wanted to see "Cameroon whoop the Netherlands." The South Africans with whom I spoke were not shy about their postcolonial motives, but such sentiments had disappeared, and some black South Africans now spewed bile at Uruguayan supporters and held up signs supporting the Netherlands, mourning Ghana, and accusing Uruguay of cheating the African continent out of a World Cup.

Still, the coming together of Africans in support of Ghana was a positive development. Given the 2008 xenophobic attacks (see the essay by Meg Vandermerwe in this volume), South African expressions of pan-African solidarity were particularly important. The making of legend has limitations, however, and the unintended consequence of black South Africans adopting Ghana was ultimately to throw many of them full-square behind a familiar European power that had once subjugated their ancestors. Only because of Uruguay did Africa's first World Cup turn out not to be another complete European carve up, something South Africans, enamored with the soft power of European football on satellite television and incensed at the sacrifice and swagger of Luis Suárez, have probably yet to fully realize.

The abuse of Uruguay was not unanimous. Lucia, a worker at a juice bar, was phlegmatic. She followed the Kaizer Chiefs, South Africa's most popular club, and had seen it all before: "Ghana man should have scored the penalty," she said. Kolade, a Nigerian academic at the University of Cape Town, said, "The problem with us Africans is that we never seem to produce players that can give it all. Suárez is a player after my own heart; he gave it all. Some say his action was reflex, but I don't think so. He took a calculated risk. He either stopped the ball with his hands, or the ball stopped Uruguay's progress. He got the red card. Ghana got the penalty. Ghana missed the penalty. Today Suárez is the hero of his nation!" Aware of Nigerians' sensibilities regarding their Black Star neighbors, I approached other seasoned African *fútbolistas* and connoisseurs in Cape Town, such as Enoch, originally from the Central African Republic, for his views on Suárez. Suárez was secondary to Enoch's disgust for those Africans—so-called superstars—whom he believed underperformed and brought disgrace to their continent. He began naming them one by one. "Assou Ekotto, Bassong, Eto'o, Yobo, Yakubu, Eboué, Zakora, Drogba, Kalou . . ." The list went on and on, a veritable who's who of English Premier League millionaires.

I felt like a millionaire mingling at the swanky Vineyard Hotel nestled in Newlands, one of Cape Town's plush southern suburbs. Word that this was the team hotel was out, and supporters soon swarmed the lush grounds, spray painting Suárez slogans on banners, leaving his name immortalized on the grass. It was the day before the semifinal, and it was then that I was reminded that all of Uruguay's luck in Soccer City had not been good. Nicolás Lodeiro had broken a bone in his foot five minutes before Gyan missed his penalty. It was bad enough that captain Diego Lugano was injured and would not play the semifinal, but here hobbling off the Uruguay bus, his leg in a cast, was the player I had expected to slice open the Oranje. I looked for reassurance from Jorge. He and his rent-a-car copilot and wife, the lovely Graciela, along with a few hundred other supporters, had helped subsidize the team's chartered plane, and they were convinced that the World Cup would be on the charter back to Montevideo. Never lost for words, Jorge assured me, "No European team has ever won the World Cup outside Europe!"

I sat with Maxi Pereira as an entourage of more than a dozen members of his family materialized, including his wife and his newborn baby. It was a wonderful moment, encapsulating the energy of the Uruguayan team. They were all together. Pereira's goal in Uruguay's 3–2 loss to the Netherlands was not enough, but that and the nature of the two goals scored in a losing effort against Germany in the third-place consolation game stood testament to what differentiated Uruguay from most other teams at the tournament. They never gave up.

NOTES

Por Oscar. Mi hermano.

1. For more on the history of Kimberley, see Robert V. Turrell, *Capital and Labour on the Kimberley Diamond Fields, 1871–1890* (Cambridge: Cambridge University Press, 1987); William H. Worger, *South Africa's City of Diamonds: Mine Workers and Monopoly Capitalism in Kimberley, 1867–1895* (New Haven: Yale University Press, 1987). On the Griqua, see Martin Legassick, *The Struggle for the Eastern Cape, 1800–1854: Subjugation and the Roots of South African Democracy* (Sandton: KMM Review, 2010).

2. Alex Bellos, *Futebol: The Brazilian Way of Life* (New York: Bloomsbury, 2003), 43.

3. Ibid., 52.

4. Ibid., 54.

5. Agence France-Presse, "Uruguay Coach Tabarez Springs Team Surprise," June 9, 2010.

6. Amnesty International, *The Amnesty International Report: June 1, 1975–May 31, 1976* (London: Amnesty International, 1976), 113.

7. Eduardo Galeano, *Soccer in Sun and Shadow* (New York: Verso, 1998), 95.

Screaming U-S-A!
(and Other Imagined Things)

Us versus Them at South Africa 2010

ANDREW M. GUEST

THERE SHOULD HAVE BEEN something discordant about finding one-self in semirural South Africa surrounded by jolly mobs of drunken Americans wearing Uncle Sam top hats complemented by sequined red, white, and blue tuxedos screaming "U-S-A" on an endless repeat. Without the proper context, it might well have been a cartoon satire on neoimperialism. Yet amid the dusty blocks of modest homes and taverns outside the Royal Bafokeng Stadium in Rustenburg for the United States–England World Cup game on June 12, 2010, it seemed just right. In fact, on that day, all the ultimately bizarre claims of nationalism somehow made sense: the American fan as a cartoonish Uncle Sam; the English fan as an aging knight in shining armor; the South African fan as a good-natured host blowing a horn and wearing a funny hat. It was an eclectic mashup of global identities of the sort that perhaps only a World Cup can supply. For a short while, it was intense and absorbing—good, silly fun.

That short while, however, was a long time coming. As a professional academic and soccer blogger with two years of Peace Corps service in Malawi and a long-standing interest in Africa, I was thrilled to have made it back for the first African World Cup. As an American soccer fan, I worried that Team USA could be in for a thrashing, but I hoped that the English would, as usual, disappoint. As a whole, when I joined the throngs of fans earlier that day shuttling by minibus from accommodations in the greater Johannesburg-Pretoria metropolis to the outskirts of Rustenburg, I felt engrossed in the peculiar excitement of a grand game.

We arrived in Rustenburg hours early, descending like a thirsty, good-natured hive of locusts onto the neighborhood around the stadium, an area on the poor side of working class without being destitute. We trampled about through dirt yards and improvised taverns full of entrepreneurial locals inviting us to eat, drink, and spend. The English congregated with their patriotic football songs and St. George's Cross, the Americans countered with stars, stripes, and loud staccato "U-S-A" chants. As an American, I wished desperately for more creativity, but I also found myself joining in periodically just to get in the spirit of things. The wide-eyed local children peering around fence posts and piles of bricks seemed to expect nothing less.

Once inside the stadium, nationalist spirit came to a crescendo with the singing of the national anthems. With the players swaying stoically in line, carefully uniformed in national colors and brands, the crowd immersed itself in "God Save the Queen" ("Send her victorious / Happy and glorious") and the "Star-Spangled Banner" ("The bombs bursting in air / Gave proof through the night / That our flag was still there"). The game itself was anticlimactic. An early positional error by the American defense led to an easy English goal. A slapstick mishandle by the English goalkeeper gifted the United States an equalizer. The rest of the game was mostly sound and fury, signifying nothing.

On the way out of the stadium, the feeling was of civil resignation, but the scene was utter confusion—the roads were a stagnant cluster of idle buses, eager hawkers, and perplexed fans. I was lucky to find my minibus shuttle after a long, lonely walk, but we were stalled against a dusty curb and a row of jacaranda trees. In the traffic and disorder, our driver seemed reasonably content to smoke and listen to radio reports of a Springbok rugby friendly from earlier in the day. He perked up when a pair of viscerally drunk American fans stumbled to his window looking for a ride to the Johannesburg airport: "500 rand [70 dollars]. Each." The rest of us had paid something like half of that for the round trip, but the two consulted only briefly before jumping in without bothering to negotiate.

One of the Americans immediately passed out in his bench back seat. The other immediately began blathering to anyone who would listen—first about the game, then into an extended discourse about himself. He was excited to realize that several of the guys on the minibus were English: though by appearance alone he looked to be no older than eighteen, he proudly explained that his large New York investment bank was transferring him to London, a place he'd never been. He insisted that the Englishmen tell him all about the best neighborhoods in London, no matter that they were from Leeds. "Leeds? Never heard of it." After several futile attempts to describe the geography of Leeds, the patient Brits asked if he had ever heard of Manchester. He had. "It's kind of near there."

As the minibus jerked and jabbed through the confused crowd, slowly finding its way out of Rustenburg on a two-lane road, the fresh-faced American banker continued his verbal assault. He interspersed brief comments about how the match had "kicked ass" before transitioning without logical segue to the secrets of his "success," the excitement of "new challenges," and how working in Manhattan with weekends in the Hamptons meant he was from "the heart and soul of America." He was a caricature of the oblivious rich American, and I felt guilty by association: Hours before, we had been screaming U-S-A together; now I wanted nothing more than to proclaim my individuality. "He doesn't represent me," I wanted to explain to the rest of the multinational passengers, to the wide-eyed commuters walking on the side of the road, to the burly, chain-smoking driver; "he doesn't represent America." But our matching Team USA jackets said otherwise.

The World Cup in South Africa, like so many global sports megaevents, was marketed as a way to "bring people together" through the power of a game. That claim was particularly appealing in a society warily negotiating the divisive legacies of apartheid and colonialism and in a contemporary global community riven by material poverty and inequality. Part of the universal appeal of football is its seeming ability to redefine those divisions: When else do whole nations with boundaries defined by sociohistorical happenstance present themselves as a unified whole? Perhaps in the United Nations General Assembly, but that doesn't make much of a show for spectators. Instead, as Eric Hobsbawm has so precisely articulated, "The imagined community of millions seems more real as a team of eleven named people."[1] But on that minibus ride, I found myself wondering more than ever whether that is necessarily a good thing.

I have long been skeptical of grand claims about the unifying power of sport. Do national rivalries like the United States versus Mexico or derbies like Rangers versus Celtic, Boca Juniors versus River Plate, and Kaizer Chiefs versus Orlando Pirates bring people together or divide them with a sharp cleaver? In fact, as an academic psychologist familiar with some research on group conflict, I have often been struck by the idea that football offers a nearly perfect context for antagonizing groups that might otherwise have much in common. The basic idea, drawing off social identity theory, is that for various evolutionary reasons, one of our most fundamentally human psychological instincts is to identify and divide the world into groups: us versus them. *Us* is good; *them* is bad. In our ancestral past, this instinct may have been oriented by clans, but now it is up for grabs—we are constantly, often unconsciously, affiliating with cities, countries, schools, political parties, genders, ethnicities, companies, teams, products, and whatever else becomes salient in our daily lives.

What's fascinating about the basic us versus them binary is how quickly and irrationally this instinct activates.[2] Start with a vague sense of commitment to a group (such as simply paying attention to a team's results), add a dash of competition (which is intrinsic to any football match), and mix in some external markers of group identity (anthems, scarves, jerseys, and flags work well), and we have a combustible blend ready to ignite at the slightest provocation. For example, I had decidedly mixed feelings about many members of both the United States and England national teams as individual players, but on that crisp night in Rustenburg, I was willing to cheer zealously for every American while barely containing a totally irrational ire toward the English.

Of course, the heightened sense of us versus them that can be so divisive between groups also has a powerful ability to unite people within abstract social groups—an ability on vivid display among South Africans at the 2010 World Cup. From a distance, in the run-up to the World Cup, we heard much oversimplified rhetoric about how soccer in South Africa was a sport for poor blacks with no appeal within the rugby and cricket worlds of white South Africans. And while there are unquestionably stark divisions and inequalities in South African society, it was equally clear during the World Cup that people across race, class, and gender lines were enthusiastically supporting Bafana Bafana. Street hawkers did a brisk business selling replica South African flags, while everyone at the malls was making a run for the bright yellow Bafana jerseys. It was oddly sweet to watch a black counter worker compliment a white shopper with a heavy Afrikaans accent on her purchase of a Bafana jersey: "Ack—400 rand [57 dollars] . . . But what can you do?" said the white woman with a shy smile.

The implicit togetherness and shared South Africanness among the local population fostered by the games occasionally seemed to translate into genuine realizations. On my way to the gleaming new Soccer City Stadium to watch Netherlands-Denmark, for example, I sat on a "soccer express" train next to two white South African thirtysomethings who had never before ridden a local train. As we passed crowded working-class townships and frenetic station platforms teeming with black commuters (no admittance to the train without a game ticket), these two men stared out the window and held a bewildered conversation: "We really do live a privileged life in our suburbs, don't we?"

That sentiment made all the more poignant the analysis of Soccer City offered by South African writer Mark Gevisser in his column in the *Mail and Guardian* on June 13, 2010. Drawing from the writings of Frantz Fanon, Gevisser observed, "What is so striking about Soccer City is that—unlike Ellis Park or the FNB Stadium which it replaces—you are entirely enclosed within the perfectly cambered calabash once you are inside; there are no vistas of the city or the world outside." For Gevisser, the stadium's architectural design may have been inspired less by ideology and more by Beijing's Olympic Stadium (the Bird's Nest), "but the effect is intense all the same; at a time when it seems increasingly difficult to hold the Rainbow Nation together, the 'African calabash' seems to provide South Africans with the fantasy of containment within a single shared national identity."[3] Of course, South Africans are not unique in maintaining the fantasy of a shared national identity. As Benedict Anderson has famously argued, all nations are "imagined communities."[4] Even when not enacted in the glorious architecture of a stadium such as Soccer City, our sense of a national *us* competing against another nation's *them* is made real primarily through symbols.

Cue the vuvuzelas. As much as the infernal noise disturbed my eardrums and even if the bleating monotone drowned out other more authentic expressions of fan culture, I came to think of the colorful plastic horns as another unifying symbol for those of us who were there. Divided in our allegiances, in defiance of television broadcasters and audiences around the world, we were united by the call of a plastic horn (and perhaps the need to buy earplugs).

The authentic feelings of national unity evoked by the shared symbols of South Africa 2010 may have been part of the reason being at this World Cup challenged my skepticism about football's ability to bring people together. But whatever the reason, in and around all the games I attended there was a surprising spirit of diplomatic understanding. I was particularly impressed after attending the United States–Algeria game, a group finale that was to determine who advanced to the knockout stage. Before the game in Pretoria, on the upmarket streets of shopping plazas and university buildings around Loftus Versfeld, the almost exclusively male Algerian fans seemed agitated—one particularly large group stationed itself in front of a Middle Eastern restaurant banging drums and defiantly waving Algerian (and a few Palestinian) flags. They seemed to be spoiling for a fight, and the rest of us gave them a wide berth. My group of American fans slipped carefully into the walled courtyard of a sports bar, singing a mix of the silly and the patriotic as we readied to march on the stadium. The game itself intensified these powerful feelings. It was an anxious, scoreless draw deep into second-half injury time, when Landon Donovan finished an end-to-end American counterattack with aplomb. 1–0: U-S-A!

After this cathartic game, back in the sports bar complex, I found myself nervously situated on a bench next to a small group of Algerian fans. We were all watching the next games on television, and I gave a tentative nod. One of the men, coiffed in a baggy green-and-white sweat suit bearing the Algerian crescent, leaned in and said in heavily accented English, "It was a good game. Both teams had chances. The U.S. just wanted it a bit more at the end." I agreed. All of us who were there agreed: It was a good game.

At the same time, it is certainly true that all was not peace and harmony around the World Cup. But when acrimony came, it was often from a far. For example, in the U.S. match against Slovenia, a potentially game-winning American goal a few minutes from the end was disallowed when the referee whistled a phantom foul. The match ended in a 2–2 draw. Those of us in attendance at Ellis Park were confused but ultimately content as the Americans had made an impressive showing by coming back from two goals down to take a valuable point and keep alive our hopes of advancing to the next round. Even watching replays on television later that evening, the disallowed goal was still just a minor talking point amid conversations about a thrilling match. It was only when I checked in online with the American media that I saw the righteous anger so familiar to perceived sporting injustice. Bloggers were calling for the scalp of Koman Coulibaly, the Malian referee, using that one peculiar judgment as an indictment of the whole developing world. Talking heads on American cable television whispered something about anti-American conspiracy. The mainstream American media were demanding retribution through official channels. Peter King, in South Africa writing for *Sports Illustrated* (the urtext of American sports journalism), used the decision to impugn entire nations in a single tweet: "Putting a ref from a small African country in charge of a vital WC game is like a Mid-American Conference ref doing the Super Bowl."[5]

The Slovenia controversy seemed to fade from the American media when Team USA went on to win that final group game against Algeria, but it was clear that the tensions of us versus them were more precarious from a distance. Even after the collective effervescence of the Algeria win, it was fascinating to read Dave Zirin, writing for the venerable liberal-progressive magazine *The Nation*, question whether fans' reactions to Team USA amounted to "joy or jingoism."[6] Though Zirin's piece was mostly a set of balanced thoughts evaluating his own reaction and that of sports radio programs in his hometown of Washington, D.C., he was immediately pilloried by other writers and online. "You must be either a biased foreigner or a self-loathing American," read a typical online comment. "If you don't take simple joy from the game," user comments seemed to be saying, "then you can't be one of us; you must be one of them." In other words, the soft power of sporting nationalism could not completely submerge the nation's internal tensions for very long.[7]

Jingoism, of course, is not just an American malaise, and its evil cousin, xenophobia, also came up for discussion in and around South Africa during the World Cup. The organizers' slogan was "Celebrate Africa's Humanity" (Does FIFA believe "Africa's Humanity" differs from other types of humanity?), but this heavily marketed ideological statement of pan-African unity and solidarity could not mask the anxiety of many Malawians, Zimbabweans, Nigerians, Mozambicans, Kenyans, and other African immigrants I talked with in South Africa. They had not forgotten the xenophobic violence of 2008 or the many instances of everyday insults and intimidation, often pitting low-wage local workers against low-wage immigrant workers in a pattern sadly familiar around the world. In the midst of a World Cup where the South African government and many of its citizens had taken seriously calls to put on their best face for the sake of projecting a positive image internationally, there was an eerie sense that further violence lay just below the surface.

Immigration denoted another virulent shifting of the us versus them dynamic. A congenial Malawian working at my guesthouse explained to me that he thought his compatriots had a relatively good reputation, "but the Zimbabweans—those ones can't be trusted." A white South African I met at a pub warned me sternly about my intention to walk home: "Don't go by that big apartment block; Nigerians live there." And, on another day, a black South African told me that the problem with the rural village he had left was "the Mozambicans; they are always just stealing." Even the concept itself was regularly assigned a definite article: "the xenophobia."[8] It was as if national identity were being infected by the plague, destroyed by the bomb, or overthrown by the army.

My Peace Corps service in Malawi had given me a special affinity for the Malawian worker who claimed that in his Johannesburg township there was much talk of many poor South Africans having been on their best behavior for the sake of the World Cup and national pride: "But they tell us, 'Wait till the World Cup ends. We're going to kick your ass.' I'm telling you, after the 11th July when you are [back in the United States]—well, just watch the news." But I have watched the news, and fortunately to this point, the more serious threats apparently have not come to pass.

South Africans seem instead to have continued living, managing like they always do, perhaps without some of the visceral bonding brought out by the hosting of the World Cup but perhaps also with a new imagining of what South Africa is. In a roundtable published in the *Financial Times* on July 10, 2010, the day before the final, Ferial Haffajee, editor of the *City Press* newspaper in Johannesburg, explained that prior to the tournament, "I was really worried about 20 years of democracy. I'm not so worried any more. I'd always thought that nationhood and non-racialism were evaporating dreams, and in fact I see they can still be made tangible and real."[9]

The World Cup was not, however, solely responsible for sharpening a sense of nationhood and making it more "tangible and real," for bolstering the imagined community of South Africa. Most of that responsibility goes to the many South Africans who embraced the event with a magnificent mix of engagement, critique, and celebration. I think here of the Muslim engineer of Indian descent, married to the daughter of an Afrikaner military man, who spent a day showing me "his" Johannesburg, an energized but familiar global city of square walled neighborhoods, leafy schools, and quiet eateries spared from FIFA's corporate partners, just because he'd read some of my pretournament blogging. I had used a throwaway line about my disappointment that international media prone to sensationalizing and stereotyping showed relatively little interest in the "normal" daily experiences of forty-nine million South Africans who somehow manage—as most people everywhere do—to muddle through. This reflection struck him as funny. I think back to the jubilant South Africans who welcomed me at a township fan park despite my being so obviously lost and out of place at the sports ground in Temba/Hammanskraal, to watch the Bafana Bafana game against France. At that point, South Africa still had an outside chance of qualifying for the knockout stage, but the team seemed not to believe it. Despite leading by two goals against a team down to ten men, the South Africans played a lackluster second half, as if beating a demoralized Les Bleus was enough. And for the crowd at the fan park that day, it was enough. Mesmerized by the beautiful game on three large portable screens spread across acres of sprawling green, a 2–1 victory over a former World Cup winner seemed to generate meaningful pride despite South Africa's dubious accomplishment of becoming the first World Cup host country not to qualify for the second round. The South African fans seemed to be saying, "It is enough just to be us."

So, did the tournament help to create a more robust version of the imagined community of South Africa or the United States of America? From up close, I have to admit that it did despite the legitimate sociological, economic, and psychological critiques of the event and its impact. The energy in and attention toward South Africa during those weeks was unlike anything I could have imagined. But at the same time, from a distance I realize that popularity risks distracting from the more serious and enduring schisms that comprise our usual social identities as rich or poor, male or female, citizen or alien, black or white. David

Goldblatt, in his magisterial history of world football, *The Ball Is Round*, quotes from Peruvian Nobel Prize laureate Mario Vargas Llosa's coverage of the 1982 World Cup: "Football offers people something that they can scarcely ever have: an opportunity to have fun, to enjoy themselves, to get excited, worked up, to feel certain intense emotions that daily routine rarely offers them." Vargas continues, "A good game of football is enormously intense and absorbing. . . . [I]t is ephemeral, non transcendent, innocuous. An experience where the effect disappears at the same time as the cause. Sport . . . is the love of form, a spectacle which does not transcend the physical, the sensory, the instant emotion, which unlike, for example, a book or a play, scarcely leaves a trace in the memory and does not enrich or impoverish knowledge. And that is its appeal; that it is exciting and empty."[10]

But while it may sound pejorative to talk of football as "empty," I prefer to think that the World Cup is only empty in the uncertainty of its potential. Like an empty signifier in semiotics, the World Cup is there to be filled in with meanings according to whoever is paying attention. From a distance, those meanings seemed potentially divisive: it was easy to imagine the games as us versus them. But in the moment, the meanings seemed genuinely unifying: We were all simultaneously imagining—together. Months later, it strikes me that those opposing impulses created an inevitable tension: Though our minds want to define us versus them, our understanding of who we are as individuals and members of a larger community depends on negotiating between *us* and *them*. And this World Cup in South Africa offered an invaluable space for that negotiation: for South Africans, for Americans, and for many of the world's imagined communities.

Going back to the end of that long day in Rustenburg for the United States–England game, after a tedious night drive listening to a young and very drunk Manhattan investment banker rambling about how he represented the "heart and soul of America," I found myself still struggling with that tension. I was still upset that he was wearing the same USA jacket as me. Fortunately, I was the first of the passengers to be dropped off in the freezing Johannesburg night, and I didn't have to suffer for long. Yet when I stumbled off the bus into the dark winter night and the banker reached out his hand to me, his fellow American, I could not bring myself to reciprocate. It was petty and unbecoming, I know, but I just turned and walked away.

NOTES

1. Eric Hobsbawm, *Nations and Nationalism since 1780* (Cambridge: Cambridge University Press, 1992), 143.

2. For a classic football travelogue that highlights conflict and rivalry, see Simon Kuper, *Football against the Enemy* (London: Orion, 1994).

3. Mark Gevisser, "A Joyous Burden," *Mail and Guardian*, June 13, 2010, http://mg.co.za/article/2010-06-13-a-joyous-burden, accessed October 19, 2012.

4. Benedict Anderson, *Imagined Communities: Reflections on the Origin and Spread of Nationalism* (1983; London: Verso, 1991).

5. Peter King, @SI_PeterKing, http://twitter.com/#!/SI_PeterKing/statuses/16499434104, accessed June 18, 2010.

6. Dave Zirin, "After Donovan's Goal: Joy or Jingoism?," June 23, 2010, http://www.thenation.com/blog/36567/after-donovans-goal-joy-or-jingoism, accessed August 9, 2011.

7. For insights on the history and culture of American soccer, see, among others, David Wangerin, *Soccer in a Football World: The Story of America's Forgotten Game* (Philadelphia: Temple University Press, 2006); Andrei S. Markovits and Steven L. Hellerman, *Offside: Soccer and American Exceptionalism in Sport* (Princeton: Princeton University Press, 2001); Franklin Foer, "Soccer vs. McWorld," *Foreign Policy* 140 (2004): 32–40.

8. Jonny Steinberg, *South Africa's Xenophobic Eruption* (Pretoria: Institute for Security Studies, 2008); Francis Nyamnjoh, *Insiders and Outsiders: Citizenship and Xenophobia in Contemporary Southern Africa* (Dakar: CODESRIA; London: Zed, 2006).

9. Richard Lapper and Simon Kuper, "Did South Africa Win the World Cup?" *Financial Times*, July 9, 2010, http://www.ft.com/cms/s/2/27b0ba2e-8a33-11df-bd30-00144feab49a.html#axzz2C2BNPh00, accessed November 12, 2012.

10. David Goldblatt, *The Ball Is Round: A Global History of Soccer* (New York: Riverhead, 2008), 904.

Official FIFA World Cup iconography, Soccer City, June 23, 2010.
(Photograph by Chris Bolsmann.)

Ghana supporter,
Soccer City, June 23,
2010. (Photograph by
Peter Alegi.)

The Alegi family with friends outside Ellis Park Stadium, Johannesburg,
June 24, 2010. (Photograph by Peter Alegi.)

The closing ceremony before the final, Soccer City, July 11, 2010. (Photograph by Chris Bolsmann.)

Makarapa Stadium, *Halakasha!* exhibition, Standard Bank Gallery, Johannesburg, June 2010. (Photograph by Chris Bolsmann.)

Detail of *Nkosi Sikelele* sculpture by Johannes Segogela, *Halakasha!*
exhibition, Standard Bank Gallery, Johannesburg, June 2010.
(Photograph by Chris Bolsmann.)

Mexico fans with masks before the opening game, South Africa versus Mexico, Soccer City, June 11, 2010. (Photograph courtesy of Wiki Commons.)

Japan fans at Soccer City, June 23, 2010. (Photograph by Chris Bolsmann.)

Spain fans pay tribute to South Africa's former president before the World Cup final at Soccer City, July 11, 2010. (Photograph by Chris Bolsmann.)

Uruguay March On, outside Royal Bafokeng Stadium, Mexico versus Uruguay, Rustenburg, June 22, 2010. (Photograph by David Patrick Lane.)

Bonds of friendship at a friendly match between England fans and inmates at Zonderwater Prison, Cullinan, near Pretoria, June 13, 2010. (Photograph by Steve McCormick.)

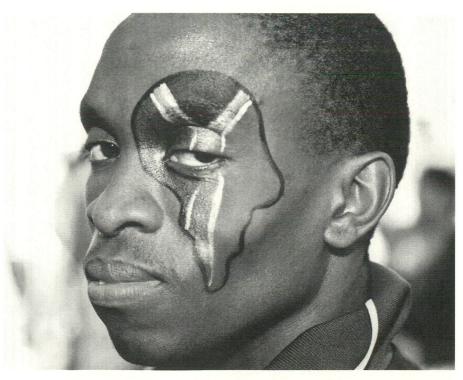

Africa's World Cup, June 2010. (Photograph courtesy of Wiki Commons.)

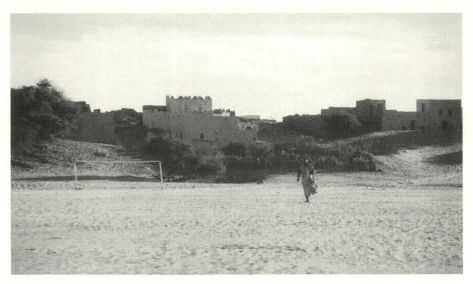

Football pitch in Chinguetti, Mauritania, January 22, 2010.
(Photograph by Anna Kayumi Kerber.)

(*Left to right*) Styles Mkhize, Thabo Dladla, and Patrick Mthembu coaching
Izichwe youths, Pietermaritzburg, July 2, 2011. (Photograph by Peter Alegi.)

Three Lions Ate My Shirt

England Fans in South Africa

MARK PERRYMAN

THE BANTER ABOUT SOUTH AFRICA began the moment that Wayne Rooney put the final goal past the opposition keeper to complete England's 5–1 rout of Croatia and clinch "our" World Cup qualification. British newspaper clichés would shortly be joined by murkier tales of spiraling murder and armed robbery rates, uncompleted stadiums, the risk of contracting HIV and AIDS, and the grinding poverty that would leave the local population resentful at best and vengeful at worst. This was a land where those of us who wear the three lions on our chest might catch a glimpse of the threesome in the wild instead. But the wildlife, the landscape, the people, and the cultures we would be experiencing scarcely earned a mention. Nor did the fact that South Africa hosted the World Cup of rugby and cricket (in 1995 and 2003, respectively), as well as thirty-five thousand fans following the other Lions (the egg-chasing variety), all with great success.

Steve Bloomfield was one of the few Western journalists to go against this flow of bad-news stories and to try to analyze why they were being written. "Like so much coverage of South Africa, stereotypes can easily take over," he wrote in the *Independent*. "Wars and humanitarian crises get far more exposure than stories about economic growth, technological advances and stability. The West's view of Africa is still seen through the prism of tragedy, meaning the story of Africa's first World Cup is read with a certain amount of cynicism. How could a continent that cannot feed itself, is ruled by despots and always at war host one of the world's largest events?"[1]

When the South African far right-winger Eugène Terre'Blanche was murdered in April 2010, the *Daily Star* front page screamed, "World Cup Fans Face Bloodbath—Race War Declared in South Africa." The group Terre'Blanche had led, the Afrikaner Resistance Movement (Afrikaner Weerstandsbeweging, or AWB), is a small white-supremacist outfit. The idea that the AWB could threaten the security of the World Cup was a sensationalist fantasy, yet the serious press followed the tabloids, giving the AWB threats a credibility they did not deserve.

The fans who followed England to South Africa were in the main experienced away travelers. We'd visited Belarus, the Ukraine, and Kazakhstan in the course of the 2010 World Cup qualifying campaign. Belarus remains Europe's last communist dictatorship; Dniepropetrovsk, where the game against the Ukraine was played, usually receives only a handful of tourists from England a year; what Kazakhstan had previously meant to most of us came from its make-believe ambassador, Borat. These are places fans visit with a mixture of eager excitement and careful caution. So why should South Africa be so different for us?

A month or so before the World Cup, I invited a panel of South Africans to address a fans' World Cup travel forum. Perhaps inevitably, the issue of the AWB came up. Audrey Brown, a South African journalist currently working for the BBC World Service, took a look around our crowd of mainly white faces: "I don't think any of you are going to be victims of a white supremacist race war, are you?" As the grin spread across Audrey's face, we could not for the life of us think why we and the media had taken the threats seriously in the first place.

In addition to these popular misconceptions about "darkest Africa," fans had to contend with FIFA's corporate vision. For FIFA, our World Cup is all about serving the association's financial interests and those of its multinational sponsors. FIFA's mission is to persuade us to travel to the other side of the world to drink Budweiser, eat Big Macs, and watch Shakira on the big screen while staying within the officially sanctioned fan parks and fenced exclusion zones around World Cup stadiums.

As a small yet conscious act of resistance to FIFA-style corporate football, we organized a send-off party in London where we drank South African beer, ate South African food, and immersed ourselves in a night of South African music, comedy, and dance. And when we arrived in South Africa and declared at every opportunity that the World Cup is not owned by FIFA but belongs to the people, the sentiment resonated with millions of South Africans who joined together to "Fick Fufa," as some locals rather wonderfully put it.

Forty-eight hours before South Africa took on Mexico in the World Cup's opening match, the wealthy Johannesburg suburb of Sandton hosted the United We Stand street party, featuring an open-top bus parade by the South African national team. Such parades usually take place after a team has lifted a trophy, not before they've even kicked their first ball. But in South Africa, they do things differently. The organizers had expected a crowd of fifty thousand, but at least twice that many turned out. In the midst of this public celebration, I met up with England fan Dave Thompson and his partner, Yazz. We thought we would drive, but the huge traffic jams overwhelmed us, and we walked. For miles around, it was one amazing party. We got caught up in groups of schoolchildren, but it was not just kids—it seemed like everyone had taken the day off. And everyone was wearing yellow Bafana Bafana shirts. This Sandton street fest also marked the first time we heard vuvuzelas. We were in our England shirts, and plenty of locals wanted to chat with us; people were friendly, full of anticipation and excitement.

DJ General S'bu had traveled from Johannesburg to London a few weeks earlier for our send-off party and to fill the dance floor with his selection of sounds. After leaving the madness of Sandton, I caught up with him on his home turf, the bohemian suburb of Melville. The General described to me what joining us to play at our party represented: "The pleasure of the World Cup is its moment of common humanity." I asked him how this connected to the intense national pride I had just witnessed in Sandton, where tens of thousands of people were succumbing to Bafana Bafana fever. The General admitted uneasiness: "The flag of the ANC, yes, that's a symbol of resistance. But a national flag, that's something I'm more uneasy with—including my own. These are symbols of exclusion, they are parochial, part of an ordering of our emotions into a hierarchy of loyalties." So far, so familiar. For years, I've been having this kind of argument with leftists in England, whenever I have championed what I call a "soft patriotism," a divorcing of pride from the prejudice too often dragged along in its wake. But in South Africa, there is another dimension to this argument that cannot be dismissed. South Africa has been forced to craft a new identity out of the legacy of apartheid, a regime that came to an end only sixteen years before the World Cup. The General had a neat way of summing up how this process is represented by the Rainbow Nation flag that would be draped, waved, and worn all over the country in the coming weeks. "Our flag? It's a compromise, a cut-and-paste job," he said.

The year 2010 was, of course, celebrated as Africa's first hosting of the World Cup, and *Times* of London columnist Simon Barnes suggests that for the English, football acts as a kind of surrogate: "Football is the last empire. In every other walk of life, we have reluctantly come to the conclusion that we no longer rule the world. Football is the one area in which the supremacy of our nation and our culture is taken for granted." He continues, "In every other sport, in every other aspect of life, we are prepared to admit the superiority of others. But in football we still, quite seriously, expect to win everything."[2]

This expectation is not based on any record of achievement. In fact, since winning the World Cup at home in 1966, England has managed only one semifinal appearance. Such overblown expectations contribute to the self-importance that at its worst, Englishness adopts—a weakness aided and abetted by the extraordinary interest in the England team around the world. This interest arises not from our World Cup success but from the global televised popularity of the English Premiership.

So perhaps I should not have been so surprised what the England end looked like at our first game versus the United States. As I looked around, I had never seen such a multicultural crowd of fans. There were hundreds of black African and Indian faces, including a group of lads wearing "South African Muslims welcome the World Cup" baseball caps. I realized that these were locals who tonight were here to support my team. And our fans had no problem with this; after all, as Robert Green's hapless goalkeeping would shortly reveal, we were going to need all the support we could get.

I found myself sitting next to a young Indian guy, so I thanked him for his countrymen's support. Mrinal looked at me blankly before proudly explaining that he was not from South Africa but from Calcutta! So how had he ended up supporting England? "World Cup 2002, Beckham's penalty against Argentina. Everything about that goal drew me to football and to becoming an England fan." Not such an easy ambition where Mrinal was growing up: almost all Bengali fans—who are unusual in India for taking their football seriously—back Brazil at World Cups. Yet for Mrinal, Beckham had sparked the original interest. "Of course I'd heard what a great player he was at Man United, but it was when I saw him in an England shirt that I felt I wanted to be part of this." Four years later, Mrinal went to England to study for his A-level exams, and the start of his new school term coincided with England's first match at the new Wembley Stadium—ironically, against Brazil. "It was a dream come true. I went to the game, and when I was there I picked up a membership form for the England Supporters Club. I joined the next day." Having grown up in Calcutta, finished his schooling in London, and attended university in New York, Mrinal has now traveled to South Africa to support my—and now his—England. (Although he does remind me, "Of course if we were playing cricket there'd be no such choice.")

The worldwide appeal of England's domestic league can inspire the kind of imperial mentality that columnist Simon Barnes describes. But the process of globalization also affects English fans' sense of belonging in a quite different manner. Race is a key element in any brand of nationalism, whether the hardened, exclusivist version or this softer, inclusive kind that I prefer. Shortly before the 2010 World Cup, journalist Gary Younge explained in the *New Statesman* what supporting the team means for a new generation of black England fans: "Supporting England is a no-brainer because English football looks more or less like the England they inhabit." He added a poignant afterthought: "Unlike boardrooms or the government, it is one in which they have seen that they have a reasonable chance of succeeding."[3] Racism can never be separated from the power that constructs it, as South Africa's recent history reminds us.

The team a nation puts on a pitch tells us a lot about the country the players come from. The 1966 World Cup Final remains English football's fondest moment, but 1966 was anything but glorious for South African football. Two years earlier, the country's white football association had been suspended for a second time. For most whites, it was inconceivable that a black player could play on the same team as a white one, let alone represent his country. For entirely different reasons, the victorious England team of 1966 also was exclusively white. The social changes that produced today's multicultural and racially diverse Eng-

land team and supporters required less pain and sacrifice than the defeat of apartheid and the building of democracy in South Africa, but the
transformation nevertheless has been momentous for all of us.

We gathered in Orlando West, one of Soweto's most historic neighborhoods, in front of Hector Pieterson's statue. "Hector Pieterson was
shot on this corner, he fell and was carried by one of his schoolmates,"
one of the students told us. Hector was killed on the morning of June
16, 1976, as more than ten thousand young students marched in protest
against the use of Afrikaans—the language of the oppressor—as a me-
dium of instruction in black schools. "I have a family member who was
shot dead that day. The white cops came here, shooting and killing the
children." To hear these children retell this violent history was deeply
moving.[4] "1994 was the year of freedom. That was when South Africa
became free. So we say as children born after 1994 we were born free,"
they told us, cheering in unison. In response, I choked back tears as I
read out the names of the players that Fabio Capello would have had
to cross off his team sheet for England's game the following day had
apartheid still been the law of the land: David James, Ashley Cole, Glen
Johnson, Ledley King, Aaron Lennon, Shaun Wright-Philips, Emile
Heskey, Jermaine Defoe. Nothing to do with injuries, loss of form or
tactics, just the dark color of their skin. We had come to South Africa to
enjoy ourselves, but having a good time does not have to force us into
compulsive forgetfulness. I will always remember the morning the 2010
World Cup opened, when the children of Soweto taught us what their
history means to them and what it should mean to us.

As fans crisscrossed the country following England match after
match, the history of South Africa was unavoidable. On the road to
Cape Town, we had a lunchtime stop in a place in the middle of nowhere called Britstown. A couple of days were spent in Kimberley, the
diamond town some of us knew as the site of a famous South African
War siege, and further down the road we stayed in Matjiesfontein in
the Karoo. In this remote spot, the Lord Milner Hotel remained rich
in imperial kitsch.

In Cape Town, we visited Robben Island, a world-famous symbol of
racial oppression in South Africa. Robben Island is also connected to
football—the reason we have traveled to South Africa. Few could fail to
make this link after meeting Chuck Korr, coauthor (with Marvin Close)
of *More Than Just a Game*, a book that tells the extraordinary tale of

how political prisoners on the island formed the Makana Football Association, complete with league and cup competitions, relegation and promotion, disciplinary hearings, and all the other paraphernalia our game demands.[5] "Playing football became a way of persevering, to keep their dignity, preserving the ideals for which they'd been locked up," said Korr.

As soon as I had finished reading *More Than Just a Game*, I contacted Chuck with an idea. He was slightly bemused: "I was both inspired and puzzled. I was so pleased that you England fans had understood what the story was all about. But I was puzzled what you might do with it. I didn't really know where you were coming from." Over the next few months, the historian got to know us better, and the plan unfolded. We decided to fill a ferry bound for Robben Island (now a museum) with one hundred fans the day before the England-Algeria game. Some of the men involved with football in the apartheid prison would join us, and on the same pitch that they had built (despite initial opposition from the prison authorities), we would present them with custom-made Makana FA team uniforms.

As the ferry left the dock at the Cape Town waterfront, the England fans, hailing from different backgrounds and inclinations, seemed unanimously proud to be making their bit of history. Joining us were Chuck and former prisoners Lionel Davis and Sedick Isaacs. As Davis patiently recounted for us what life had been like on the island, there was no danger that the story of him and his mates playing football would somehow transform the oppressive prison regime into some kind of penal holiday camp. As we listened in respectful silence, none of us would make that gross error. The prisoners had to campaign for years, facing opposition and disappointment over and over again, to do what we take for granted—the right to kick a football, organize a team, wear their colors, mark out a pitch. "The fans I spoke to crossing over, they told me how much they were looking forward to being on the island," Korr said. "But these weren't any ordinary tourists. They were fans, to them football really matters. They'd come to South Africa for the football, and they understood why this sport mattered so much to those locked up by the apartheid government, too." At the end of the visit, we presented Lionel Davis and Sedick Isaacs with their shirts. We had designed an FA crest for Makana, too, and underneath, where "England vs Algeria" and the match date would be embroidered on the shirts of Rooney and the team the following night, we had sewn "Football vs Apartheid, 1969–1990." What we learned there about the prisoners' battle with the violent and racist regime that ruled South Africa with an iron fist for half a century will stick in our memories, I suspect, a lot longer than England's pitifully poor 0–0 draw with Algeria in Cape Town.

After Cape Town, England's qualification for the knockout stages was secured and hopes were briefly raised, only to be dashed in spectacular fashion at Bloemfontein with a 4–1 thrashing by the Germans. England fans have had plenty of time to learn to live with disappointment. However, the team's performance this time round was so dismal it might finally begin to lift the burden of expectation they have carried to every tournament since 1966.

For traveling England supporters, South Africa 2010 was another stage in the journey away from a viciously offensive brand of popular English nationalism that revolves around football. At a South African football culture exhibition entitled *Halakasha!* at the Standard Bank Gallery in Johannesburg (see the essay by Fiona Rankin-Smith in this volume), I found a sentence that captured this process of increasing detachment of patriotic pride from prejudice among England fans: "The field of play it produces stretches far beyond the boundaries of its goal posts and pitches," states Prishani Naidoo in the official exhibition catalog, "fields of play that sometimes bring into question the 'taken-for-granted,' 'the natural,' the ways in which 'we are meant' to be in society."[6] For many England fans, this was the core of our World Cup experience in South Africa: It provided us with a different way to consume our football. As we boarded the plane home at Oliver Tambo International Airport the day after the final, we were happy to have caught Bafana Bafana fever. We knew we—and maybe South Africa, too—would never be the same.

NOTES

1. Steve Bloomfield, "Football Needs to Tackle Its Stereotyping," *Independent*, June 12, 2009. See also Steve Bloomfield, *Africa United: Soccer, Passion, Politics, and the First World Cup in Africa* (New York: Harper Perennial, 2010).

2. Simon Barnes, "England Remain in Fantasy Football Land," *Times* (London), July 9, 2009. Using football experience, population size, and per capita income as key indicators, Kuper and Szymanski looked at the country's international results

between 1872 and 2001 and concluded that "England was not underperforming at all. Contrary to popular opinion, it was overperforming" (Simon Kuper and Stefan Szymanski, *Soccernomics* [New York: Nation Books, 2009], 37).

3. Gary Younge, "How I Finally Learned to Cheer for England," *New Statesman*, July 6, 2010.

4. For further details, see Khangela Ali Hlongwane, Sifiso Ndlovu, and Mothobi Mutloatse, eds., *Soweto '76: Reflections on the Liberation Struggles* (Houghton: Mutloatse Arts Heritage Trust, 2006).

5. Chuck Korr and Marvin Close, *More Than Just a Game: Football v. Apartheid* (London: Collins, 2008).

6. Prishani Naidoo, "A Field of Play," in *Halakasha!*, ed. Fiona Rankin-Smith (Johannesburg: Wits Arts Museum, 2010).

Mexi-co, Mexi-co, Ra, Ra, Ra!

Invented Traditions and the Cultural Performance of Mexican Fans at the 2010 World Cup

SERGIO VARELA HERNÁNDEZ

JUNE 22, 2010: Rustenburg, 120 kilometers west of Johannesburg. It's a fast-growing city, home to nearly four hundred thousand people and to the largest platinum mines in the world and the scene of the worst performance of El Tri—Mexico's national team—at the 2010 World Cup. Two days earlier, Elena, a Mexican living in Johannesburg and married to Herb, a South African, had contacted me to organize a group trip. We gathered thirteen people willing to pay 200 rand (29 dollars) each and hired a minibus and driver to take us from Johannesburg to Rustenburg and back. We began our journey at nine in the morning on match day.

An odd mix of nationalities made the trip: Juan, a Nicaraguan based in Mozambique; Roger, a Honduran; Andy, Herb, and the driver (all South Africans); Diego and Raul from Spain; and seven Mexicans—Elena, Ernesto, María, Bere, Cris, Roberto, and me. I knew none of the Mexicans before I arrived in South Africa.

The departure from Johannesburg was slow, much like a family outing. As we left the city's skyscrapers behind us, bottles of Castle, a popular South African beer, began to circulate.[1] Bere was wearing a "Made in China" Mexican flag as a cape and a bandana wrapped around his head. Elena carried another pair of flags in her backpack. Bere and Elena decided to hang one *tricolor* on the rear window of the microbus.

For Mexicans, the tricolor flag is a very important element of national identity. The vertical green, white, and red are *criollo-mestizo* in origin, while the coat of arms in the center of the flag, as generations of Mexican schoolchildren have been taught, represents the indigenous past. An eagle perched on a *nopal* (an edible local cactus) sprouting out of an island in the middle of the lake where the Aztecs, so the legend goes, founded the ancient city of Mexico-Tenochtitlán, the center of the Aztec Empire.

On the road to Rustenburg, a strange and special international dialogue unfolded. That is, my fellow travelers launched into conversations that began in the same way: "In Mexico . . . ," "In Nicaragua . . . ," and so on. As if it were an awkward, somewhat stiff television sketch, we Mexicans started communicating and, in the process, performing and inventing our Mexicanness.

The Mexican contingent launched into a folk-ranchero classic, "Cielito Lindo": "Ay, ay ayay, canta y no llores. Porque cantando cielito lindo." Others sang some *corridos* (Mexican folk songs) that I did not know, with Elena's parents, Ernesto and Maria, from Durango, a northern state of the republic with a rich folk and ranchero tradition, humming along. Nowadays, there is a broadly popular *norteño* (northern) folk music style known as *paso duranguense* (Durango dance). Herb, Bere's South African husband, exclaimed, "Viva Mexico, cabrones" in a South African English–accented and quasi-authentic Mexican Spanish.

As we continued down the freeway, Bere, Elena, Maria, Ernesto, and Cris tried to coordinate a kind of Mexican line to follow. Then suddenly it was the old-fashioned war chant of Mexican fans that enveloped us: "Chiquitibum a la bim bom ba, Mexico, Mexico, ra, ra, ra!"[2] This chant was interspersed with one verse of "El Rey," a song composed by José Alfredo Jiménez, another famous Mexican folk-ranchero musician.

After a fuel stop, it was time for an "El Rey" reprise. Bere pulled out a lipstick in the green, white, and red of the Mexican flag and began to apply stripes on the cheeks of all the passengers. Again, the obsession with the flag!

We finally made it to Rustenburg in the early afternoon, though we still had a good distance to cover before reaching the stadium. I was resigned to being late for kickoff. We were on "Mexican time"—that is, not just fashionably late, but following a Mexican tradition of refusing to be punctual for an appointment. At about 3:45 p.m. we reached the Park and Ride, a heavily policed official parking area where fans boarded buses for the Royal Bafokeng Stadium.

As the 4:30 kickoff approached, I arrived at the "FIFAland" fence with my ticket in hand. The fenced borders of the area surrounding the stadium had an obvious organizational purpose (crowd control and spectator safety) but had disciplinary effects as well. South Africa's World Cup venues, in other words, were organized to coercively and noncoercively produce symbolic and economic homogeneity. In a way, the discipline and organization of the event "invented" the fans themselves.

After about three minutes of waiting, we got on the bus that would take us to the stadium; thus, I crossed the first filter for the site. Only ticket holders were allowed on the bus, so with few exceptions, the guests at FIFA's party were a privileged minority with Internet access, credit cards, and disposable income. On the bus, we mingled with people from around the world, including many children and elderly persons. Chants and jokes made for a friendly atmosphere, with no hints whatsoever of tension or violence. "Hey you Uruguayans, are you ready to go back to South America?" a cheeky Mexican supporter asked a pair of Uruguayans. "You have to score first and Chicharito [Mexican striker Javier Hernández] will not score a goal," replied one of the Uruguayans with a smile in his face.[3]

After about fifteen minutes, the bus arrived at its destination, a fifty-thousand-seat stadium is in the middle of a sparsely populated area. Renovations for the World Cup cost $50 million and transformed the ground into an impressive, modern stadium that contrasted starkly with the empty land around it.

As I approached the Royal Bafokeng Stadium, the social technology used for organizing the event seemed to be consistent with the provisions of the state of security and disciplinary control. This did not mean that at all times and in every space, fans were forced into the designs and desires of FIFA and its corporate allies. Fortunately, certain expressions and practices suggested the possibility of slipping through the net of control. For example, dozens of informal vendors were selling knockoff T-shirts, flags, scarfs, hats, *makarapas* (decorated hard hats), and vuvuzelas.

Another example of FIFA's lack of total control was the vibrant black market for World Cup tickets. Despite the governing body's centralized ticket-selling system, tickets could easily be found online and on the streets. Using some personal connections, I bought a match ticket from a scalper who said he had obtained them from South African organizers cashing in on complimentary tickets allotted to them by FIFA.

Closer to the stadium, metal fences and metal detectors discouraged fans without tickets from approaching. My two Spanish fellow travelers and I got out of the bus and walked toward the gates under direction of dozens of World Cup volunteers and police officers. We passed the first crowd filters a few hundred meters from the stadium's main gate. A policeman conducted the first search and cut the bottom of the ticket. It was virtually impossible to enter with food or beverages, nor were spectators permitted to carry signs, badges, or clothing that might visibly affect the marketing interests of the sponsoring companies. Sportswear brands other than Adidas could be forfeited if a security officer deemed the items "ambush marketing." Any kind of commercial or "ideological" propaganda, including political demonstrations, was strictly forbidden. Thus, FIFA's corporate machinery influenced the construction and performance of World Cup fandom and efficiently managed it to exploit its vast commercial potential.[4]

After crossing the final security checkpoint, we were in the heart of FIFAland, a theme park landscape choreographed with officially branded stores, banners, trademarks, sponsors, slogans, and music. The overwhelming commercial character of FIFAland intensified as one penetrated further into the stadium. Fans and their passion were almost trapped by trade, police and private security guards, and, of course, hundreds of members of the media, who attracted much attention from fans. The opportunity to be seen on television shaped many Mexican fans' conduct and performance styles. Dressed in colorful clothes and adorned with accessories, Mexicans aspired to see their image beamed on television screens in the stadium and around the world or perhaps reproduced in the pages of a magazine or newspaper.

Finally, I entered the seating area. My pace quickened. It was already 4:10. My seat was on the second level, very close to the northwestern corner of the pitch, near the Uruguayan goal in the first half. The athletics track surrounded the pitch, putting the crowd far away. I was seated in the midst of a sea of my countrymen and -women. I turned and viewed the amazing spectacle of thirty thousand Mexicans in the middle of the South African countryside, 14,000 kilometers (8,750 miles) from the motherland. Crazy! The insanity of it all was kept in check by tested systems of spectator control: Any "embarrassing" action could be prosecuted and punished. According to the terms and conditions printed on the back of my expensive ticket, activities or symbols that were ostentatiously "racist, xenophobic, altruistic, or ideological" were banned. Any kind of organized collective action potentially beyond FIFA's control was considered suspicious or dangerous. Even solidarity statements, such as AIDS-awareness messages, were prohibited. Such prohibitions were a powerful symbol of the highly individualistic and commercialized ethos of the tournament.

Within this context, Mexican supporters inside the Royal Bafokeng Stadium wore wrestlers masks, *ranchero* hats, and *sarapes* (traditional blankets) and proudly waved tricolor flags and the seemingly obligatory green-and-black Adidas football shirts. Chants of "Cielito Lindo" and "Mexico, Mexico, ra, ra!" sounded intermittently. The hats and wrestler masks, worn at previous matches and in the streets of South African cities, were understood as emblematic of Mexicanness. These invented "traditional" symbols of Mexican national identity and culture were, of course, manufactured in China.

Mexican fans practiced a series of performances that placed them into two paradoxical categories: fans and Mexicans. Being a fan involves the invention of a particular socioeconomic behavior within the constraints set by state security forces, corporate commercial imperatives, and FIFA-accredited media conglomerates.[5] To be Mexican at the 2010 World Cup meant to practice one of the aspects of commercial impulse, the nationalist-chauvinistic one, which is essentially a discourse that appeals and recourses to certain "traditions"—symbols, myths, rituals, and choreographies invented by and for the exaltation of modernity itself. *Sarapes*, *ranchero* hats, and wrestler masks, along with "Cielito Lindo" and "El Rey," filled Mexicans' need to differentiate themselves from supporters of other nations precisely as Mexicans. By drawing on superficial yet popular idioms, the huge number of Mexican fans in South Africa became an important part of the media circus covering the World Cup. In doing so, the agency of Mexican fans played out in a frame created and defined by global capitalism.

As the teams walked out on to the field to the tune of the newly composed FIFA anthem, Mexican fans seemed nervous and worried. But Mexicans did what they did at other matches during the World Cup: They stood up, put their right hands on their chests, and bellowed the lyrics. They belted the usual *porras*—stadium chants or cries—and performed their typical rituals, such as waving their hands and outstretched arms and shouting "puto" (loosely translated as sissy) at the goalkeeper about to kick the ball into play. Many South Africans enjoyed this novelty and joined in.

With the score still 0–0, the euphoria of Mexico's impressive victory over France five days earlier had disappeared, replaced by a collective sense of impending defeat. Indeed, the specter of Mexico's failure and possible elimination loomed over Royal Bafokeng Stadium. Making matters worse for the Mexican fans, vuvuzelas blared at the news of South Africa's first goal against France in Bloemfontein. Goal differential might decide who went home and who progressed to the next round. Again the vuvuzelas; South Africa's second goal. Then two minutes before halftime, striker Luis Suárez scored for Uruguay.

Out of a group of white and very drunk Mexican young men, barechested and with painted faces, a bottle of beer flew onto the pitch. Those around them singled him out and chastised him. The culprit, an overweight, tall, twenty-year-old, faced his critics but remained silent. Other fans shouted "Pinche naco" (fucking Indian) and "pendejo" (idiot) at him. Fatalism took over. Even obvious inebriation was incapable of resurrecting the euphoric nationalistic spirit that had been present a few days earlier at the match against France.

The second half in Rustenburg went by without emotion and precious few scoring chances. The bad Mexican play was surpassed only by Uruguayan brusqueness. A cry of "Get the Guille out" was heard. Mexican fans often criticized Guillermo "Guille" Franco, a Mexican striker picked by coach Javier Aguirre, because of the player's Argentinean origin. During the World Cup, Guille was also booed and targeted by homophobic insults. As we waited for the final whistle, the welcome news spread (through cell phones) that France had scored a consolation goal against South Africa. South Africa would have to score a miraculous three additional goals to eliminate Mexico. It did not happen. The good news was that despite losing 1–0 to Uruguay, Mexico would still advance to the round of sixteen. The bad news was that our squad would face Argentina, one of the favorites to win the World Cup.

I left the stadium and went in search of my traveling companions. Along the way, a comedian named Derbez, the jester of the Mexican network Televisa, conducted interviews among a handful of drunken

Mexicans. Nearby, a group of Uruguayans jumped and shouted in unison, "*Celeste*, I'm blue" (the color of the Uruguayan flag and team jersey). They were happy. Their squad had defied the odds and won the group, avoiding a face-off against Argentina in the next round. Thousands of Mexicans left the stadium in a hurry. That day there was nothing to celebrate.

In the end, chauvinist feelings among Mexican fans—both Mexicans and Mexican Americans—stemmed mostly from "global" dynamics tied to forms of masculinity and class identity. Drinking alcohol, for example, is a quintessential component of fans' masculinity, but it also conveys class status as it gives an individual the opportunity to show off an ability to spend freely on steeply priced beer sold in and around the stadium. Fueled by alcohol, many Mexican supporters at the World Cup in South Africa embraced an invented Mexican "way of life" that most of the time is frowned upon because of its association with the rural, Indian, and mestizo past and present. But conversely, to be perceived as "real" Mexicans, fans could not simply rely on "modern" Mexican symbols such as highways, railroads, airports, smartphones (even if made in Mexico) as symbols of Mexicanness. Caught in this contradiction, Mexican fans combined symbols of campesino folk culture (sombreros, ponchos, songs) and global urban symbols (wrestlers and their masks) to "become" Mexicans. This creative performance transfigured these disparate symbols and inserted them into a global network of manufactured national identities influenced by commercial forces and FIFA with the generous and willing assistance of the South African hosts.

Mexican football nationalism is embedded in global competition, which has historically brought rare glorious victories and many discouraging defeats. In South Africa as so many times before, Mexican fans channeled their disappointment at losing to Argentina in the round of sixteen by blaming the corrupt Mexican political system, psychological (almost innate) weakness, and underdevelopment. "Common sense" explanations were deployed, too: "Les faltaron huevos" (They lacked balls). As the insults against Franco demonstrated, many Mexican fans turn to homophobic and misogynist discourses to explain the team's lackluster performance. Other Mexican fans in South Africa walked away uttering the sports fan's undying hope that "someday" Mexico will—indeed, must—succeed.

Ultimately, the thousands of Mexicans and Mexican Americans who traveled to South Africa for the 2010 World Cup were "closet Mexicans," to borrow a description from the writer Carlos Monsiváis.[6] That is, they represented Mexican men and women who express their nationalistic impulses under the guidance of big business (and triggered by copious amounts of alcohol) during glamorous and expensive events, but they do so without recognizing Mexico's complex history, particularly the struggles of workers, farmers, intellectuals, and political leaders. In the end, closet Mexicans in South Africa never went beyond performing a banal and superficial sense of nationhood best captured by the ever-present chant, "Mexi-co, Mexi-co, ra, ra, ra!"

NOTES

1. See Anne Mager, *Beer, Sociability, and Masculinity in South Africa* (Bloomington: Indiana University Press, 2010).

2. "México, México, Ra, Ra, Ra!" is an old-fashioned chant used to cheer on Mexican teams in international competitions.

3. For a general overview, see Rory M. Miller and Liz Crolley, eds., *Football in the Americas: Fútbol, Futebol, Soccer* (London: Institute for the Study of the Americas, 2007).

4. On commercialism and international soccer, with special emphasis on FIFA, see Barbara Smit, *Pitch Invasion: Adidas, Puma, and the Making of Modern Sport* (London: Lane, 2006).

5. For a detailed ethnography of Mexican fan culture, see Roger Magazine, *Golden and Blue Like My Heart: Masculinity, Youth, and Power among Soccer Fans in Mexico City* (Tucson: University of Arizona Press, 2007).

6. Carlos Monsiváis, *Los Rituales de Caos* (México, D.F.: Ediciones Era, 1995), 187.

The Road to 2010

*A Soccer Journey from
Marrakech to Johannesburg*

NIELS POSTHUMUS AND ANNA MAYUMI KERBER

THE IDEA CAME UP while we were living and working in Johannesburg in 2008: Let's drive a car all the way from Europe through Africa to the 2010 World Cup. It sounded like a crazy idea, and, in fact, it was. To make the best of our journey, given our limited time and means, we soon decided to focus on the region that produced Roger Milla, Michael Essien, and Emmanuel Adebayor and that, with North Africa, is the most accomplished in the continent's soccer history: West Africa.[1]

At the end of 2009, we bought the cheapest sport utility vehicle we could find—a Suzuki Vitara—and packed our bags. We put spare tires in the trunk, waterproofed an old tent, and were ready to leave. Somehow it all felt strangely logical. A Dutch reporter and football fan and a slightly less soccer-obsessed Austrian photojournalist on the road to 2010, driving from Amsterdam southward, through Belgium and France, to a ferry near Spanish Algeciras four days later, and into the African continent to write stories about soccer for the next six months on our way to the first World Cup on African soil.

We came to West Africa to study its soccer culture. What explained its importance in the societies of this vast and diverse region? Ivory Coast, Ghana, Nigeria and Cameroon had all qualified for the World Cup 2010 in South Africa. This meant that four of the tournament's six African participants were located in the West African area along the Gulf of Guinea. Did soccer in this region mean more than just sport?

176

We thought of a poster in Cape Town that stated, "In Africa, soccer is no religion; it is what any religion should be." Still, we wanted to search for more than stories of African soccer success and the game's social resonance. We also were keen to learn more about failures and the shadowy aspects of soccer. What explained the rapid decline of a Togolese national team that had been so successful in 2006? And how had Morocco, arguably Africa's strongest national side for much of the 1970s, turned into a national disgrace?

We crossed into Morocco from the rock of Gibraltar in December 2009. We expected to find soccer madness in the country because the African Nations Cup was due to start in two weeks in Angola. We expected everyone to be fully absorbed by the impending competition, but Moroccans seemed not to care. On the day of the opening match, it was dead quiet at the Montreal, a coffeehouse in the Djemaa el Fna, Marrakech's central square, bustling with street vendors and tourists, surrounded by souks and the town's tallest minaret. The coffeehouse's television was switched off. The rundown Hotel Tiza, just behind the square, was doing brisk business because local folks had gathered there to watch a Spanish La Liga game between Barcelona and Tenerife.

Local disinterest in the African Nations Cup, explained Youssef Ahenguir as he brought us tea, stemmed from Morocco's failure to qualify for the tournament. Once among Africa's most powerful and feared soccer teams, Morocco would not challenge for the continental title for the first time since 1996, when South Africa won the competition on home soil. Moroccan soccer, Youssef told us, was in deep crisis. It had gone sharply downhill after 2004, when the country lost the bid to host the 2010 World Cup.

The FIFA executive committee vote had been close. South Africa edged out Morocco 14–10; three more votes for Morocco, and the newly built stadium just outside Marrakech would have been the arena for a World Cup semifinal. "But after losing the 2010 bid, everything went wrong," according to our interlocutor.[2] Morocco failed to qualify for the 2006 World Cup and was eliminated in the first round in both the 2006 and 2008 African Nations Cup tournaments. The Atlas Lions, as the national team of Morocco is known, reached their nadir in 2010, failing to reach the Nations Cup in Angola and the World Cup in South Africa.

Morocco's exclusion from the 2010 World Cup was especially painful. "We were the first African country to top a group at the World Cup," Youssef said proudly. That result had been achieved in Mexico in 1986 when Morocco beat Portugal 3–0 and drew 0–0 against England and Poland. "The Africa Cup is no big deal," he continued; "Moroccans feel more European than African anyway." A handful of customers at the Montreal coffeehouse, who by this time had joined the conversation, agreed. King Hassan II, the country's former monarch, is reputed to have said, "Morocco is like a tree of which the roots are planted firmly in Africa, but which has its branches in Europe."

Looking at contemporary Moroccan soccer, Hassan's insight seems prescient. For example, the question vexing Moroccan soccer fans was not only whether FAR Rabat, Wydad Casablanca, or Kawkab Marrakech would top the national league but whether one supported Real Madrid or Barcelona. Tellingly, local kids solely wore the football shirts of Barcelona's Lionel Messi and Real Madrid's Kaká and Cristiano Ronaldo, never Atlas Lions stars such as Marouane Chamakh (2009 Player of the Year in France now with Arsenal) or Mounir El Hamdaoui (2009 Dutch Player of the Year and top scorer, currently with Fiorentina).

The problem, the men at the Marrakech coffeehouse said, was that neither Chamakh nor El Hamdaoui were real Moroccans. Born and raised in Europe, Chamakh in France and El Hamdaoui in the Netherlands, their hearts and loyalty allegedly rested in Europe; they lacked passion for the Moroccan national team. These critical fans had their suspicions confirmed when El Hamdaoui refused to give an interview in Arabic, choosing to explain the latest defeat in English, a language neither widely used nor widely understood in Morocco. Six national coaches over the past five years had been unable to replant Afro-European stars into Moroccan soccer soil, the fans explained. In the end, the recent dismal, humiliating qualification campaigns produced only indifference and resignation.

Trying to dust off Morocco's soccer disappointment, we drove further south toward Mauritania, where the Sahara desert took over the landscape. Trees and green bushes disappeared; sand in a million shades of gray, yellow and white came into sight. Seemingly endless panoramas of dusty nothingness enveloped the perfectly tarred road on which we drove.

Except for some desolate soccer fields, there was no evidence of life in this thinly populated area. But when we stopped at a tiny village, as the sun set and a cool breeze took away the heat of the day, faint dark silhouettes appeared from the shadows and started kicking around a soccer ball made out of a bundle of old rags. A small crowd of spectators followed minutes later. At nightfall, the desert suddenly seemed to have more inhabitants than one could possibly imagine in the daytime. Soccer seemed to bring the desert to life.

In Nouadhibou, the Mauritanian port city near the border with Western Sahara, sixteen-year-old Abou Amadou Sy took a deep breath as he walked onto a pitch that was nothing more than a golden strip of plain sand on the shores of the Atlantic Ocean on an early Saturday morning. Abou quickly looked at the rusty goalposts at both ends. He gazed at the lines marking the pitch, black as if they were scratched into the sandy soil with a piece of charcoal.

It looked as if Abou was imagining a freshly cut grass pitch, perhaps one of country's two turfed soccer venues, located 300 miles (479 kilometers) down the coast in the capital, Nouakchott. It was about 10:00 in the morning. The muezzin had called for the second prayer of the day not too long before. It had been a piercing call, sounding almost desperate. Abou was the captain of his team. He gathered together his players, who were completing their pregame stretching exercises on the side of the pitch, just as he had done with the squad at a Koranic school earlier that morning. The religious school had functioned as a dressing room.

Abou was one of the country's most gifted soccer talents. In the near future, he was likely to sign his first professional soccer contract for ASC SNIM of Nouadhibou, the Mauritanian champions at the time, yet he still insisted on attending school every day. He was religiously observant, but the main reason for attending Koranic school was to learn about the Islamic prohibition of slavery. It was an important lesson because master/servant relationships are still common in Mauritania despite a 2007 government law criminalizing slavery. This recent law freed as many as five hundred thousand people (about one in five Mauritanians) from bondage. Therefore, Abou's religious education not only enabled him to play soccer but also taught him the difference between right and wrong. Asked what he liked most about soccer, Abou replied softly that he cherished the equality on the pitch, the fact that once the ball was rolling, individual achievement and team success were based mainly on technical skills and tactical insight, not skin color or social status.

After the game, when the city's muezzins had made up their way to the top of the minaret and had called for the day's midday prayer, the young footballers walked back home together through the sand dunes. The pitch changed back into nothing more than a piece of desert flatland, its red corner flags and goalposts the only clue about its exciting and worthwhile purpose. Walking home, the boys talked about various subjects, but not about the upcoming World Cup in South Africa. They did not seem to dream of playing in the tournament—probably a wise omission, since Mauritania has never come even remotely close to qualifying. Desert sand is not fertile soil for soccer success. For Mauritanian youths such as Abou and his comrades, soccer was not about winning trophies: Simply playing the game and exercising their right to play was a victory.

Two months later, in April 2010, we were in the luscious confines of Togo's forests and tropical palm beaches. It was again a Saturday, and we were sitting in the Kégué Stadium in Lomé, the country's capital. It had a capacity of about thirty-five thousand spectators, but only a tenth of it was filled for the national team's match against Ivory Coast. "A couple of months earlier the stadium would have been packed," said Joseph Müller Afanyagbe, the cofounder of radio channel Sport FM and a West African with German ancestors, "but the fans are frustrated with their leaders now and disappointed by fate." Joseph had taken us to the game in the Kégué Stadium. An authority on African soccer, he had advised local government about sport policy and had been a soccer analyst for the BBC. "The dream of a whole generation has been smashed," he said. Togo had been struggling with awful political leadership for years. Politics had damagingly interfered with soccer since independence from France in 1960, but in recent years Togolese soccer had suffered a staggering amount of bad luck and experienced a calamitous decline.

What made this misfortune especially frustrating for Togo fans was that it came so soon after Togolese football had skyrocketed in the world rankings. In 2006, the national team, nicknamed Les Eperviers (the Sparrow Hawks), had surprised pundits by qualifying for the World Cup in Germany. Although the team lost all three of its group matches, many observers predicted a glorious future for the young and obviously talented team. But the fairy tale of the "golden generation" did not last long.

Popular expectations had reached fever pitch during the qualifying stages of the 2008 African Nations Cup in neighboring Ghana. With only two matches remaining, Togo headed its qualification group after beating Sierra Leone away. However, just hours after the June 3, 2007, game, a helicopter transporting Togolese soccer officials and politicians home crashed outside Freetown. More than twenty people died in the accident, including sports minister Richard Attipoe.[3] The team and the nation were devastated. Friends of the players and coaches had died in the air crash. Emotionally ruined by the disaster, Togo lost its next two matches and did not qualify for the Nations Cup. "It was a huge slap in the face," said Joseph, who had been in Freetown as a media analyst and reporter. Yet even the most pessimistic could not have envisioned the rapidity of the Sparrow Hawks' fall from grace.

As if Togo wanted to wash away the bad taste of its absence in Ghana, the Sparrow Hawks qualified for the 2010 Nations Cup hosted by Angola, an oil-rich country recovering from two decades of civil war. But before the ball was kicked, tragedy struck again. On the way to the opening match in Cabinda, close to the Angolan border with the Democratic Republic of the Congo, terrorists from an armed wing of the Forces for Liberation of the State of Cabinda, a separatist group, attacked the national team bus. Three people died in the attack: the driver and two team officials, one of them Stan Ocloo, the team's spokesperson and a good friend of Joseph's.[4]

The tragedy made news headlines worldwide, with the more cynical media wondering whether South Africa was safe enough to host the World Cup. That Luanda, Angola's capital, is fifteen hundred miles (twenty-four hundred kilometers) from Johannesburg, did not seem to matter. The Togolese government immediately withdrew its national team from the tournament; in response, the Confederation of African Football (CAF) fined Togo and banned the country from international competition for four years. "The government had been affronted," said Joseph while the small crowd in the Kégué Stadium celebrated a wonderful opening goal for Togo. "They were affronted because CAF had not sent any delegation to Togo to express its condolences after the incident." FIFA later rescinded the punishment, perhaps sensing a public relations disaster. Togo seemed pacified by the decision, but Joseph believed that the reinstatement might have sent the wrong message to the troubled Togolese government. "Politics and soccer should not mix," he said.

But in Togo, more than anywhere else in the world, politics and football are closely linked. Soccer, we discovered, is an especially tricky, sometimes dangerous business in West Africa. The czar of Togo soccer was none other than Colonel Rock Gnassingbé, son of General Gnassingbé Eyadéma, Togo's dictator from 1967 until his death in 2005, and brother of Togo's current president, Faure Gnassingbé. In Togo, soccer did not mix with political affairs, it *was* politics. In fact, Togo's qualification and solid performance in the 2006 World Cup in Germany had given President Faure's government a valuable opportunity to restore its popularity, which had waned as a result of his autocratic, violent rule. In 2007, Joseph quit his job at Sport FM as a consequence of the ongoing political interference. "It is not easy to work within sports business if you don't belong to the right party," he said. He would not have been allowed to criticize Rock Gnassingbé. "But that colonel had no clue what he was doing," Joseph argued. "He is a military commander, not a soccer expert. One does not deal with players like one does with soldiers."

Back in Kégué Stadium, Ivory Coast mounted a comeback and scored the winning goal in the last minute of the game. Joseph shook his head. "With all this corruption and leaders like that, how are we ever going to motivate all the young talents we still have?"

Our interlocutor might be underestimating the special motivation of many young boys in Togo. In Kara, the northern Togolese hometown of the ruling Gnassingbé family, nineteen-year-old Issa Yerima would have done anything to become a professional soccer player. He had even left home, ostensibly to attend college in Lomé, but his parents ordered him to return home when they found out he was in the capital only to play soccer. Now he spends lots of time surfing the Internet in search of football schools in Europe—Belgium and France in particular—to make his dream come true. It just did not seem to occur to wide-eyed youngsters like Issa that they might be not as talented (or fortunate) as their idols: Drogba, Essien, Yaya Touré, Eto'o, Adebayor.

Since the early 1990s, European clubs had become increasingly interested in cheap African talent, especially players competing in lower leagues and in less wealthy countries.[5] Not only were kids like Issa easy prey for shadowy player agents and talent scouts scavenging West Africa for a quick profit, but "a lot of schools in Africa didn't care much about their students' needs," University of Ulster researcher Paul Darby, an expert on African player migration, told us. These academies focus on making financial profit from the children, not educating them or equipping them to become good citizens and productive members of the community. In fact, studies show that hundreds of soccer academies lack genuine educational programs. Young players who fail to meet expectation are kicked out, sometimes after years of neglecting their formal education, leaving them without a future. Some academies are nothing more than scams run out of agents' living rooms.

Even so, a small number of elite African soccer academies do offer a combination of professional and academic training. Darby suggested we have a look at the Right to Dream academy outside Accra, Ghana. The main criterion for admission to Right to Dream is soccer talent, but founder Tom Vernon, an Englishman and former Manchester United scout, raises fifty thousand dollars per student to fund five years of education at the academy. Graduates can obtain scholarships to British and American universities, facilitated by Vernon's international connections and professional networks. Right to Dream seeks to develop not only top footballers but well-educated individuals, because Ghana, Vernon said, needs a new elite.

But even with such genuine interest and tangible investment in schooling, soccer remained central at the Right to Dream academy. "Everybody wants to become a professional soccer player at this school," said fifteen-year-old Joshua Waro. He had grown up on the streets of Kumasi, the Asante capital, 73 miles (117 kilometers) north of Accra; his parents were too poor to buy him shoes. "But you never know what could happen. I was injured for six months last year. Bad luck can end my career. Anyone needs a Plan B." No outlook could please Tom more.

In Johannesburg one month later, however, a Plan B was exactly what we lacked when the big screen at Melrose Arch mall turned black on July 11, 2010. It happened during the second minute of extra time of the World Cup final between the Netherlands and Spain. Thousands of people screamed in despair. Panic-stricken fans scurried around in search of televisions behind apartment windows on the upper floors of the crescent-shaped buildings around the square. The timing of the blackout could not have been worse. Regular power outages had been common in the years before the World Cup. When we lived in Johannesburg, our neighborhood usually lost power on Thursday evenings. But after traveling through so many African countries on the road to

2010, we believed it was going to be, it *had* to be, different during those 120 historic minutes in soccer history.

It was dead quiet on the open square at Melrose Arch. Even the flags were motionless, as if waving would make too much noise. Who had ever imagined listening to rather than watching the climax of the 2010 World Cup final, especially so close to the actual sporting battlefield? Would a crowd gathered in the host nation's largest city miss the decisive minutes of the first World Cup final in Africa? The technicians ran around the stage to find that presumably disconnected cable. In an extraordinary scene, Spanish and Dutch fans helped each other gather as much information about the game as possible through mobile phones and the game sounds coming out of the speakers. We were in disbelief. Could it be that we had driven more than 12,500 miles (20,000 kilometers), only to miss the tournament's decisive moments?

We heard that Spanish substitute Cesc Fabregas had had a scoring chance saved by Dutch goalkeeper Martin Stekelenburg. For a second we were happy not to be watching. How long could this televisual darkness last? Finally, we found a tiny television in an apartment on the third floor of the building right behind us. Lurking in the window, we saw another Spanish substitute, Jesús Navas, shoot wide of the net. Then Fabregas missed the target. Both times Dutch supporters sighed with relief, though we could not tell just how close those shots had come to giving Spain the lead. The main thing some of us could decipher by peering at the minute screen in the distance was whether the Dutch orange or Spanish dark blue were attacking.

Suddenly, a collective explosion of joy welcomed the reappearance of the game on the big screen! Flags were frantically waving again. Spanish and Dutch fans went back to shouting at each other, others nervously chewed on their nails. One of the first things we saw was English referee Howard Webb showing a red card to Dutch defender John Heitinga. When he was sent off in the 109th minute, Dutch fans almost wished the screen would go black again. It did not look good for "us." When Iniesta finally scored the winning goal on a Fabregas pass in the 116th minute, our world collapsed. We turned our backs to the screen. The disappointment was utterly profound, though we took some comfort in "seeing" this historic event.

During our seven-month journey through Africa, we had not watched a lot of television. We peeked at screens in Moroccan teahouses,

Senegalese bars, and Ghanaian restaurants. We paid a couple of cents to enjoy a game at a dodgy theater in Togo, but we did not catch any televised football at all in Burkina Faso and in Mali. It was as if the short yet dramatic blackout in Johannesburg was a way of demonstrating that soccer in Africa is far from perfect. Even so, the South African technicians at Melrose Arch beamed with pride as the final whistle blew, capturing the resilience of African soccer and the power of the World Cup to vindicate the continent and its people.

NOTES

1. Peter Alegi, *African Soccerscapes: How a Continent Changed the World's Game* (Athens: Ohio University Press; London: Hurst, 2010); Susann Baller, *Spielfelder der Stadt: Fußball und Jugendpolitik im Senegal seit 1950* (Cologne: Böhlau, 2010); Bea Vidacs, *Visions of a Better World: Football in the Cameroonian Social Imagination* (Berlin: LIT, 2010).

2. Scarlett Cornelissen, "'It's Africa's Turn!': The Narratives and Legitimations Surrounding the Moroccan and South African Bids for the 2006 and 2010 FIFA Finals," *Third World Quarterly* 25, 7 (2004): 1293–1310.

3. Xinhua News Agency, "Togo Mourns for Victims of Freetown Helicopter Crash," *People's Daily Online*, June 9, 2007, http://english.peopledaily.com .cn/200706/09/eng20070609_382483.html, accessed December 2, 2011.

4. "Assistant Coach among Dead in Attack on Togo Team," *CNN.com*, January 11, 2010, http://www.cnn.com/2010/SPORT/football/01/09/angola.african .nations.cup.togo/index.html, accessed January 13, 2010.

5. Raffaele Poli, "Migrations and Trade of African Football Players: Historic, Geographical, and Cultural Aspects," *Africa Spectrum* 41, 3 (2006): 393–414; Paul Darby, Gerard Akindes, and Matthew Kirwin, "Football Academies and the Migration of African Football Labor to Europe," *Journal of Sport and Social Issues* 31, 2 (2007): 143–61.

 *PART 4*

Political Discourses and Economic
Rationales of World Cup Hosting

Worlds Apart?

*The 1995 Rugby World Cup
and the 2010 FIFA World Cup*

ALBERT GRUNDLINGH AND JOHN NAURIGHT

WHILE SOUTH AFRICA HAS HOSTED numerous sports events since the end of apartheid, two events stand out far above the rest: the 1995 Rugby World Cup, recently rememorialized in the movie *Invictus,* and the 2010 FIFA World Cup in association football. Perhaps not coincidentially, *Invictus* was released in the lead-up to 2010, increasing the comparisons in the minds of some analysts. The two events meant quite different things for South Africans and perhaps even for the global community, but is important to go beyond the mystique of 1995, as memory can play tricks on the present-day mind, as can Hollywood.

SATURDAY, JUNE 24, 1995, was a red-letter day in South Africa. Before a capacity crowd at Ellis Park Stadium in Johannesburg and with millions watching on television, the Springbok team narrowly managed to beat the much vaunted New Zealand All Blacks team to win the finals of the Rugby World Cup. The margin of victory came in extra time through a drop goal by the fly-half, Joel Stransky. South Africa was the new rugby champion of the world. On hand to present the Cup to the victorious captain, Francois Pienaar, was South Africa's most celebrated former prisoner, President Nelson Mandela, decked out, in an unmistakable show of identification and support, in Pienaar's spare number 6 jersey. It was the perfect climax to a tournament that saw South Africa taking pride of place in the rugby world after the international sports isolation of the apartheid years.[1]

Unprecedented scenes of mass euphoria followed the Springbok victory—a celebration of exhilarating excess, of hugs and hurrahs, of merriment and madness. From the usually staid tree-lined, predominantly white suburbs to dusty black township streets, black and white South Africans seemed to have discovered a sense of common unity as the victory was toasted across the land. For a country with a long and painful history of division and conflict, and with rugby perceived as the game of the Afrikaner oppressors, such celebrations were thrillingly extraordinary. The occasion was later re-created in a film, *Invictus*, that imparted and popularized the feel-good dimension of the event on a global scale.[2]

But the euphoria also needs to be explained in a rational manner. What underlying factors accounted for the outcome? A fuller understanding of the contextual forces that helped to shape the public sphere during the time of the World Cup has to begin with an examination of the attempts to remodel the Springbok rugby ethos along appropriate postapartheid lines.

Springbok rugby has long been associated with Afrikaners and apartheid. The unification process between antiapartheid rugby organizations and establishment mainly white organizations that followed political changes after 1990 was a painful and slow process. The South African rugby hierarchy was alive to the problems and the real possibility that the tournament could be disrupted by dissent and conflict. Louis Luyt, president of the South African Rugby Football Union, was not a man who easily tolerated failure. For all his bluster and at times bombastic behavior, he fully understood the need to work in a different political environment after the 1994 elections. For the World Cup to be a success, one of the prerequisites was that rugby had to project a more positive image of embracing the new order in South Africa, which had enabled the country to host the tournament. According to the February 12, 1995, issue of the Johannesburg *Sunday Times*, "Rugby, it was reported, is known to be keen to improve its poor image and portray itself as a catalyst for change." To this end, a new management structure had to be deployed; stodgy Afrikaner functionaries of the old order had to be replaced with more progressive officials.

Out of a thousand applications, Edward Griffiths, a noted sports journalist, was appointed to the position of CEO. It was a significantly different type of appointment. Such positions usually had been reserved for Afrikaans-speakers from the inner circle of rugby administrators with years of service to the game. Griffiths was English-speaking and, at thirty-two, young. However, he had written a number of critical yet constructive articles on South African rugby that brought him to the attention of rugby officials. Louis Luyt, so often in the center of public relations disasters, was impressed, seeing in Griffiths the ideal person to refashion the image of South African rugby during the forthcoming World Cup tournament.

Another significant appointment was that of manager Morné du Plessis. Du Plessis, a Springbok rugby captain from 1975 to 1980, was one of the few apartheid-era players who was sensitive to the iniquities of the system and the rationale behind the sporting boycott. Du Plessis's appointment further enhanced the image of Springbok rugby. Equally important was the marketing potential of Francois Pienaar, the 1995 Springbok captain, who was friendly, accessible, and articulate; enjoyed a good relationship with President Mandela; and was well aware of the wider ramifications of his role.

With the key personnel in place, the rugby show embarked on what Griffiths later described as "an exemplary public relations campaign."[3] Writing in the *Sunday Times* on November 19, 1995, Griffiths explained that he considered the Springboks to be in the "entertainment industry" but that their responsibility extended "far beyond the rugby field." In the world of public relations, where perceptions tend to determine reality, the Springboks had to project an image of being humble, excited, and proud of their new democracy, and this message had to be repeated, Griffiths emphasized, at every press conference and public appearance.

Rugby officials also perceived the need to add a distinctive African dimension to South African rugby, even if only symbolic. The tournament was taking place in a "new" *African* country. A good starting point was to ensure that the Springboks knew the words of the "new" part of the national anthem, "Nkosi Sikelel' iAfrika," as well as they knew the "old" part, "Die Stem," which many South Africans associated with the apartheid order (see the essay by Chris Bolsmann in this volume). Television close-ups zooming in on players' facial expressions before kickoffs, at times embarrassingly revealed that some players regarded

"Nkosi" at best as superfluous or at worst with disdain. Du Plessis was determined that such attitudes would change. "Most of the guys can't even remember the words of pop songs," he said, "but they will know the words of the anthem."[4]

In a further bid to lend more African color to the team, an African work song, "Shosholoza" (literally meaning "pushing" or "running" together) was adopted as a theme song. It was also widely publicized that the Springboks supported a community-driven campaign, Masakhane (Let us build together) in the black townships. The Africanization drive received an unexpected boost when a black newspaper, the *Sowetan*, coined the term *Amabokoboko* for the Springboks. This African-derived name rapidly gained currency, possessing an implicit degree of cultural fusion that helped to contribute to the subsequent retention, amid some controversy, of the springbok as an official emblem of South African rugby despite the symbol's associations with apartheid. Dovetailing with these developments, the Springboks also had to be seen as standard-bearers of national unity, and the squad's official slogan was "One Team: One Country." These strands neatly tied together in the notion of South Africa as a "Rainbow Nation," a metaphor that was much peddled by one of South Africa's Nobel Peace Prize laureates, Archbishop Desmond Tutu (see the essay by Daniel Herwitz in this volume).

While the refashioning of the symbolic imagery of South African rugby was meant to showcase the changes in the country's internal emphases, these claims would ring hollow if the Springbok rugby team consisted only of white men. In stepped Chester Williams, a colored winger from Western Province. Williams was certainly a good enough player to qualify on merit, but he was a priceless asset as the new face of South African rugby. Despite his reserved nature, Williams, known routinely as the "Black Pearl," received a disproportionate amount of media attention. The only black player on the Springbok squad, he was the emblem of achievement, hope, reconciliation, and recognition for the fledgling nation.

The tournament's opening ceremony would serve as the principal vehicle for the self-representation of a newly born society. Given the country's deeply divided past, the ceremony had to be drained of history as much as possible. On a bright, sunny Cape day, a colorful pageant of happy, smiling, and dancing South Africans of all ethnic groups cavorted around the field, representing the Rainbow Nation, while the official World Cup song, "A World in Union," was belted out. When President Nelson Mandela appeared on the field to make a short speech, he was warmly and enthusiastically welcomed. The entire enterprise represented a well-choreographed public spectacle that gave the dark and dangerous South African past a wide berth, thereby creating the illusion of a new country born and received without sin.

But the repackaging of South African rugby ideology only partially explains why the South African public so enthusiastically endorsed the refashioned product. Careful repackaging of a product will not necessarily affect the cultural marketplace.

In this respect, events on the rugby field itself were tremendously important. The fact that the Springboks won all their games kept alive public interest. If the team had performed poorly, the nation would have had little cause for celebrations. Moreover, the victory was achieved in South Africa's first participation in the World Cup tournament.

And the prevailing public mood at the time was one of optimism and buoyancy and of relief at the end of apartheid: In 1995, Griffiths recalled, "if ever a country was in need of a party, a good time . . . it was South Africa."[5] Public spaces had opened up for interaction on a different level than had been possible under apartheid. Rugby enabled blacks and whites to express a common sentiment without either side sacrificing or risking too much.

Most Afrikaners, excluding those on the right, adapted much more quickly to the new dispensation than many observers had anticipated. In part, Afrikaners still perceived that political negotiations had worked to their advantage and saw parallels in the connections between sport and society. There was more than an element of truth in journalist Patti Waldmeir's observation that "Afrikaners had swapped apartheid for rugby, and there was every sign they thought it a fair deal."[6]

The African National Congress (ANC), in turn, had just assumed office, and its leaders still had to demonstrate that they had effectively made the transition from a liberation movement to a responsible government committed to order and reconciliation. Furthermore, as far as economic and social policies were concerned, Michael Macdonald has noted how the ANC was put on "capitalist probation and subjected to unrelenting pressure to prove its reliability to business interests that [would] help shape its fate."[7]

Mandela of course played a central role in the new government's blessing of the World Cup tournament. The South African rugby team stood to gain more by association with Mandela than the other way around. Mandela already had a long-established international reputation as an antiapartheid icon, while the Springboks still had to prove their international credibility. Mandela's strategic appearances and his identification with the team helped elevate the Boks to a symbol of nationhood.

It turned out to be a marketing masterstroke. One media specialist commented that Mandela—"he of the perpetual smile and the studied stoop of humility"—had "instilled and enthused the brand image of South Africa with his personality."[8] Mandela's involvement with the team and the tournament generally can also be seen as an excursion into the field of cultural politics. The closed cultural space occupied by rugby, hitherto a predominantly Afrikaner preserve, was sufficiently prised open to allow at least a partial reinscription of the game's narrow cultural identity. Moreover, the "public ownership" of rugby was symbolically democratized and extended. Afrikaner claims of possession were compromised by Mandela's anointment of the game; the metaphorical message was that the game belonged to the new South Africa and the old order had passed.

South Africa repeated its Rugby World Cup win in 2007, though because the tournament was held in France, the games were more removed from everyday South African life, and the Springbok victory failed to re-create the mythological narrative of 1995. The 2007 win was also overshadowed by the upcoming 2010 FIFA World Cup. While rugby is now accepted as a major sport in South Africa, it is nowhere near rivaling soccer as the country's most popular sport.

FAST-FORWARD TO 2010, and we see a very different scene from that of just fifteen year earlier. The dramatis personae have changed, Mandela is now an aged nonagenarian former president who made only a brief appearance at the final between Spain and the Netherlands, doing a lap of honor in a golf cart before the kickoff. Jacob Zuma, South Africa's current president, does not carry the same pan–South African popularity as Mandela but was ever-present throughout the buildup to the tournament and during the event itself. Zuma is more of a self-styled "people's president" than his predecessor, Thabo Mbeki, who brought the World Cup to South Africa. South Africa had sought to host the FIFA World Cup and the Olympics as part of an events-driven global public relations strategy that accelerated after the success of the 1995 Rugby World Cup. Cape Town bid for the 2004 Olympics and did quite well in the competition before losing out to sentimental favorite Athens.[9] South Africa, this time a sentimental favorite, was not selected to host the 2006 FIFA World Cup by one vote under decidedly shady circumstances. And South Africa demonstrated its ability to host international sporting events with its successful African Nations Cup and Cricket World Cup.

Since 1990, structural changes have shifted the balance of power from host nations and cities to the organizations that own the brand-names of global megaevents.[10] In the realm of football, FIFA's monopoly power is well known; the same holds true for the International Olympic Committee (IOC) and much of global sport. As with the Olympic Games, the World Cup is a unique event, likely to attract exceptional audiences. It has a de facto monopoly on supply, since there is no rival or substitute competition. As a consequence, countries wishing to host FIFA-controlled events must follow the organization's policies. FIFA, for example, holds all rights to the use of its brand.

FIFA president Sepp Blatter clearly stage-managed the event with the assistance of capable FIFA executives and support from President Zuma, World Cup Local Organising Committee head Danny Jordaan, and other South African political and sports officials. The images of Blatter and Zuma holding hands in a pose reminiscent of two political teammates at the final draw ceremony in Cape Town in December 2009, followed by Blatter leading Zuma along with the trophy after the final, allowing Zuma a role in handing the trophy to Iker Casillas, the Spanish captain and goalkeeper, provided clear visual imagery of the power relations between the president of sub-Saharan Africa's largest economic state and the president of one of the world's two most powerful sporting organizations. Zuma was incorporated because Blatter permitted it, quite a different situation from Mandela presenting the Webb Ellis Trophy to Francois Pienaar at Ellis Park in 1995, where the president was very much front and center, dwarfing the international rugby officials around him. That Zuma was complicit in his secondary role suggests both the power of FIFA and the difference between South Africa's standing in the global soccer hierarchy and its position in global rugby. In addition, FIFA and its global sponsors fully controlled the content of the event. Budweiser was the only beer sold at World Cup stadiums, though unbranded beer produced by SABMiller was sold at the Fan Fests as a consequence of the American brewer's lack of capacity within South Africa. While local traders were marginalized in favor of multinational corporations that paid FIFA for the rights to exclusive access, the organizers allowed a few local traders to have stalls within the economic exclusion zones around World Cup match venues.

At both South African World Cups, most locals in attendance were white. Unlike the Rugby World Cup, however, in 2010 the overwhelming majority of fans in the stadiums were foreigners supporting their teams or merely experiencing Africa's first World Cup. While South Africans expressed widespread support for the tournament and for Bafana Bafana, the instant carnival generated in 2010 felt more managed and corporatized, like going from Rainbow Nation to Rainbow Nation Inc. Thus, the success of 2010 did not depend as heavily on the performance of the national team, which played creditably but did not advance out of the opening round group stage.

What will be remembered most from 2010? Certainly not a moment of national reconciliation or the political and cultural triumph of an iconic figure. The iconic image of this tournament was the vuvuzela, which defined South African fandom to the global community and became, for good or ill, the single-most-important thing that made this World Cup "African." Though the vuvuzela did not become popular until the late 1990s, boosters attempted to frame it as having a long history that provided continuity between Africa's "tribal" past and its modern present. (For a different perspective, see the essay by Solomon Waliaula in this volume.) As with 1995, a careful stage-managing of history took place as a way to sell a distinctive brand to the world. The U.S. television broadcasts of the football World Cup portrayed an idealized vision of Africa. Each one began with an African man standing on a mountain blowing a kudu horn, the invented traditional antecedent of the vuvuzela, as he called in the world via panoramic aerial camera shots, inviting viewers first to South Africa and then into the stadiums.

The atmosphere we observed in Cape Town, Johannesburg, and Port Elizabeth was electric, but other than the vuvuzela, the Africanness of the event was not readily evident inside the stadiums. Outside of the stadium precincts, the genuine embrace of the World Cup and the excitement generated by thousands of international visitors was clearly evident from coffee shops to informal traders to restaurants and bars. Was it like 1995? Yes and no. The embracing of a global event was similarly evident, but the relationship of the national and the global was clearly different.

As with 1995, key elements of popular culture surrounded the Cup in 2010. The Diski Dance was promoted as the World Cup dance with South African dance moves given soccer names or created for the dance, such as "Table Mountain" which mimics a player trapping the ball between the shoulders with the body shaped like Cape Town's famous backdrop. The official World Cup song was recorded by Colombian megastar Shakira and the global anthem "Wavin' Flag" was recorded by Somali-born Canadian K'Naan, with a Spanish-language version adding David Bisbal. In 1995, a South African version of the World Cup theme song "The World in Union" appeared, and the country's Ladysmith Black Mambazo recorded "Shosholoza," the South African team song, which became the Cup's unofficial anthem. By 2010, the global had subsumed the local in the trappings of World Cup presentation.

The FIFA World Cup has been to Africa and is now setting off to rediscover South America in the global soccer heartland of Brazil before attempting to conquer Russia and the Middle East. The Olympics are going to South America for the first time in 2016, leaving Africa and the Middle East as the primary regions where the games have never been held. As a result, new countries are scrambling to bid to host the Olympics. Unlike rugby and soccer World Cups, however, the Olympics are hosted by single cities, meaning that Johannesburg, Cape Town, and Durban would have to bid individually. By 2011, it had become evident that South African efforts to win a Summer Olympics would focus on Durban, at least in the near future.

It is clear that the South African government and major business interests have succumbed to the global sport-media-tourism-events complex as part of an overall ideology of growth. Whether the legacies generated from any or all of these events have any lasting impact throughout society remains suspect. The 1995 World Cup used existing facilities, though it sparked some infrastructural improvements. The 2010 Cup, by contrast, led to the construction of several new stadiums in major cities, though the post–World Cup viability of these facilities remains questionable. The capacity of the glimmering new stadiums in

Cape Town and Durban has been reduced to fifty-five thousand seats in the hopes of maintaining an international standard venue that will not be too large for local audiences. Management of the Cape Town venue initially went to a partnership between a local South African company and the French company that manages Paris's Stade de France. In October 2010, however, the joint venture pulled out of the contract.[11]

More likely than the Olympics are a series of events in single sports such as the cricket and rugby World Cups. Indeed, South Africa has emerged as the favorite to host the 2023 Rugby World Cup, which will be awarded in 2013. The euphoria created in 1995 and again in 2010 certainly created moments of joy throughout much of South African society, but neither Cup did much in a measurable sense to address issues of poverty and unemployment. As Andrea Giampiccoli and John Nauright argue, the World Cup will likely prove detrimental to local tourism development initiatives, particularly those located well away from larger centers enveloped in the global sports-media-tourism complex.[12] South Africa has become a society of the spectacle in which, according to Guy Debord,

> The spectacle presents itself simultaneously as all of society, as part of society, and as instrument of unification. As a part of society it is specifically the sector which concentrates all gazing and all consciousness. Due to the very fact that this sector is separate, it is the common ground of the deceived gaze and of false consciousness, and the unification it achieves is nothing but an official language of generalized separation.
>
> The spectacle is not a collection of images, but a social relation among people, mediated by images. The spectacle cannot be understood as an abuse of the world of vision, as a product of the techniques of mass dissemination of images. It is, rather, a Weltanschauung which has become actual, materially translated. It is a world vision which has become objectified.[13]

While the 2010 World Cup concentrated "all gazing and consciousness" across the nation and much of the world, many South Africans barred from the stadiums and the exclusion zones found ways to both celebrate and profit from the massive influx of international tourists and money into the country in ways that both challenged the official confines of the event and created avenues of carnivalesque expression.

Now, after years of preparation and expectation, the World Cup has ended; the hard realities of sustaining a meaningful legacy for the nation remain the real challenge. The moment of national celebration generated in 1995 lasted for a short time before South Africa returned to the task of rebuilding a society torn apart by centuries of segregation and exploitation. We will watch with great interest to see if other variables can prolong the 2010 moment.

NOTES

1. See also Albert Grundlingh, André Odendaal, and Burridge Spies, *Beyond the Tryline: Rugby and South African Society* (Johannesburg: Ravan, 1995); David Black and John Nauright, *Rugby and the South African Nation* (Manchester: Manchester University Press, 1998).

2. *Invictus* was directed by Clint Eastwood and starred Matt Damon as François Pienaar, captain of the Springboks, and Morgan Freeman as Nelson Mandela. It was based on the book by John Carlin, *Playing the Enemy* (New York: Penguin, 2008).

3. Edward Griffiths, *One Team, One Country: The Greatest Year of Springbok Rugby* (London: Viking, 1996), 114.

4. "Rugby's New Songs," *Economist*, May 27, 1995, 132.

5. Griffiths, *One Team, One Country*, 51.

6. Patti Waldmeir, *Anatomy of a Miracle: The End of Apartheid and the Birth of the New South Africa* (New York: Norton, 1997), 269.

7. Michael Macdonald, "Power Politics in the New South Africa," *Journal of Southern African Studies* 22, 2 (1996): 227.

8. Quoted in Albert Grundlingh, "From Redemption to Recidivism?: Rugby and Change in South Africa during the 1995 Rugby World Cup and Its Aftermath," *Sporting Traditions* 14, 2 (1998): 77.

9. Harry H. Hiller, "Mega-Events, Urban Boosterism, and Growth Strategies: An Analysis of the Objectives and Legitimations of the Cape Town Olympic Bid," *International Journal of Urban and Regional Research* 24, 2 (2000): 439–58.

10. For a deeper analysis of this trend, see John Nauright, "Global Games: Culture, Political Economy, and Sport in the Globalized World of the 21st Century," *Third World Quarterly* 25, 7 (2004): 1325–36.

11. See Peter Alegi, "Jumping Off the Green Point Bandwagon," *Cape Argus*, October 18, 2010.

12. Andrea Giampiccoli and John Nauright, "Problems and Prospects for Community Based Tourism in the New South Africa: The 2010 FIFA World Cup and Beyond," *African Historical Review* 42, 1 (2010): 42–62.

13. Guy Debord, *The Society of the Spectacle*, 1967, http://www.marxists.org/reference/archive/debord/society.htm, accessed December 3, 2011.

South Africa Welcomes the World

The 2010 World Cup, Xenophobia, and South Africa's Ubuntu *Dream*

MEG VANDERMERWE

"KE NAKO (IT IS TIME): Celebrate Africa's Humanity" was the official 2010 FIFA World Cup slogan, announced on November 25, 2007.[1] Conscious of the superficial and negative way that Africa is so often portrayed in the world media—a backward place of poverty, conflict, dictatorships, and corruption—designers picked a slogan that would defy such associations and portray a more hospitable image of the continent: one of unity, humanity, and African humanism, or *ubuntu*. *Ubuntu* is a concept among speakers of Bantu languages, such as isiZulu and isiXhosa, commonly defined by a saying, "Umuntu ngumuntu ngabantu" (A person is a person through other people).[2] In recent years, this African ethic has gained global popularity as a phrase and ideology. It has entered the lexicon of politicians, rock stars, sports coaches, philanthropists, corporate managers, advertisers, and computer users who rely on the Ubuntu operating system, available for free and in an open access format.[3] No African country has been keener to claim an affinity with *ubuntu* than postapartheid South Africa. The country's self-professed identity as the continent's "Rainbow Nation," embodying racial and cultural diversity yet embracing unity and tolerance, highlights this position, as does South Africa's liberal constitution, one of the most inclusive and human-rights-based in the world.

Of course, all of this emphasis in South Africa on the *ubuntu* ideal is a response not only to general assumptions about Africa's inhumanity but also to a very particular desire to distinguish our postapartheid identity from its evil predecessor. If South Africa prior to the elections of 1994 was a country synonymous with white supremacy, crimes against humanity, ignorance, divisions, and intolerance, then the new democratic South Africa strives to be associated with their opposites. This desire is not just political propaganda or canny government marketing designed to attract foreign investment and tourism to what has become, in the minds of many, Africa's showcase democracy. Rather, it reflects a very real desire and even need on the part of many South Africans.

Indeed, for many of us living in South Africa, our self-christening as an *ubuntu* Rainbow Nation during the Mandela presidency and in the wake of the Truth and Reconciliation Commission was an essential step in the nation-building process. Without it, we might not have achieved the extraordinary and relatively peaceful transition that we did. Nor might we have been able to begin to forgive ourselves or each other for the many moral transgressions of our collective past. Now, nearly two decades on, the *ubuntu* dream is no less vital. No one can deny that South Africa has experienced many disappointments and setbacks in recent years—widespread poverty and inequality, the HIV/AIDS pandemic and the government's initially wholly inadequate response to it, continuing high levels of crime, a faltering education system, and seemingly endless tales of fat-cat political corruption. Yet the *ubuntu* Rainbow Nation dream lives on. Many of us continue to cling to it, believing that it is an ideal that we still can and must realize.

In the months leading up to the 2010 World Cup opening ceremony, the government called on us via our televisions, newspapers, and radios to use the megaevent as a motivation to put recent differences and disappointments aside and reconnect with the dream—Welcome the world, they told us, and embrace and celebrate your fellow South Africans. Perhaps because we maintain the Rainbow Nation dream, we threw ourselves into the task with an almost religious intensity.

From South Africa's ubiquitous rainbow-like flags, scarves, hats, wigs, and car ornaments to our national team's yellow football jerseys becoming obligatory wear on Fridays in many workplaces, the message to ourselves and to the rest of the world seemed clear: While the last sixteen years have had their highs and lows, the World Cup has reignited our dream of a united and more humane South Africa. Even the vuvuzela, an instrument that until the 2010 World Cup was commonly

seen and heard only at local soccer games and church events patron-
ized by black South Africans, became a means of communicating the
entire population's seemingly reenergized commitment to the pursuit
of *ubuntu*. Forty-eight hours before the official opening ceremony in
Johannesburg, state and private television and radio broadcasts encouraged South Africans to blow their vuvuzelas at noon. This collective
blast was a symbolic gesture, signifying our national unity and goodwill
toward one another in anticipation of the greatest sporting event ever
held on the African continent as well as a loud welcome to our foreign
guests. Millions of South Africans from all walks of life heeded the call,
reveling in the sense of solidarity and jovial optimism that it created.

Nelson Mandela first understood the potential for sport to unify
and reconcile a South Africa at odds with itself. By donning the national
rugby jersey during the 1995 rugby World Cup, the president showed
a nervous white community that he was committed to building bridges
of understanding. This gesture smoothed what was still a fragile and
fraught transition, and its importance cannot be overestimated.

No doubt the current government hoped to achieve similar mir-
acles, and it initially seemed to get them. Newspapers, officials, and
individuals could not help but wonder whether this constituted a new
beginning for the new South Africa? Had the World Cup really given
the country a desperately needed national boost? Were South Africans
finally back on the road to becoming the *ubuntu* Rainbow Nation of the
1990s after seeming to have lost our way in recent years? Many people
certainly dared to articulate their belief that maybe, just maybe, "we"
were doing just that, or at least reimagining that possibility.

However, at the same time as the nation was patting itself on the
back, another more sinister side of the rainbow was casting its shadow
and already making a mockery of such optimistic hopes. A rumor was
rumbling across the black townships and into the inner-city high-rises,
which many of the nation's poorer African foreign nationals call home.
Come the World Cup, these immigrants and refugees were being told
by many of their black South African hosts, a clock will start ticking:
one month, thirty days. Thirty days to pack your bags. Thirty days to
prepare to go. After the World Cup final, when the football fans have
returned home, you must go, too. Those stubborn enough to remain,
they were warned, would be attacked.

This was not the first time that South Africa had experienced a spike in xenophobic tensions.⁴ In May 2008, at least sixty-two African foreign nationals (mostly Zimbabwean and Somali) were murdered, as were a handful of South Africans who were mistaken for foreigners.⁵ More than one hundred thousand people were displaced as xenophobic attacks erupted in working-class townships from Johannesburg to Cape Town. Women were raped, homes and businesses were looted, and people were beaten, burned, and tortured to death. However, it seemed a cruel irony that potential perpetrators were rumored to have chosen the 2010 World Cup, a time when we as a nation were supposedly celebrating our humanity and hospitality, as the time to warn of another widespread attack.

This fearmongering resulted in a shameful schism of experience during the tournament itself. While most South Africans greeted each new match with a mixture of trepidation and excitement, a Congolese man pointed out that for him and many other African foreign nationals living in South Africa, each new match represented a kind of perverse countdown to when their lives might again be in jeopardy.⁶ He also found it hard to swallow that while the nation was falling over itself to extend a warm and welcoming hand to its visiting soccer guests, the same hand of hospitality did not extend to many of South Africa's foreign African residents.

The irony of this dual World Cup narrative was not lost on all observers. A well-known and irreverent South African political cartoonist, Zapiro, captured this terrible irony with a cartoon published in the weekly *Mail and Guardian* newspaper on July 9, 2010. The drawing depicts the members of a dismayed Somali family huddling together in the foreground. On the left is Johannesburg's Soccer City Stadium, where the World Cup final would soon take place. On the right, beside township shacks, lurks an angry machete- and axe-toting mob labeled *Xenophobia*. "Feel it, it is here," says the Somali family's speech bubble, a reference to one of the popular unofficial 2010 World Cup slogans. However, Zapiro's clever triptych leaves the viewer in no doubt that the "it" in this context is not just the World Cup but also South Africa's xenophobia.

Yet Zapiro was in the minority. Most national media outlets turned a blind eye to the stark contradictions that were fast overshadowing the legacy of what could have and should have been one of postapartheid South Africa's very proudest moments. For example, the front page of the June 10, 2010, issue of the *Cape Times* reported that the World Cup Opening Ceremony "will celebrate the world coming home to Africa." The same article went on to quote the organizing committee's chief of marketing, Derek Carsten: "We are celebrating the world coming home. . . . This is where it all started. Look at the Cradle of Humanity. We are saying to everyone, celebrate that Africanness."[7]

However, on page 3 of the same newspaper, a large spread reports the story of a Burundian woman allegedly attacked by black South African train staff for being a *makwerekwere*, the derogatory local term for African foreigners. The Burundian woman describes how immediately after the attack, other black locals did not come to her aid but surrounded her screaming, "You must all go home before July 11, out of our country, or we (are) going to kill you door by door."[8] Here, within a few columns of print of each other, were the two faces of the World Cup in South Africa. One was the official "Ke Nako" 2010 spin; the other made a mockery of it. Yet few seemed willing to articulate this contradiction. So desperate were South Africans for a bit of patriotic *ubuntu* cheer and a potentially lucrative slice of positive marketing internationally that the disconnect between rhetoric and reality went largely unmentioned.

Of course, the ongoing tensions between local South Africans and African immigrants is just one of many divisions threatening our *ubuntu* dream. Race, too, continues to be an issue, High crime rates as well as affirmative action and black economic empowerment policies contribute to the emigration of high numbers of white South Africans.

Other minorities also continue to find themselves marginalized, even victimized despite a democratic dispensation. The "corrective rape" and murder of lesbians in townships by black South African men who claim they intend to "cure" the women of their homosexuality has, for example, been a worrying trend for many years and has been documented by a courageous Gauteng-based photographer, Zanele Muholi. But only recently have such attacks begun to find their way into mainstream headlines. Among the victims is Eudy Simelane, a promising young female footballer who played midfield for Banyana Banyana, the women's national team. In April 2008, however, she was found raped and stabbed to death in an apparent hate crime a mere two hundred yards from her home.[9] Women and children—in particular, poor women and children—also continue to be subject to shaming levels of physical abuse and sexual violence. According to the Saartjie Baartman Centre in Cape Town, national levels of violence have reached a "crisis" point. "South Africa has all the constitutional and government mechanisms to address the status of women," writes academic and social commentator Rhoda Kadalie, "but it has failed spectacularly to improve the lives of poor women."[10]

Given the violence and looting that broke out in the Western Cape after the Cup's closing ceremony, the xenophobic threats provided further examples of how South Africans continue to fall short of the *ubuntu* dream in spite of our initial hopes to the contrary. To better understand how World Cup xenophobia compromised *ubuntu*, we need to examine what is one of xenophobia's key root causes.

The reasons given for 2010 World Cup xenophobic attacks, like the reasons given after the 2008 attacks, were manifold. At one extreme were those who argued that such attacks are an unavoidable legacy of apartheid, of the negrophobia and black self-hatred that are inevitable consequences of internalized colonial assumptions of black inferiority fostered during the predemocratic years. "Westernness and whiteness remain imprimaturs in the scale of human worthiness," blogged Malawian-born and U.S.-based academic Paul Tiyambe Zeleza; they help to explain "why shades of blackness have become a shameful basis for distinguishing African immigrants among black South Africans, why the latter's xenophobic rage is not directed at white immigrants but at 'those Africans,' the despised *makwerekwere.*"[11]

Officials at the highest levels of the South African government dismissed the localized violence and looting as the acts of a small but powerful criminal force rather than xenophobia. As reported in the *Cape Argus*, hundreds of African nationals fled their homes and barricaded their businesses in Western Cape townships after a spate of violence in the province. Police minister Nathi Mthethwa shrugged off the "so-called" xenophobia, telling the media that the violence could be attributed to "criminality disguised as xenophobia."[12] In contrast, Western Cape premier Helen Zille of the Democratic Alliance, the main opposition party, insisted that the problem of xenophobia was real and needed to be addressed.

While these and many of the other explanations offered may possess elements of truth, they fail to take into account a number of complexities. Most notably, narrow explanations fail to consider why, during the

World Cup, as in 2008, the threats and ultimate violence exclusively targeted those African nationals living and working in the poorest areas of South Africa. This is not to suggest for a moment that xenophobic sentiment is exclusively a problem among the black poor. Indeed, a 2008 study conducted by the Southern African Migration Project revealed that xenophobic sentiments are in fact more widespread in the country than initially assumed.[13] According to this comprehensive study, xenophobic prejudice if not violence has infiltrated to varying extents people and communities across racial and socioeconomic lines. Government and official institutions such as the army and police are also not immune to such prejudice. Even so, acts of violence perpetrated against African foreign nationals took place in poor and mostly black communities in both May 2008 and again in July 2010 in areas of the Western Cape including the informal settlement of Du Noon and parts of the Cape Flats, including Khayelitsha. And so we edge toward the real shame and travesty of World Cup 2010. Writing in the wake of the xenophobic attacks of 2008, Zimbabwean writer and academic Nhamo Anthony Mhiripiri explained, "Some elements in the South African under-classes are the most xenophobic and equally attack the most vulnerable, because they have been systematically forgotten and excluded from sharing the national cake."[14]

Mhiripiri's insight is just as relevant for what happened or was threatened in the aftermath of the World Cup. In short, South Africa's African migrants and immigrants have become scapegoats for the nation's failure to deliver basic services and social uplift to the very poorest and most disenfranchised communities in society. Criminologist and author Jonny Steinberg has reached essentially the same conclusion: "The violence has become the site of a skirmish between classes. We are sending back and forth a series of angry and fearful missives, and they are written in the blood of foreign nationals."[15] Deprived of power and excluded from the decision-making process, our nation's poorest used threats of xenophobic violence after the World Cup to assert their presence on the political radar at a time when they knew the eyes of the whole world would be watching. Steinberg believed that one of the messages behind the threatened violence was, "We can leave our mark on this event by writing our anger all over it. Look at how you rush to bring in the army. Look at how we have made you jump."[16]

Some progress has certainly been made since 2008 with regard to tackling xenophobia. In 2010, the attacks were less widespread than initially feared, thanks in part to a quicker government response as well as to greater affinities between South Africans and people from other African nations. Yet one cannot help but wonder what the impact on xenophobic resentments and ultimately on the violence itself might have been if even a small percentage of the forty billion rand spent on World Cup stadiums, new and upgraded airports, roads, and fan parks had instead been used to improve basic services such as schools, hospitals, and housing and to create sustainable jobs for the country's poorest. It might have meant a slightly less comfortable stay for our flyby football guests but would also certainly have ensured a better situation for our most vulnerable African nationals as well as for the poor South African majority who have turned such nationals into scapegoats for their socioeconomic discontent.

The foreigner, as Jacques Derrida has noted, is a destabilizing presence in our communities: "By his mere presence amongst us, he is posing questions—questions not only of who he is and what his presence signifies, but ultimately of who 'we' are and what we signify in relation to him."[17] So in the end, what lessons did the Africans from north of the Limpopo River teach South Africans during the 2010 World Cup? Perhaps one lesson learned is that a celebration of Africa's and South Africa's supposed *ubuntu* humanism cannot be just about spectacles, slogans, and marketing schemes or even good intentions. We are an extraordinary nation, and we have much to be proud of about post-1994 South Africa and about how we hosted the continent's first football World Cup. However, if we are going to claim that such an event will celebrate not only our skills as event managers but also our humanity, then we had better make sure that it does just that. Such an achievement will not be easy. It will require that, among other things, proper and concerted government initiatives address the underlying socioeconomic inequalities that feed xenophobic resentment and violence. Until such initiatives are put into place, however, should another sporting megaevent come our way, politicians and advertisers must think up another slogan.

NOTES

1. On the bidding process, see Peter Alegi, "'Feel the Pull in Your Soul': Local Agency and Global Trends in South Africa's 2006 World Cup Bid," *Soccer and*

Society 2, 3 (2001): 1–21; Chris Bolsmann, "Mexico 1968 and South Africa 2010: Sombreros and Vuvuzelas and the Legitimisation of Global Sporting Events," *Bulletin of Latin American Research* 29, 1 (2010): 93–106; Scarlett Cornelissen, "'It's Africa's Turn!': The Narratives and Legitimations Surrounding the Moroccan and South African Bids for the 2006 and 2010 FIFA Finals," *Third World Quarterly* 25, 7 (2004): 1293–1310.

2. C. L. Sibusiso Nyembezi, *Zulu Proverbs* (Pietermaritzburg: Shuter and Shooter, 1990), 49.

3. See, for example, M. D. Giardina, "One Day, One Goal?: PUMA, Corporate Philanthropy, and the Cultural Politics of Brand 'Africa,'" *Sport in Society* 13, 1 (2010): 130–42; Mzamo P. Mangaliso and Mphuthumi B. Damane, "Building Competitive Advantage from 'Ubuntu': Management Lessons from South Africa (and Executive Commentary)," *Academy of Management Executive* 15, 3 (2001): 23–34; "Doc Rivers on Celtics and 'Ubuntu,'" June 3, 2008, http://www.necn.com/Boston/Sports/Doc-Rivers-on-Celtics-and-ubuntu/1212541255.html, accessed December 5, 2011.

4. For an overview, see Michael Neocosmos, *From "Foreign Natives" to "Native Foreigners": Explaining Xenophobia in Post-Apartheid South Africa: Citizenship and Nationalism, Identity and Politics* (Dakar: Council for the Development of Social Science Research in Africa, 2010).

5. Agence France Press, "Toll from Xenophobic Attacks Rises," *Mail and Guardian Online*, May 31, 2008, http://mg.co.za/article/2008-5-31-toll-from-xeno phobic-attacks-rises, accessed June 1, 2008. See also Jonny Steinberg, *South Africa's Xenophobic Eruption* (Pretoria: Institute for Security Studies, 2008).

6. Palesa Morudu, "Across the Gulf of South Africanness," *Mail and Guardian*, July 2–8, 2010, 32.

7. "Opening Ceremony 'Will Celebrate the World Coming Home to Africa,'" *Cape Times*, June 10, 2010, 1.

8. Michelle Pietersen, "Metrorail Officers Beat Burundian Woman for Being a 'Makwerekwere,'" *Cape Times*, June 10, 2010, 3.

9. John Turnbull, "Remembering Eudy, KwaThema's Brightest, Killed on Its Darkest Night," *Global Game*, August 30, 2009, http://www.theglobalgame.com/blog/2009/08/south-africa-remembering-eudy-kwathemas-brightest-killed-on-its-darkest-night/, accessed November 7, 2009.

10. Rhoda Kadalie, "Call to Women in Power," *Big Issue South Africa*, December 3 2010, 10.

11. Paul T. Zeleza, "The Racialized Complexes of Xenophobia," *Zeleza Post*, May 26, 2008, http://www.zeleza.com/blogging/african-affairs/racializedcom plexes-xenophobia, accessed June 16, 2008; reprinted in Paul T. Zeleza, *Barack Obama and African Diasporas: Dialogues and Dissensions* (London: Ayebia Clarke; Athens: Ohio University Press, 2009), 201–3.

12. *Cape Argus*, July 17, 2010.

13. See Jonathan Crush, "South Africa: Policy in the Face of Xenophobia," Southern African Migration Project, July 2008, http://www.migrationinformation.org/Feature/display.cfm?ID=689, accessed November 30, 2011.

14. Nhamo Anthony Mhiripiri, "Under Fire Essay: From May Shame to 2030

or There About: A Tale of Xenophobia, Zimbabwe, and Fictive Identities," *Critical Arts* 24, 2 (2010): 289.

15. Jonny Steinberg, *Big Issue South Africa*, December 3, 2010, 7.

16. Ibid.

17. Andrea Castle, Miki Flockemann, Kudzayi Ngara, and Wahseema Roberts, "The Everyday Experience of Xenophobia: Performing the Crossing from Zimbabwe to South Africa," *Critical Arts* 24, 2 (2010): 246.

In the Theater of the World Cup

LAURENT DUBOIS

THE WORLD CUP is the largest theater that has ever existed in human history. It produces a powerful monthlong narrative in which all those who watch and participate largely follow one plotline. The features of football itself guarantee a gripping drama that invariably includes heroism, tragedy, unfairness, massive blunders by referees, and an exhausting yo-yoing between utterly tedious and totally exhilarating and even redemptive play. In the midst of the tournament, it seems all-encompassing, irreducible, and indeed—during a particular riveting game or a particularly boring one—like it might never end. But almost immediately after the final whistle, the contest comes to seem strangely fleeting, ethereal, a little unbelievable. Did I really spend several weeks in South Africa—having planned to do so for literally several years—going to games? What for? And what remains?

The answer to that question lies partly in the crowds generated by the World Cup, both at the tournament and among viewers throughout the globe, which are unlike those generated by any other event I can think of. At games I met a bewildering array of people—South Africans, of course, plus Irish, Japanese, Haitian, Argentinean—all participating in a very specific set of expectations, worries, and pleasures. The flags and banners and face paint were never limited to the teams that were playing or even to teams in the tournament: People come decked out in their national colors, with club jerseys, regional flags, and curious get-ups of all sorts. Wandering about before and after the games is part of the terrific pleasure of the whole thing. As I wandered around at the final, for example, I kept seeing an odd expression on people's faces,

210

and then I realized it was the same one I had on mine: a slightly-crazed, elated grin that simply said, "I can't believe I'm here." And—absurdly, perhaps—I have incredibly fond memories of waiting in line to go to the bathroom at the World Cup, standing with people draped in all colors, sometimes elated, sometimes despairing, but always extremely chatty, with sudden communities formed for the time of the line, then disappearing back into the vastness of the stadium.

That rare and fleeting reality remains a kind of reservoir, almost painful but also sustaining to recall, especially since outside of the time of the World Cup, it seems so surreal and evanescent. So here are a few snapshots, drawn from dispatches from the World Cup originally posted on my *Soccer Politics* blog and offered as traces of the event.[1]

AFTER THE SIXTEEN-HOUR nonstop flight from the United States to South Africa, I arrived just in time to catch the United States–Ghana round-of-sixteen game at a restaurant in Melville, a bohemian neighborhood in Johannesburg. Everything was incredibly efficient at the airport, so much so that I'd like to propose that South Africa send a commission to explain to the French how to run an airport.

I was coming from Durham, North Carolina, where watching the United States–Algeria match in a packed bar had been the most exciting football-viewing experience I'd ever had at home: muttering, stomping, shouting, and finally, as Landon Donovan scored the winner with time running out, complete elation, hugs from random strangers. That night we were, for the briefest of moments, in precisely the right place, glowing in an experience that we'll carry that with us for a long, long time. Before that instant of ecstasy, there had been the bemusing buzz around our referee-induced victimization during the United States–Slovenia game (when the referee wrongly disallowed a goal that would have given us a victory), which had in its own way confirmed a certain type of belonging for fans in the United States: We have our own flare-ups and debates about things that no one else is even paying that much attention to, which also means we were participating fully in the swirling global theater of the World Cup.

Now, though, I was in South Africa. And while I found a lot of affection for the U.S. team—"You guys have done well," I heard several times, with a slightly condescending but sincere pat on the back—there was little ambiguity about who needed to win the game. I was torn

212 • AFRICA'S WORLD CUP

about the match, wanting the United States to win but also wanting Ghana to win—it turns out that's a little tough in football. The restaurant, with the exception of a few despondent U.S. fans at our table, had no such uncertainty: Everyone supported Ghana, all the way, and delighted at the flash of Asamoah Gyan's second goal in extra time. It was tough to feel too down about the U.S. elimination in the midst of the happy crowd or while walking home through vuvuzela-blowing, Ghanaian-flag-waving fans on the street. The only African team to make it out of the group phase, Ghana had made one more step. Would they beat Uruguay? "No chance," said a Spaniard at the table with us. "Of course," said a South African.

I HAD BEEN WELCOMED in South Africa by Achille Mbembe, a prominent Cameroonian philosopher, and Sarah Nuttall, a South African cultural studies professor, both of Stellenbosch University, who were hosting a kind of wandering seminar on the World Cup at their Johannesburg home. On June 27, before heading to the Soccer City Stadium for Argentina-Mexico, I watched that afternoon's England-Germany game with Joseph-Antoine Bell, Cameroon's outspoken goalkeeper of the 1980s and early 1990s. After the Indomitable Lions' elimination in the first round of the 1998 World Cup, Bell had publicly "claimed that Cameroonian players were just not as good as their opponents, and that crying racism was a way to hide the inefficiency and corruption of the Cameroonian football establishment, and of Cameroon in general."[2] Bell also provided an instant philosophical analysis of why England's keeper, David James, had allowed a crucial goal in the 4-1 loss to Germany: "C'est que, malheureusement, les hommes sont programmés pour faire des exploits" (Unfortunately, men are programmed to try to be heroes). James had tried to put himself in a position to make an impressive save, diving and catching the ball to his right, but in the process had left an opening for the ball to slip to his left. Bell's reflection on the difficulty of being a goalie captured the terrifying psychological experience of being the last chance. He told us that what makes a good keeper is the ability to direct his players around the goal and to inspire the confidence that produces an effective defense. In "Alone in the Woods: The Literary Landscape of Soccer's 'Last Defender,'" John Turnbull agrees with Bell: "A goalkeeper lives with the unbridgeable distance between interior landscapes of fear and what he permits the world to see."[3]

Then, out into the night. On the double-decker bus from the northern part of the city to the stadium near Soweto, we met a seven-year-old local boy and his father. The two black South Africans were heading to their sixth game, and the child looked determined and cool as he headed into a long night. The father was yawning. The next day, they were headed to Durban. As a simple answer to all the questions and cost-benefit analyses of whether the World Cup is good or bad for South Africa, there was this. The boy would never have been able to see the tens of thousands of people and tongues, Messi on the pitch, if the Cup had not come to South Africa.

Wandering the two dusty miles to the stadium from the bus drop-off was itself an unexpected pleasure. I had been reading and talking with colleagues and students during the previous year about the fact that FIFA would not allow any kind of "unofficial" merchandising around the World Cup venues, that the governing body had trademarked pretty much anything with the words *South Africa, 2010,* and *World Cup.* But the organizers were unable to trademark what people really wanted to buy on the way to a game: national colors on scarves and flags or the all-important vuvuzelas (or earplugs). That night, local vendors seemed to be transacting more business than the overpriced official stores within the stadium complex.

When I finally got to my seat inside the enormous stadium, a friendly Irishman draped in his national flag asked if I would swap seats with his buddy a few rows down so they could sit together. I accepted, figuring it was fair penance for being a fan of the French team and Thierry Henry, who in the last minutes of a crucial qualifying playoff match against Ireland had used his hand to set up France's decisive goal. Somehow I felt a little responsible for the fact that the Irish were there with their flag but not their team. As a result, I watched the match next to a chain-smoking sixtysomething Argentinean from Rosario, Lionel Messi's hometown, who let out of string of harsh and unprintable insults at his team for nearly the entire ninety minutes. On my right was a quiet, long-haired Japanese man wearing a hood and glasses who erupted into nods and cheers with each goal.

My Argentinean friend smiled a little at his team's three unanswered goals. But he complained (quite rightly, as it turned out) that they really were not playing well on defense, pointing out each time they failed to keep their tactical shape or scrambled to cope with Mexican attacks. An Australian in front of us told him he was not allowed to smoke, but the man from Rosario pointed to sky and said, "We're outside. What's the big deal?" After stadium security made him put out his cigarette, the man from Rosario ate cough drops for the rest of the match. He seemed pleased—a little—when I told him I thought his team would probably win the Cup. "We'll beat Germany," he said, "and I'm not worried about Brazil. It's Spain I'm worried about."

Facing elimination, thousands of Mexican fans, beautifully decked out and spirited at kickoff, turned gloomy. The South African police officers in charge of security at the stadium (private security guards had walked off the job in a dispute over wages) had the unenviable task of dealing with various tussles between a tightly packed group of intertwined Mexico and Argentina fans. A bit of beer was thrown at one unfortunate policeman, who was impeccably controlled about the whole thing. Then—as if out of a FIFA brochure or one of those World Cup commercials—some Mexico fans waded into the Argentinean side of the standoff and began waving flags and jumping up and down, patting the enemy fans on the back. This conciliatory move seemed to calm everyone down.

FOOTBALL, I LEARNED the night during the Ghana-Uruguay game a few days later, is one of the most effective tools for mass torture ever devised by the human race. A vast majority of the more than eighty thousand fans at Soccer City, plus millions of viewers throughout the world, were left speechless and unwound by what we saw unfold. For me, a devout fan of France, it was a little bit like reliving the final of the 2006 World Cup. An early euphoria followed by an equalizer, then a game agonizingly dragging on and on, with Gyan's missed penalty in the last minute of extra time playing the role of Zidane's head-butt as the dramatic and decisive instant of the night, regardless of the outcome of the dreaded penalty shootout. The sorrow, the indignity, the sense of unfairness of Ghana's loss were too much even to contemplate. For all those who hoped that 2010 would be the year an African team would go further than any had before, the remaining games seemed somehow sapped of meaning.

The night had begun very differently. The atmosphere in Johannesburg was electric, with everyone in South Africa seemingly behind Ghana (rechristened BaGhana BaGhana) and the country's flags and emblems everywhere. The symbolism was of course great. Half a century earlier, Ghana's independence signaled a wave of decolonization on the continent. In 1966, Ghana's president, Kwame Nkrumah, led a boycott of the World Cup by African nations unhappy with the fact that African, Asian, North and Central American, and Caribbean teams had no guaranteed berths in the sixteen-team competition. The boycott was successful, setting in motion a long process during which African countries have gained more power within FIFA.[4] The South African World Cup was in some sense the culmination of that long process. For Ghana to become the first African team to advance to the semifinals would have been a fitting and inspiring confirmation that things have changed and that they can change even further in the football world.

Most Ghana supporters had thrown caution to the wind. Street vendors sold a few small Uruguay flags on the way into Soccer City, but mostly it was every kind of merchandise in Ghana's red, yellow, and green. Fans from all over the world—not just Africans—decked themselves out in Ghana scarves (I picked up a nice one), Ghana hats, Ghana gloves, and Ghana face paint and waved small and large Ghanaian flags. There were also groups of the famous stalwart Black Stars fans. Everyone knew what the "right" outcome should be, it seemed. And as the game began, it seemed like Ghana would win. The Black Stars played beautifully. They were exciting to watch. The Ghanaians attacked, probing for openings in the tough Uruguayan defense and appearing technically superior. As if to validate Ghana's superiority, Sulley Muntari scored on a thunderous blast from forty yards out just before halftime.

The rest of the story is one I cannot quite bear to recount: Forlán curled a free kick into the net to draw the teams level. Then, in the final minute of extra time, Uruguayan Luis Suárez kept the ball out of his team's goal with his hands. He was promptly ejected, and a penalty kick was awarded to Ghana. But Gyan missed. His failure to convert the penalty crippled the Ghanaian team, and Uruguay went on to win in a penalty shootout. Despite the cacophony of the crowd and the millions of prayers, among them mine, the result of all of that support was unbearable. To watch Gyan, sobbing uncontrollably, consoled by his teammates on the pitch, was—like the entire match—purely gut-wrenching.

After the game, I went through several possible responses. The first, certainly the most reasonable, was simply to forever swear off football. This approach had several advantages. After all, we let it into our lives and let it torture us, so we should have the power to politely show it the door and ask it to take its leave. Doing so would save a lot of money and time and would allow some of us to devote ourselves to nobler causes or to the pleasures of gardening or spending time with family. I seriously considered this option for about as long as it took to get home that night.

One could also, of course, consider putting the disappointment into proper perspective. On the long walk back to the buses from Soccer City, surrounded by a lugubrious atmosphere among the fans, I tried to take consolation from remembering the many World Cup matches that had similarly been determined by the crime against humanity that is the penalty shootout: West Germany–France, the 1982 World Cup semi-final, for example, when Michel Platini's generation of French players perhaps came closest to winning the World Cup. Gyan had taken his place among many generations of stars who suffered the same fate. But, unlike some of them—like Roberto Baggio of Italy in the 1994 final against Brazil—Gyan was still young, and he and his teammates have much ahead of them that may come to surpass, if never erase, this memory.

In truth, I would not have traded anything for having been *fully* at Soccer City the night of July 2, part of the crowd witnessing the Ghanaians and Urguayans fight for a place in the final four. During the penalty kicks, I literally sat down on my seat with my head in my hands, unable to watch. I relied on the sound of the crowd to tell me what was going on. I knew when things looked up, briefly. And I knew "we" had lost when, in the stadium, after hours of constant and intense noise, there was nothing but the sound of tens of thousands of sighs. The whole experience was both unbearable and irreplaceable. And, in the end, it was probably best to have company, to hug friends afterward, to commiserate with strangers as we left the stadium.

In the end, I found the best solution—one that is, after all, the only approach to surviving in life with some sense of balance and joy—is perhaps to hold on tightly to a particular time from that match: between Muntari's forty-fifth-minute goal and Forlán's fifty-fifth-minute strike, when there was a buzz of hope, tempered by an undercurrent of fear, the time when what is now impossible briefly seemed possible.

THE URUGUAY-NETHERLANDS semifinal in Cape Town brought with it another lesson: football's limited power to offer moral clarity. After the Ghana match, I intended to take out my rage and spleen at the Uruguayans in the next game, savoring their defeat by the Dutch. But a conversation with a ten-year-old stalwart Uruguayan fan on the plane to Cape Town softened my position. Friends lamented the real possibility that European teams would contest the title, so Uruguay became the last hope of the rest of the world. In the end, I did not lament Uruguay's 3–2 defeat in a captivating match. The crowd in the Cape Town stadium was more posh than at previous games. Cape Town's stadium, too, was strikingly attractive, and watching the game there was a different kind of experience than I had had in Soccer City: riveting and peaceful but somehow slightly more aloof.

Returning to Johannesburg from Cape Town, I could feel that the end of the tournament was near: a few World Cup–themed advertisements on the highway had already been replaced with the more perennially useful advertisements for funeral services. On the eve of the final, the state of exception of the World Cup in South Africa, fixated on the incredible liveliness of a common narrative, of the actions of players and the life of crowds, had ceded to more banal, grinding realities.

TWO DAYS AFTER SPAIN'S first World Cup triumph (and after I had survived an encounter with baboons in the hills outside Johannesburg), I was on my way home to North Carolina, and the World Cup experience seemed slightly surreal. Critics of the World Cup and the enthusiasm it inspires often insist that for all the talk of football creating understanding, tolerance, and communication, this global tournament is ultimately a brief moment, even a fantasy, with little broader impact on structures of oppression and domination. Some observers point out the ways in which the tournament reproduces those structures. All of this is quite right, yet it misses another point: The World Cup is what it is precisely because it is slightly out of time and out of place in the world. What do all those people who watched World Cup games, near and far, take from this? We disperse, individually carrying this massive collective experience. We have glimpsed an alternative space, one composed of people from all over sharing a common story, full of absurdities and twists and turns, random, even futile, yet perfect because it is common ground. We came like pilgrims looking for something but perhaps returned not precisely sure of what we found.

NOTES

1. *Soccer Politics*, http://sites.duke.edu/wcwp/author/wcwp/, accessed December 5, 2011.

2. Bea Vidacs, "The Postcolonial and the Level Playing-Field in the 1998 World Cup," in *Sport and Postcolonialism*, ed. John Bale and Mike Cronin (Oxford: Berg, 2003), 156.

3. John Turnbull, "Alone in the Woods: The Literary Landscape of Soccer's 'Last Defender,'" *World Literature Today* 84, 4 (2010): 19–22.

4. For more details, see Peter Alegi, *African Soccerscapes: How a Continent Changed the World's Game* (London: Hurst; Athens: Ohio University Press, 2010), 68–77; Paul Darby, *Africa, Football, and FIFA: Politics, Colonialism, and Resistance* (London: Cass, 2002), 36–40.

Forum on the 2010 World Cup

Perspectives from South African Practitioners

CONVENOR AND MODERATOR: PETER ALEGI
WITH THABO DLADLA, MOHLOMI KEKELETSO
MAUBANE, AND RODNEY REINERS

The 2010 World Cup in South Africa was widely celebrated as a huge success. What did the event mean to you?

MOHLOMI KEKELETSO MAUBANE: To better understand what the World Cup meant to me, I'd like to go back to 1990. I was staying in a rural township called Bapong, just outside Brits in what is now the North West Province. I was in Standard 4 (Grade 6), and my daily routine entailed going to school, coming back home to do my chores, like fetching water from the communal tap, and then going to "Ellis Park," the neighborhood sandlot, to play soccer. I enjoyed imitating my favorite players: Doctor Khumalo, Mark Tovey, Marks "Go Man Go" Maponyane, Reggie Jantjies, Tebogo Moloi, and Innocent Mayoyo. When darkness fell, I would return home to do homework.

At the time, only a few people in Bapong had electricity in their homes, and most families did not own TV sets. However, Thabo, one of the older boys at Ellis Park, had a small black-and-white TV powered by a car battery, and we would watch big matches at his place. I remember watching a final between Kaizer Chiefs and Moroka Swallows—I think it was the Castle Challenge Cup Final when Noel "Phinda Mzala" Cousins scored for the Dube Birds [Swallows] in the first minute. But typical of the Kaizer Chiefs teams of that era, Shane MacGregor equalized in the last minute, before Fani Madida scored the winning goal in extra time as Amakhosi clinched yet another trophy.

In the final years of isolation from FIFA, football on South African television meant the National Soccer League (NSL). That was it! No World Cup, no African Nations Cup, no European Cup. Despite the lack of television coverage, I already knew about Pelé and Maradona. My father liked telling my brother and me football stories from back when he was still a young man growing up in Soweto. He told us about past South African greats like Chippa Moloi, Al Die Hoekies, Dharam Mohan, Alfred "From Russia with Love" Jacobs, Ratha Mokgoathleng, and many, many others. I suspect that it is from my father that I first heard about Maradona and Pelé.

Since only a handful of households in Bapong had electricity and television sets, a culture developed of people visiting their "well-off" neighbors to watch TV. This was done mostly on Tuesdays and Thursdays, when the local African-language drama or soap opera was screened. My folks, especially my mother, were not too keen on this, and so my grasping of the *Lesilo Rula* or *Ululu Ubuyile* story line was often courtesy of a narration from a classmate who, in the oral tradition of our ancestors, in turn might have been told the plot of the previous night's episode by a friend who watched the drama at their neighbors' place.

Suddenly, one Saturday evening, our parents for the first time granted my three siblings and me permission to watch TV at a friend's home. Not only was this the very first time we were allowed to venture out at night, the special occasion was the opening match of Italia 1990 between world champions Argentina and the Indomitable Lions of Cameroon.

This was the very first time a World Cup match was broadcast live in South Africa. It was also the first time I saw Maradona with my own eyes. By the end of the match, Cameroon had won my heart. I only watched two other games during Italia '90, the West Germany versus England semifinal and the final. By the end of the tournament, I had new heroes: Cameroonian Roger Milla, and AC Milan's Dutch trio of Frank Rijkaard, Marco van Basten, and Ruud Gullit. I have been an AC Milan fan since then and have always had a soft spot for the Indomitable Lions. That Argentina versus Cameroon match signaled the beginning of my relationship with the World Cup.

By 1994, at home and in South Africa, things had improved. By then, we were staying in Lebanon Township in Mabopane. Our home was the quintessential four-roomed *kasi* (house) you find in black townships in South Africa, and though modest, it was much better than our previous place in Bapong. We had running water in the house, electricity, and our own TV. I only missed one USA 1994 match: Russia 6, Cameroon 1.

Between 1990 and 1994, my grasp of international football improved tremendously. BOP TV, one of the local stations, had an Italian Serie A highlights show. So names like Baresi, Maldini, Papin, Albertini, Asprilla, and Dino Baggio became familiar. BOP TV also used to broadcast a football show called *Futbol Mundial* which I never missed.

My favorite team at USA '94 was Italy, and Roberto Baggio was my hero. I have never seen a player singlehandedly lift a team like that in a major tournament. Even though the Divin Codino (Divine Ponytail) and Italy lost the final against Brazil on penalties, my sadness was tempered by the fact that every neutral fan is also a fan of Brazilian football. During the 1998 and 2002 World Cups, I watched as many matches as possible so when South Africa bid for the 2006 World Cup, I was ecstatic about the prospect of my country hosting the tournament.

My friend, Lucky, and I hatched a crazy plan: We were going to work our way into the Bafana Bafana squad. Growing up, we were talented footballers but never pursued football careers. By talented footballers, I don't mean we were like Samuel Eto'o or anything like that. In fact, we were not even the best in Mabopane, but we were good enough. (The standards were pretty high in Mabopane. To this day, some of the best players I have seen in South Africa, across all levels, were amateur footballers I crossed paths with in that township, now part of Limpopo Province.) The plan was to take a year to reach peak physical fitness level, join the Mabopane Young Masters team in the Mvela League (the second tier of professional football), then move into the Premier Soccer League (PSL), and finally win a call-up to the national team.

In July 2000, on the day the host country of the 2006 World Cup was announced, I was with Lucky and other members of the Hungry Lions—the moniker of our childhood crew—watching the live feed of the announcement from Zurich. To many South Africans, the voting seemed like a mere formality. The 2006 World Cup was going to be ours. Mark Gleeson was one of the two commentators narrating the proceedings from Zurich. During the last round of voting, Gleeson made an insightful observation: that during the final round of voting, Germany and South Africa would be tied at twelve-all, leaving FIFA president Sepp Blatter to cast the deciding vote. Blatter had positioned himself as the crusader behind Africa's bid to host the World Cup, and the general expectation was that he would vote for South Africa. But, as Gleeson presciently noted, things might not get to that stage if Oceania decided to abstain from voting.

I don't know what sparked the idea in Gleeson's mind, but as things turned out, Germany won the bid thanks to the abstention of Charles Dempsey, Oceania's representative on the FIFA Executive Committee. Dempsey became Public Enemy Number 1 in South Africa, but FIFA was also criticized. This painful moment signaled my loss of faith in the upper echelons of world football governance. I was fuming. These Europeans colonized us, took our land, severely altered our way of life, and now they won't even give us a chance to host a World Cup!

However, a couple of years later, when FIFA announced that it would rotate the World Cup among the continents, starting with Africa in 2010, I knew that South Africa would be first in line. When we won the bid to host the 2010 World Cup, it seemed like compensation for FIFA's earlier mistake. The shenanigans of the 2006 World Cup bid decision opened my eyes to the politricks behind the world game. In the build-up to 2010, I learned even more about FIFA's dark side. Nevertheless, I am glad we won the bid and hosted the World Cup successfully.

THABO DLADLA: It was a highlight of one's sporting life. It was the first time I experienced the senior World Cup live in the stadium. I had had the privilege of going to Malaysia (as an assistant coach) with the South African under-twenty team for the FIFA Under-Twenty World Cup [in 1997], where we faced big teams like Brazil and France. But this time, being in the stadium with fans coming from different countries watching foreign teams—I never got the opportunity to watch South Africa—it was quite an experience, quite an experience.

Everything went smoothly in this World Cup. On the sporting side, it went very well. We had some very exciting matches. The first match I attended was Australia versus Germany; then I went to Spain against Switzerland (both played in Durban). People never thought that Spain, playing in their intelligent way, would end up winning the event after losing that first match. From the business side of things, I don't think people gained much financially, except a few fat cats in South Africa. Unfortunately, the majority of ordinary people did not make any money, and they were not able to go and watch the matches. Only a privileged few could afford even the cheapest tickets. But following it on television and on the radio, people felt like they were part of the action because the tournament was happening in their country.

RODNEY REINERS: As a South African, the World Cup made me very proud. Considering where this country has come from—once a pariah of the world, then the miracle of democratic change, and the enduring negativity of Afro-pessimism—we showed that "Africa can do world class," in the words of Danny Jordaan (South African Local Organising Committee CEO).

Back in my playing days, when this country was in the vise grip of the apartheid machine, when football was a neglected and barely tolerated sport, much sacrifice was made. We never had the money, the glitz or the glamour of today's Premier Soccer League. I played for Santos in Cape Town, and it was bread-and-butter stuff, all for the love of the game. We'd travel to away matches in rickety vans or ramshackle buses and endure many, many hours on the road to Johannesburg to play matches in the nonracial Federation Professional League (before the days of football unity in South Africa). Looking back on this rough past, when the World Cup landed on our shores, it made all that sacrifice worth it.

Covering the 2010 World Cup as a member of the media gave me a tremendous sense of pride and achievement, especially in my country. The World Cup brought the nation together, even if only for a brief while before we retreated back to our respective enclaves. The tournament showed the potential that lies locked, ready to be unleashed, in this most frustrating of countries. The solution to a peaceful racial future in South Africa is there; it's almost tangible yet is so far away. The World Cup gave just a quick insight into how, when this nation pulls together for a common cause, we can get there.

What was your favorite moment of the tournament?

RR: The football, what else? I'm a football man at heart, and despite all the glitz and philosophizing and fandom and unity and political pandering, it's the game that moves me. As a Capetonian through and through, the best moment for me was the opening game at the Cape

Town Stadium. Don't even ask me who played—it wasn't important. What mattered on that day was that *the World Cup* had come to Cape Town! I never even bothered with a media parking ticket. I wanted to be in the crowd on the Cape Town Stadium Fan Walk. I wanted to feel the vibe and the buzz of the evening. I parked my car several miles away from the stadium. Then I joined the throng in central Cape Town heading to Somerset Road in Green Point and slowly inched toward the ground. It was an occasion to savor: the noise of the vuvuzelas, the color, the vibrancy, the music, the chatter, the anticipation, the enjoyment. And not a hint of the class, social, and racial problems that bedevil us in South Africa on a daily basis. For a brief while, I was in Eden—but only for a brief while, of course!

MKM: The buildup to the opening game was memorable. On June 11, 2010, I mysteriously became "sick" and could not report to work. Together with a group of friends, we stocked up on consumables of our choice and during the few hours before the kickoff of South Africa versus Mexico, that is when it actually sunk in that the 2010 FIFA World Cup was about to kick off right here in my country! Those four hours or so of anticipation and excitement leading to the opening match are a moment I will always cherish. The World Cup about to kick off in Africa.

TD: My favorite moment was the semifinal match between Spain and Germany. I had wanted to see how effective the German counterattack would be against a team with such intelligent, highly technical players like Spain. That night at Mabhida Stadium had quite a number of interesting moments. The quality of the technique, the quality of the passing game of the Spanish team, the level of patience is something to behold, you know. Spain reminded us that the game is not just about physical speed, it's also about mental speed. In the end, it was good that the Spanish won this World Cup; I'm hoping that in South Africa and maybe the rest of the world, people will start believing that constructive, beautiful football can be successful.

Did the World Cup change the way South Africans relate to each other and to their nation?

RR: It was amazing how for an ephemeral yet joyful moment, so many South Africans found the time to put aside their petty prejudices and naked ambitions and reach out to each other.

MKM: Like Rodney said, the World Cup brought us together for a brief moment. But it was superficial. Diverse Mzansi people [South Africans] with faces painted in the colors of the national flag, clad in yellow Bafana T-shirts, and blowing vuvuzelas are a rarity and a sight to behold. But after the final whistle, we went back to our different ways. In South Africa, we enjoy remembering how events like the 1995 Rugby World Cup and the 2010 FIFA World Cup united us. But if these events unite us, what is it that divides us when they are over?

TD: It is unfortunate that we tend to wait for big events to develop a sense of nationhood, to temporarily come together, only to go back to the old way of doing things as soon as the event is gone. Maybe we need to have a World Cup every day in this country! Then people can realize that there is much that they can learn from living together, interacting, that people of different races and cultures can enrich each other and improve the quality of life for everyone.

   During the World Cup, the spirit of nationhood was huge, but unfortunately as we previously saw with the rugby World Cup, the African Nations Cup, we still look at things mainly in terms of race. . . . We have not succeeded in building a united sense of nationhood in South Africa; we continue to live in our own compartments.

How would you rate the performance of the six African teams?

RR: Ghana's Black Stars were by far the best African team. Fueled by the adrenalin of being World Cup hosts, Bafana showed some promise. But the South Africans lacked a cutting edge as well as player quality to compete at the highest level. Cameroon, Algeria, Ivory Coast, and Nigeria were disappointing, none doing justice to their considerable potential.

TD: As a South African who has been involved in football development since the birth of SAFA [the South African Football Association] in the early 1990s, I know that we haven't moved fast enough in development. Looking at the team we had, I did not expect Bafana Bafana to compete with the big boys. Besides the tough group they were drawn in, the quality of planning was not there. Two years is not enough time to prepare for a World Cup. It was always going to be an uphill battle for us. In the buildup to the World Cup, expectations for Bafana were not high. Most of the talk revolved around whether the team would make it into the second round. In the end, Bafana did as much as I expected.

I thought Ivory Coast would do better than they did, given the caliber of players like Didier Drogba, men who are competing week in and week out against some of the best players in the world in the Premier League and in the Champions League. Even the best African team, Ghana, was very lucky along the way. The Black Stars played well, but if you look at their matches, their opponents got red cards, conceded key penalties, and Australia held them to a draw despite playing a man down most of the match. Finally, had Australia not defeated Serbia in the final group match, Ghana would have been knocked out in the first round.

The main reason why African teams struggle in the World Cup is poor administration. Ivory Coast and Nigeria, for example, changed head coaches a few weeks before the World Cup, which reduced their chances of doing well. The heart of the problem is that African football administrators are always looking for instant success. They don't understand the game and don't have passion for the game. They have passion for money, power, glory.

MKM: Let me use my relationship with Bafana Bafana to answer this question. After winning the 1996 African Nations Cup, South Africa participated in the Confederations Cup in Saudi Arabia in 1997. The team gave a good showing, winning the accolades of Brazilian coach Mario Zagallo and others, but was knocked out of the tournament partly due to their inability to convert their scoring chances.

Once the tournament ended, SAFA fired Clive Barker despite the fact that the Nations Cup, the COSAFA Cup [a regional competition], and the World Cup were coming up in the next six months. In came Jomo Sono. For good measure, he gave a chance to players like Quinton Fortune and Benni McCarthy whom Barker had overlooked in favor of his tried and tested soldiers. Jomo Sono guided the team to the finals of the Nations Cup in Burkina Faso in 1998, losing in the final against the Pharaohs of Egypt. Yet it was not Jomo who steered the Bafana Bafana ship at the World Cup four months later, it was Frenchman Phillip Troussier, who liked to call himself the White Witch Doctor. Three coaches in less than six months, each with a different coaching philosophy and method, tactics, and player preference. In the end, Troussier proved not to have the right *muthi* [traditional medicine] at France 1998: Bafana lost to France and drew twice and was eliminated in the first round.

This recent history is strikingly similar to what happened to African teams at the 2010 World Cup. Newly appointed European coaches guided Cameroon, Ivory Coast, and Nigeria. Cameroon was most disappointing, losing all three matches; Ivory Coast was once again unlucky to be drawn in a "group of death," while Nigeria was characteristically inconsistent. Algeria looked as if it had already achieved its objective by beating Egypt in a tense playoff match to earn a trip to South Africa. Bafana Bafana was never going to be in it. As Thabo Dladla noted, the overall problem with the performance of the African sides is closely connected to the actions of myopic men in suits who administer the national associations.

The 2010 World Cup had the second-lowest ever goals-per-game average in World Cup history (2.27, behind Italia 1990's 2.21). How would you rate the quality of play?

MKM: The quality was not as good as I had expected. I would say the standard of play at the European Championships and at the UEFA Champions League is much higher than what I saw at the World Cup. Spain to me never played to their full potential or displayed the majestic football they did at Euro 2008. Germany is the team that I think played the best football.

RR: There were some good games. Germany's 4–1 demolition job of England was particularly satisfactory, with the emergence of Thomas Müller a joy to watch. The Spanish were magnificent (except in their opener against Switzerland), with my favorite footballer Xavi excelling and Sergio Busquets behind him playing brilliantly.

But overall, the quality of play was not terribly entertaining. It seemed that far too many national teams came to South Africa with a defensive mind-set. Do we need to mention the "let's just kick 'em" effort by the Dutch against Spain in the final? That game proved to be an embarrassment to world football when it should have been the showpiece of Africa's first World Cup.

TD: There were many disappointing matches. Aside from Spain, Mexico was entertaining, vibrant, dynamic. Argentina looked promising initially, but their organization really let them down. Maradona lacked a good technical staff to help him get the most out of the team's quality players. Germany's style was more attacking, partly a reflection of the kind of football many German clubs play in their domestic league. Unfortunately, Brazil under Dunga played very direct, simple football. Holland has a reputation as a passing team, but even the Dutch were conservative throughout the tournament. The coaches were very conservative, and so they are to blame for the poor quality of play at the 2010 World Cup.

To what extent was South Africa 2010 an "African" World Cup?

TD: South Africa is a country in Africa, but I don't think that South Africa fully embraced the continent's people. Maybe the national government has done so at the diplomatic level, first with Thabo Mbeki and his dream of an African Renaissance and now with President Zuma. South Africans, unfortunately, have not been exposed to Africans as much as they have been exposed to Europeans and Americans, mainly because of the apartheid history. This past also explains the xenophobic threats circulating before and even during the World Cup against other Africans. People here have not yet embraced the idea that they are part and parcel of Africa, . . . maybe because most South Africans have not traveled to other African countries.

As much as the tournament organizers purported to stage an "African" World Cup, I don't think many of our African brothers and sisters had the means to come here as fans. It wasn't easy for an ordinary supporter from Ghana or Cameroon to travel to South Africa. Maybe others did not have the courage to come here after what had happened recently with xenophobic violence. It was an elitist World Cup. I saw many rich white and Indian people at the games in Durban. But if this week you go to Chatsworth in Durban to watch the PSL [Premier Soccer League] game between Golden Arrows and Sundowns, you'll maybe see 99 percent blacks, even though Chatsworth is an Indian township.

MKM: It was an "African" World Cup only because it was played on these shores. Except for the vuvuzela, there is nothing that made the 2010 World Cup an African World Cup.

RR: The inspiring manner in which South Africans got behind Ghana after the elimination of Bafana Bafana showed that the World Cup was not just about South Africa but also about Africa's success and solidarity.

Do you see FIFA's role in organizing the World Cup in South Africa as positive or negative?

RR: FIFA's role was positive. Whatever the criticism that went before, the World Cup in South Africa created the opportunity for the government to shift into high gear on delivering public projects and improving roads and infrastructure. At the same time, FIFA gave South Africans—and the continent—a glimpse of their true potential. This contribution was crucial because in South Africa and in Africa as a whole, personal agendas, individual greed, and power-mongering hold sway, and the ordinary, important things in life are too often overlooked.

TD: For FIFA, the World Cup is a business. Bringing the World Cup to Africa, particularly South Africa, was important to Sepp Blatter and the FIFA Executive Committee. South Africa 2010 was a legacy to them because no one before had brought the tournament to Africa. It was a calculated risk since South Africa has a well-developed infrastructure and cities comparable to other major world cities. The large profits that FIFA made out of this World Cup show that it was a risk worth taking.

The FIFA World Cup helped the country. The world sees South Africa differently after the tournament: Fewer people overseas think of South Africa as a "bush country," and more people know that there are some decent human beings living here, not just lions and wild animals. To an extent, the World Cup has changed the way people view South Africa and in doing so allowed the country to rebrand itself.

MKM: FIFA bulldozed South Africa into doing what it wanted. I remember the very first speech a FIFA official made in South Africa after we won the 2010 bid. Jerome Valcke [FIFA general secretary] told a full session of Parliament that this was not South Africa's World Cup, it was FIFA's World Cup, which South Africa just happened to be hosting. Valcke also added that FIFA had the most sophisticated lawyers in the world and would not tolerate the undermining of any of his organization's objectives, rules, and procedures.

I appreciate the significance of the World Cup to FIFA's brand and financial bottom line, but the tone of Valcke's speech was paternalistic and condescending toward the South African taxpayers who paid most of the hosting costs. He sounded like a schoolmaster laying down the law to schoolkids. Of course, FIFA played a leading role in ensuring that the tournament was a success. But FIFA came to South Africa with preconceived notions and imposed them on us. If FIFA gave South Africa a nine out of ten as World Cup hosts, I give FIFA a five out of ten.

Since the World Cup ended, most of the new stadiums are sitting empty. Ticket prices have doubled. The minister of tourism stated that foreign tourist arrivals, while substantial, were much lower than expected. And the grassroots game is still struggling. What is the longer-term impact of the World Cup on South Africa?

MKM: As with other aspects of the tournament, the tourism benefits were slightly overstated. More importantly, what on earth was the benefit of building the Mbombela Stadium in Nelspruit, capital of Mpumalanga Province that does not have a team in the PSL? There was also no need to build the Peter Mokaba Stadium in Polokwane or the Moses Mabhida Stadium in Durban.

As far as increased ticket prices go, I am in a go-slow mode; I choose which matches to attend. It can be boring to go to the stadium alone, so I normally go with a group of friends. For the recent Orlando Pirates versus Kaizer Chiefs derby, for instance, seven of us wanted to go to the game together. In the past, the ticket prices would have cost a total of 140 rand [20 dollars]. But for this game, the cost was 280 rand [40 dollars] for the tickets alone, and we still had to travel to Soccer City and get things like cigarettes and beverages on top of that. In the end, we decided not to attend the match and instead bought some meat, had a *braai* [barbecue], drank beer, and watched the game on TV. The sad thing is that the people who decide on hiking ticket prices are officials who don't have to pay to watch games at the stadium. This ticket pricing thing is crazy. I stay in Orlando West, Soweto. In the past with just 100 rand [14 dollars], over a weekend I could walk to Orlando Stadium to watch Pirates on Saturday and then the next day walk to Dobsonville to watch Swallows. Now I can watch one match for the price of two! The people who inflated the ticket prices can go watch the matches and cheer the players themselves.

As far as grassroots-level football is concerned, at the official presentation of Pitso Mosimane as the new coach of Bafana Bafana, SAFA's CEO said that Mosimane was appointed to ensure that Bafana Bafana made it to the 2014 World Cup in Brazil. That was SAFA's primary vision; nothing else was said of the other national teams. There was lip service paid to soccer development, but no specifics about how SAFA was going to go about doing this.

In December 2010, SAFA held its annual general meeting, and Kirsten Nematandani, SAFA president, was quoted as saying, "We have just hosted a successful World Cup, and we need to take advantage of that." But a different SAFA official pointed out that "the buses from the World Cup are gathering dust, and we need to start making a profit from them. They have been parked at Soccer City since the competition ended." For an organization to be admitting to such things after hosting a megaevent shows that it has no plan whatsoever. A week after this meeting, we learned that the Under-twenty-three national team would not be participating in the upcoming All-Africa games because SAFA did not send a fax confirming the team's participation.

As far as the long-term effects of the World Cup in South Africa, the World Cup will prove to be a turning point in South Africa as a whole, and not only for the football community. After 1994, the mantra in South Africa was "Madiba magic" and how we were a Rainbow Nation. It was an era of reconciliation, and we were the world's miracle country [see the essay by Daniel Herwitz in this volume]. But South Africa is a country with fundamental problems, and the "Madiba magic" should have been tempered with a dose of reality. There is no magic wand to wave and solve the enormous challenges we face, so the rhetoric should have been accompanied by the more realistic assertion that it's not yet *uhuru* [freedom]. Furthermore, reconciliation the way it was discussed in South Africa was fundamentally flawed. It is black people who are preaching reconciliation when it should be the other way round. It's akin to a rape victim saying they forgive their rapist when the former is not even bothered to acknowledge the heinous deed they committed, let alone show remorse for it.

Despite Mandela and his spirit of forgiveness, the first years of a "new South Africa" did not unshackle people from the chains of material hardship. Then came the 2010 World Cup. Not only were we going to watch Brazil playing right here in our country, hosting the tournament was going to afford ordinary people the chance to strike it rich. But the so-called man on the street struggled not only to buy tickets to watch World Cup matches; vendors could not sell pap and vleis [stiff cornmeal porridge and grilled meat] and other goods outside the stadiums. The World Cup took place in the First World parts of South African cities while the Third World parts were left on the periphery, at best to serve as tourist attractions.

In the end, South Africa remains a sharply unequal society, as demonstrated by the one mile that separates luxurious and overwhelmingly white Sandton and the impoverished and historically black Alexandra. The powers that be often make the mistake of thinking that marginalized people are not perceptive or have scant understanding of what is going on in the country. Yet a simple visit to even the remotest or [most] impoverished corner of the country will expose one to the reality that being poor does not translate to being dumb. The newly empowered elites are too busy chest thumping, brandishing their struggle credentials, and purging the country's resources and don't have their ear on the ground. There is a simmering class struggle in South Africa, as so-called service delivery strikes demonstrate.

More than a marketing exercise and a soccer tournament, the World Cup was dangled as a carrot to the poor, as a beacon of hope and the answer to their material hardships. Now that the tournament has come and gone, it is clear that millions of people still struggle to make ends meet. What is the ruling class now going to dangle? The 2020 bid for the Olympics in Durban?

In the end, the 2010 World Cup was more than just a football tournament. Despite my misgivings, it was one of the most important undertakings by African people in modern times. So in conclusion, my utmost thanks to Irvin Khoza, Danny Jordaan, and everyone who played a part in bringing the tournament to South Africa. Thank you also to all the people who visited our country during the tournament. Hope you enjoyed your stay and that you took home a vuvuzela and great memories. I also hope you will come back in the future.

RR: From a Cape Town point of view, because that is where I live, the road improvements were especially welcome, and as a result, in some areas it is now much easier to get around. The city's new World Cup Stadium, while expensive, has provided a superb venue for local professional clubs. The games staged there this season have sparked new interest in Cape Town football. For example, the season-opening doubleheader in August 2010 drew forty-five thousand people. More recently, the stadium hosted a match between Ajax Cape Town and Kaizer Chiefs, the biggest team in the country, and drew a crowd of forty-five thousand again. The Chiefs match was a magnificent event, with the football on show of a high quality and the response of people to the media very positive. In this city, where rugby and cricket are still very popular, the new stadium has provided an opportunity for new people to come into the sport of football. No longer is local football fobbed off as a nuisance; there is respect and a renewed interest in the game.

The new stadium has also provided the Mother City with a suitable venue to attract Bafana, who were often loath to come to Cape Town before. The sold-out Nelson Mandela Challenge match against the United States in November 2010 is a case in point. Cape Town Stadium has also allowed the city to bring in top music bands like U2 and Kings of Leon, thus giving Capetonians the opportunity to see world-class international acts. Of course, the financial viability of the stadium will always be in question, but if it is managed in the right way, then it has the capacity to play a vigorous and rewarding role in ensuring that the Mother City becomes one of the top tourist destinations in the world.

TD: If I can take the example of Pietermaritzburg (the capital of KwaZulu-Natal Province), where I live, politicians talked about the World Cup leaving a legacy in terms of new infrastructure set aside for long-term use by local people. Millions were spent to refurbish Harry Gwala Stadium, but only Maritzburg United [in the Premier Soccer League] plays there now. The ground was rebuilt with taxpayers' money, but ordinary people have not had the privilege to use it for football. Before the World Cup, Harry Gwala was used by many local teams, but Vodacom League games and school tournament finals are no longer held there. It seems that the culture of reserving the best facilities for the elite endures. This means that the World Cup did not change a lot for the ordinary person.

Looking back to 2010, there's been lots of talk about the profits that FIFA would be giving the national football association (100 million dollars) but for me that is neither here nor there. Because every day we delay providing opportunities for young people to play, we lose them to crime, we lose them to AIDS, we lose them to many other social ills. I had expected that long before the World Cup kicked off, concerted investments in terms of providing the facilities, providing equipment, providing the coaches for the kids would have occurred all over South Africa. This grassroots development would have been the biggest legacy of the World Cup. But we did not do that. We only look at sports at the elite level; we don't look at sports at the grassroots level. But that's where life is: People live at grassroots level, not elite level. The World Cup was successful, but too many young people in this country still have no hope, they have no future.

Selected Bibliography

Adekeye, Adebajo, Adebayo Adedeji, and Chris Landsberg, eds. *South Africa in Africa: The Post-Apartheid Era*. Scottsville: University of KwaZulu-Natal Press, 2007.

Alegi, Peter. *African Soccerscapes: How a Continent Changed the World's Game*. London: Hurst; Athens: Ohio University Press, 2010.

Alegi, Peter. "'Feel the Pull in Your Soul': Local Agency and Global Trends in South Africa's 2006 World Cup Bid." *Soccer and Society* 2, 3 (2001): 1–21.

Alegi, Peter. *Laduma!: Soccer Politics and Society in South Africa, from Its Origins to 2010*. Scottsville: University of KwaZulu-Natal Press, 2010.

Alegi, Peter. "'A Nation to Be Reckoned With': The Politics of World Cup Stadium Construction in Cape Town and Durban, South Africa." *African Studies* 67, 3 (2008): 397–422.

Alegi, Peter. "The Political Economy of Mega-Stadiums and the Underdevelopment of Grassroots Football in South Africa." *Politikon* 34, 3 (2007): 315–31.

Alegi, Peter, and Chris Bolsmann. "From Apartheid to Unity: White Capital and Black Power in the Racial Integration of South African Football, 1976–1992." *African Historical Review* 42, 1 (2010): 2–18.

Alegi, Peter, and Chris Bolsmann, eds. *South Africa and the Global Game: Football, Apartheid, and Beyond*. London: Routledge, 2010.

Anderson, Benedict. *Imagined Communities: Reflections on the Origin and Spread of Nationalism*. London: Verso, 1991.

Attali, Jacques. *Noise: The Political Economy of Music*. Manchester: Manchester University Press, 1985.

Bakhtin, Michael. *Rabelais and His World*. Trans. Helen Iswolsky. Cambridge: MIT Press, 1968.

Baller, Susann. *Spielfelder der Stadt: Fußball und Jugendpolitik im Senegal seit 1950*. Cologne: Böhlau, 2010.

Bass, Orli. "Aiming for Africa: Durban, 2010, and Notions of African Urban Identity." In *Development and Dreams: The Urban Legacy of the 2010 Football World Cup*, edited by Udesh Pillay, Richard Tomlinson, and Orli Bass, 246–65. Cape Town: HSRC Press, 2009.

Bellos, Alex. *Futebol: The Brazilian Way of Life*. New York: Bloomsbury, 2005.

Berger, Guy. "Image Revisions: South Africa, Africa, and the 2010 World Cup." *Ecquid Novi: African Journalism Studies* 31, 2 (2011): 174–90.

Bickford-Smith, Vivian, Elizabeth van Heyningen, and Nigel Worden. *Cape Town in the Twentieth Century: An Illustrated Social History.* Claremont: David Philip, 1999.

Birmingham, David. *Kwame Nkrumah: The Father of African Nationalism.* Athens: Ohio University Press, 1998.

Black, David R., and John Nauright. *Rugby and the South African Nation.* Manchester: Manchester University Press, 1998.

Black, David R., and Janis van der Westhuizen. "The Allure of Global Games for 'Semi-Peripheral' Polities and Spaces: A Research Agenda." *Third World Quarterly* 25, 7 (2004): 1195–1214.

Bloomfield, Steve. *Africa United: Soccer, Passion, Politics, and the First World Cup in Africa.* New York: Harper Perennial, 2010.

Bolsmann, Chris. "The 1899 Orange Free State Football Team of Europe: 'Race,' Imperial Loyalty, and Sports Spectacle." *International Journal of the History of Sport* 28, 1 (2011): 81–97.

Bolsmann, Chris. "Mexico 1968 and South Africa 2010: Sombreros and Vuvuzelas and the Legitimisation of Global Sporting Events." *Bulletin of Latin American Research* 29, 1 (2010): 93–106.

Bolsmann, Chris. "Representation in the First African World Cup: 'World-Class', Pan-Africanism, and Exclusion." *Soccer and Society* 13, 2 (2012): 156–72.

Bond, Patrick. *Elite Transition: From Apartheid to Neoliberalism in South Africa.* London: Zed, 1999.

Bond, Patrick, and Eddie Cottle. "Economic Promises and Pitfalls of South Africa's World Cup." In *South Africa's World Cup: A Legacy for Whom?,* edited by Eddie Cottle, 39–71. Scottsville: University of KwaZulu-Natal Press, 2011.

Bongmba, Elias K. "Reflections on Thabo Mbeki's African Renaissance." *Journal of Southern African Studies* 30, 2 (2004): 291–316.

Booth, Douglas. *The Race Game: Sport and Politics in South Africa.* London: Cass, 1998.

Campbell, Horace. *Barack Obama and 21st Century Politics: A Revolutionary Moment in the USA.* London: Pluto, 2010.

Carlin, John. *Playing the Enemy: Nelson Mandela and the Game That Made a Nation.* London: Atlantic, 2008.

Castle, Andrea, Miki Flockemann, Kudzayi Ngara, and Wahseema Roberts. "The Everyday Experience of Xenophobia: Performing The Crossing from Zimbabwe to South Africa." *Critical Arts* 24, 2 (2010): 245–59.

Chapman, Michael, ed. *The Drum Decade: Stories from the 1950s.* Pietermaritzburg: University of Natal Press, 2001.

Cornelissen, Scarlett. "'It's Africa's Turn!': The Narratives and Legitimations Surrounding the Moroccan and South African Bids for the 2006 and 2010 FIFA Finals." *Third World Quarterly* 25, 7 (2004): 1293–1310.

Cottle, Eddie, ed. *South Africa's World Cup: A Legacy for Whom?* Scottsville: University of KwaZulu-Natal Press, 2011.

Crush, Jonathan. "South Africa: Policy in the Face of Xenophobia," Southern African Migration Project, July 2008, http://www.migrationinformation.org/Feature/display.cfm?ID=689, accessed November 30, 2010.

Darby, Paul. "Africa and the 'World' Cup: Politics, Eurocentrism, and Resistance." *International Journal of the History of Sport* 22, 5 (2005): 883–905.

Darby, Paul. *Africa Football and FIFA: Politics, Colonialism, and Resistance*. London: Cass, 2002.

Darby, Paul. "'Go Outside': The History, Economics, and Geography of Ghanaian Football Labour Migration." *African Historical Review* 42, 1 (2010): 19–41.

Darby, Paul, Gerard Akindes, and Matthew Kirwin. "Football Academies and the Migration of African Football Labor to Europe." *Journal of Sport and Social Issues* 31, 2 (2007): 143–61.

Debord, Guy. *The Society of the Spectacle*. Detroit: Black and Red, 1983.

Degen, Monica. "Fighting for the Global Catwalk: Formalizing Public Life in Castlefield (Manchester) and Diluting Public Life in El Raval (Barcelona)." *International Journal of Urban and Regional Research* 27, 4 (2003): 867–80.

Desai, Ashwin, ed. *The Race to Transform: Sport in Post-Apartheid South Africa*. Cape Town: HSRC Press, 2010.

Desai, Ashwin. *We Are the Poors: Community Struggles in Post-Apartheid South Africa*. New York: Monthly Review Press, 2002.

Dietschy, Paul, and David Claude Kemo-Keimbou. *Africa and the Football World*. Paris: EPA, 2008.

Dobson, Paul. *Rugby in South Africa: A History, 1861–1988*. Cape Town: South African Rugby Board, 1989.

Dubin, Steven. "Review." *Art South Africa* 9, 1 (2010): 72–76.

Dubois, Laurent. *Soccer Empire: The World Cup and the Future of France*. Berkeley University of California Press, 2010.

Farred, Grant. *Long Distance Love: A Passion for Football*. Philadelphia: Temple University Press, 2008.

Fletcher, Marc. "'You Must Support Chiefs: Pirates Already Have Two White Fans!': Race and Racial Discourse in South African Football Fandom." In *South Africa and the Global Game: Football, Apartheid, and Beyond*, edited by Peter Alegi and Chris Bolsmann, 79–94. London: Routledge, 2010.

Flyvbjerg, Bent. "Macchiavellian Mega Projects." *Antipode* 37, 1 (2005): 18–22.

Foer, Franklin. *How Soccer Explains the World: An Unlikely Theory of Globalization*. New York: HarperCollins, 2004.

Foer, Franklin. "Soccer vs. McWorld." *Foreign Policy* 140 (2004): 32–40.

Galeano, Eduardo. *Soccer in Sun and Shadow*. New York: Verso, 1998.

Giampiccoli, Andrea, and John Nauright. "Problems and Prospects for Community Based Tourism in the New South Africa: The 2010 FIFA World Cup and Beyond." *African Historical Review* 42, 1 (2010): 42–62.

Giardina, Michael D. "One Day, One Goal?: PUMA, Corporate Philanthropy and the Cultural Politics of Brand 'Africa.'" *Sport in Society* 13, 1 (2010): 130–42.

Giulianotti, Richard. "Supporters, Followers, Fans, and Flaneurs: A Taxonomy of Spectator Identities in Football." *Journal of Sport and Social Issues* 26, 1 (2002): 25–46.

Goldblatt, David. *The Ball Is Round: A Global History of Soccer*. New York: Riverhead, 2008.

Griffiths, Edward. *One Team, One Country: The Greatest Year of Springbok Rugby.* London: Viking, 1996.

Grundlingh, Albert. "From Redemption to Recidivism?: Rugby and Change in South Africa during the 1995 Rugby World Cup and Its Aftermath." *Sporting Traditions* 14, 2 (1998): 77–86.

Grundlingh, Albert, André Odendaal, and Burridge Spies. *Beyond the Tryline: Rugby and South African Society.* Johannesburg: Ravan, 1995.

Haferburg, Christoph, Theresa Golka, and Marie Selter. "Public Viewing Areas: Urban Interventions in the Context of Mega-Events." In *Development and Dreams: The Urban Legacy of the 2010 Football World Cup,* edited by Udesh Pillay, Richard Tomlinson, and Orli Bass, 246–65. Cape Town: HSRC Press, 2009.

Hare, Geoff. *Football in France: A Cultural History.* Oxford: Berg, 2003.

Hiller, Harry H. "Mega-Events, Urban Boosterism, and Growth Strategies: An Analysis of the Objectives and Legitimations of the Cape Town Olympic Bid." *International Journal of Urban and Regional Research* 24, 2 (2000): 439–58.

Hlongwane, Khangela Ali, Sifiso Ndlovu, and Mothobi Mutloatse, eds. *Soweto '76: Reflections on the Liberation Struggles.* Houghton: Mutloatse Arts Heritage Trust, 2006.

Hoberman, John. "France's Soccer Debacle Lifts Lid on Racial Tensions." *Foreign Policy,* July 2010. http://www.foreignpolicy.com/articles/2010/07/01/le_scandal, accessed July 29, 2011.

Hobsbawm, Eric. *Nations and Nationalism since 1780.* Cambridge: Cambridge University Press, 1992.

Hook, Derek, and Michele Vrdoljak. "Gated Communities, Heterotopia, and a 'Rights' of Privilege: A 'Heterotopology' of the South African Security-Park." *Geoforum* 33 (2002): 195–219.

Hornby, Nick. *Fever Pitch.* London: Penguin, 2000.

Hunter, Mark. *Love in the Time of AIDS: Inequality, Gender, and Rights in South Africa.* Bloomington: Indiana University Press, 2010.

Jacobs, Sean. "'It Wasn't That I did not like South African Football': Media, History, and Biography." In *South Africa and the Global Game: Football, Apartheid, and Beyond,* edited by Peter Alegi and Chris Bolsmann, 95–104. London: Routledge, 2010.

Kathrada, Ahmed. *Memoirs.* Cape Town: Zebra, 2008.

Korr, Chuck, and Marvin Close. *More Than Just a Game: Football v. Apartheid.* London: Collins, 2008.

Kuper, Simon. *Football against the Enemy.* London: Orion, 1994.

Kuper, Simon, and Stefan Szymanski. *Soccernomics.* New York: Nation, 2009.

Legassick, Martin. *The Struggle for the Eastern Cape, 1800–1854: Subjugation and the Roots of South African Democracy.* Sandton: KMM Review, 2010.

Macdonald, Michael. "Power Politics in the New South Africa." *Journal of Southern African Studies* 22, 2 (1996): 221–33.

Magazine, Roger. *Golden and Blue Like My Heart: Masculinity, Youth, and Power among Soccer Fans in Mexico City.* Tucson: University of Arizona Press, 2007.

Mager, Anne. *Beer, Sociability, and Masculinity in South Africa.* Bloomington: Indiana University Press, 2010.

Makgoba, Malegapuru William, ed. *The African Renaissance: The New Struggle*. Johannesburg: Mafube and Tafelberg, 1999.

Mandela, Nelson. *Long Walk to Freedom*. Boston: Back Bay, 1995.

Mangaliso, Mzamo P., and Mphuthumi B. Damane. "Building Competitive Advantage from 'Ubuntu': Management Lessons from South Africa (and Executive Commentary)." *Academy of Management Executive* 15, 3 (2001): 23–34.

Marais, Hein. *South Africa: Limits to Change—The Political Economy of Transition*. Cape Town: University of Cape Town Press; London: Zed, 2011.

Markovits, Andrei S., and Steven L. Hellerman. *Offside: Soccer and American Exceptionalism in Sport*. Princeton: Princeton University Press, 2001.

McKinley, Dale T. "Mbombela: Corruption, Muder, False Promises, and Resistance." In *South Africa's World Cup: A Legacy for Whom?*, edited by Eddie Cottle, 281–311. Scottsville: University of KwaZulu-Natal Press, 2011.

Merrett, Christopher. "From Non-Racial Sport to the FIFA World Cup: A Tale of Politics, Big Business, and Hope Betrayed." In *Sport versus Art: A South African Contest*, edited by Chris Thurman, 74–82. Johannesburg: Wits University Press, 2010.

Mhiripiri, Nhamo Anthony. "Under Fire Essay: From May Shame to 2030 or There About: A Tale of Xenophobia, Zimbabwe, and Fictive Identities." *Critical Arts* 24, 2 (2010): 284–97.

Miller, Rory M., and Liz Crolley, eds. *Football in the Americas: Fútbol, Futebol, Soccer*. London: Institute for the Study of the Americas, 2007.

Monsiváis, Carlos. *Los Rituales del Caos*. México, D.F.: Ediciones Era, 1995.

Mudimbe, Valentin, Y. *The Idea of Africa*. Bloomington: Indiana University Press, 1994.

Murray, Bruce, and Christopher Merrett. *Caught Behind: Race and Politics in Springbok Cricket*. Johannesburg: Wits University Press; Scottsville: University of KwaZulu-Natal Press, 2004.

Murray, Martin J. "Building the 'New South Africa': Urban Space, Architectural Design, and the Disruption of Historical Memory." In *History Making and Present Day Politics: The Meaning of Collective Memory in South Africa*, edited by Hans Erik Stolten, 227–47. Uppsala: Nordiska Afrikainstitutet, 2007.

Murray, Martin J. *City of Extremes: The Spatial Politics of Johannesburg*. Durham: Duke University Press, 2011.

Naidoo, Prishani. "A Field of Play." In *Halakaska!*, edited by Fiona Rankin-Smith, 15. Johannesburg: Wits Arts Museum, 2010.

Nauright, John. "Global Games: Culture, Political Economy, and Sport in the Globalized World of the 21st Century." *Third World Quarterly* 25, 7 (2004): 1325–36.

Nauright, John. *Sport, Cultures, and Identities in South Africa*. London: Leicester University Press, 1997.

Neocosmos, Michael. *From "Foreign Natives" to "Native Foreigners": Explaining Xenophobia in Post-Apartheid South Africa: Citizenship and Nationalism, Identity and Politics*. Dakar: Council for the Development of Social Science Research in Africa, 2010.

Nesbitt, Francis Njubi. *Race for Sanctions: African Americans against Apartheid, 1946–1994*. Bloomington: Indiana University Press, 2004.

Nyamnjoh, Francis. *Insiders and Outsiders: Citizenship and Xenophobia in Contemporary Southern Africa*. Dakar: CODESRIA; London: Zed, 2006.

Nyembezi, C. L. Sibusiso. *Zulu Proverbs*. Pietermaritzburg: Shuter and Shooter, 1990.

Otter, Steven. *Khayelitsha: uMlungu in a Township*. Johannesburg: Penguin, 2007.

p'Bitek, Okot. *Artist the Ruler: Essays on Art, Culture, and Values*. Nairobi: East African Education, 1986.

Poli, Raffaele. "Migrations and Trade of African Football Players: Historic, Geographical, and Cultural Aspects." *Africa Spectrum* 41, 3 (2006): 393–414.

Posel, Deborah, and Graeme Simpson, eds. *Commissioning the Past: Understanding South Africa's Truth and Reconciliation Commission*. Johannesburg: Wits University Press, 2002.

Prashad, Vijay. *The Darker Nations: A People's History of the Third World*. New York: New Press, 2007.

Preller, Karin. "Review." *de Arte* 82 (2010): 66–71.

Rathbone, Richard. *Nkrumah and the Chiefs: The Politics of Chieftaincy in Ghana, 1951–60*. Accra: Reimmer; Athens: Ohio University Press; Oxford: Currey, 2000.

Roberts, David. "Durban's Future?: Re-Branding through the Production/Policing of Event-Specific Places at the 2010 World Cup." *Sport in Society* 13, 10 (2010): 1462–73.

Roche, Maurice. *Mega-Events and Modernity: Olympics and Expos in the Growth of Global Culture*. London: Routledge, 2000.

Saunders, Christopher. "Cape Town and New Orleans." *Safundi* 1, 1 (2000): 1–6.

Schoonbee, Karen, and Stefaans Brümmer. "Public Loss, FIFA's Gain: How Cape Town Got Its 'White Elephant.'" In *Player and Referee: Conflicting Interests and the 2010 FIFA World Cup*, edited by Collette Schulz Herzenberg, 133–67. Pretoria: Institute for Security Studies, 2010.

Schulz-Herzenberg, Collette, ed. *Player and Referee: Conflicting Interests and the 2010 FIFA World Cup*. Pretoria: Institute for Security Studies, 2010.

Seekings, Jeremy, and Nicoli Nattrass. *Class, Race, and Inequality in South Africa*. New Haven: Yale University Press, 2005.

Sellström, Tor, ed. *Liberation in Southern Africa: Regional and Swedish Voices*. Uppsala: Nordiska Afrikainstitutet, 1999.

Silverstein, Paul. "The Tragedy and Farce of French Football Politics." *Social Text*, 2010. http://www.socialtextjournal.org/periscope/2010/07/the-tragedy-and-farce-of-french-football-politics.php, accessed August 24, 2011.

Smit, Barbara. *Pitch Invasion: Adidas, Puma, and the Making of Modern Sport*. London: Lane, 2006.

Sole, Sam. "Durban's Moses Mabhida Stadium: Arch of Hope or Yoke of Debt?" In *Player and Referee: Conflicting Interests and the 2010 FIFA World Cup*, edited by Collette Schulz Herzenberg, 169–201. Pretoria: Institute for Security Studies, 2010.

South Africa. Truth and Reconciliation Commission. *Truth and Reconciliation Commission of South Africa Report*. 5 vols. Cape Town: Juta, 1998.

South African Democracy Education Trust. *The Road to Democracy in South Africa*. Vol. 3, *International Solidarity*. Pretoria: University of South Africa Press, 2008.

Southall, Roger. "The ANC and Black Capitalism in South Africa." *Review of African Political Economy* 31, 100 (2004): 313–28.

Sparks, Allister. *Tomorrow Is Another Country: The Inside Story of South Africa's Negotiated Revolution.* Johannesburg: Struik, 1994.

Steinberg, Jonny. *South Africa's Xenophobic Eruption.* Pretoria: Institute for Security Studies, 2008.

Stiebel, Lindy, and Liz Gunner, eds. *Still Beating the Drum: Critical Perspectives on Lewis Nkosi.* Johannesburg : Wits University Press, 2006.

Surplus People Project. *Khayelitsha: New Home, Old Story.* Cape Town: Surplus People Project, 1984.

Swanepoel, De Wet, and James W. Hall. "Football Match Spectator Sound Exposure and Effect on Hearing: A Pretest–Post-Test Study." *South African Medical Journal* 100, 4 (2010): 239–42.

Swanepoel, De Wet, James W. Hall, and Dirk Koekemoer. "Vuvuzela—Good for Your Team, Bad for Your Ears." *South African Medical Journal* 100, 2 (2010): 99.

Thompson, Glen. "Making Waves, Making Men: The Emergence of a Professional Surfing Masculinity in South Africa during the Late 1970s." In *Changing Men in Southern Africa*, edited by Robert Morrell, 91–104. London: Zed; Pietermaritzburg: University of Natal Press, 2001.

Thompson, Glen. "Reimagining Surf City: Surfing and the Making of the Post-Apartheid Beach in South Africa." *International Journal of the History of Sport* 28, 15 (2011): 2115–29.

Thurman, Chris. "Poor Relations?" In *Sport versus Art: A South African Contest*, edited by Chris Thurman, 8–33. Johannesburg: Wits University Press, 2010.

Tiyambe, Paul Zeleza. *Barack Obama and African Diasporas: Dialogues and Dissensions.* Banbury: Ayebia Clarke; Athens: Ohio University Press, 2009.

Turnbull, John. "Alone in the Woods: The Literary Landscape of Soccer's 'Last Defender.'" *World Literature Today* 84, 4 (2010): 19–22.

Turrell, Robert V. *Capital and Labour on the Kimberley Diamond Fields, 1871–1890.* Cambridge: Cambridge University Press, 1987.

van der Merwe, Justin, and Janis van der Westhuizen. "The Branding Game: The Role of Sport in South African Foreign Policy." *Global Insight* 67, 1 (2006): 1–3.

van der Westhuizen, Janis, and Kamilla Swart. "Bread or Circuses? The 2010 World Cup and South Africa's Quest for Marketing Power." *International Journal of the History of Sport* 28, 1 (2011): 168–80.

Vasili, Phil. *The First Black Footballer, Arthur Wharton, 1865–1930: An Absence of Memory.* London: Cass, 1998.

Vidacs, Bea. "The Postcolonial and the Level Playing-Field in the 1998 World Cup." In *Sport and Postcolonialism*, edited by John Bale and Mike Cronin, 147–58. Oxford: Berg, 2003.

Vidacs, Bea. *Visions of a Better World: Football in the Cameroonian Social Imagination.* Berlin: LIT, 2010.

Vokes, Richard. "Arsenal in Bugamba: The Rise of English Premier League Football in Uganda." *Anthropology Today* 26, 3 (2010): 10–15.

Waldmeir, Patti. *Anatomy of a Miracle: The End of Apartheid and the Birth of the New South Africa.* New York: Norton, 1997.

Wangerin, David. *Soccer in a Football World: The Story of America's Forgotten Game.* Philadelphia: Temple University Press, 2006.

Wilson, Jonathan. *Inverting the Pyramid: The History of Football Tactics.* London: Orion, 2008.

Worger, William H. *South Africa's City of Diamonds: Mine Workers and Monopoly Capitalism in Kimberley, 1867–1895.* New Haven: Yale University Press, 1987.

Zaaijman, J. du T. "Vuvuzelas: *Ex Africa Semper Aliquid Novis*—Again?" *South African Medical Journal* 100, 9 (2010): 546.

Contributors

Simon Adetona Akindes is an associate professor at the University of Wisconsin, Parkside. His most recent publication is "Elections in Côte d'Ivoire: The Contrasting Colors of Democratization," in *West Africa's Quest for Democracy: Lessons in Elections, Liberalization, and Democratization, 1990–2009* (2011). In 2007, he was a guest editor of a special issue of the journal *West Africa Review* focused on Benin and Ivory Coast. Akindes is a former player on Benin's national football team and has published on a variety of topics, including photography, visual culture, education, and music. He is a cofounder of Tous au Sport, a nonprofit organization that aims to expand physical activity and sports for health, a better environment, and safe communities (http://usa.tousausport.org/).

Peter Alegi is a professor of history at Michigan State University. He is the author of *African Soccerscapes: How a Continent Changed the World's Game* (2010) and *Laduma!: Soccer, Politics, and Society in South Africa*, 2nd ed. (2010). He has also coedited, with Chris Bolsmann, *South Africa and the Global Game: Football, Apartheid, and Beyond* (2010). He hosts the "Africa Past and Present" podcast with Peter Limb (http://afripod.aodl.org) and blogs at *Football Is Coming Home* (http://www.footballiscominghome.info). In 2010, he was Visiting Fulbright Professor of History at the University of KwaZulu-Natal.

Orli Bass is a senior project officer at the Centre for Critical Research on Race and Identity at the University of KwaZulu-Natal. With Udesh Pillay and Richard Tomlinson, she coedited *Development and Dreams: The Urban Legacy of the 2010 Football World Cup* (2009), and her research interests include cities and culture, African identity and cities, and megaevents.

Chris Bolsmann is a senior lecturer in sociology at Aston University. His research focuses on the transformation and marketization of higher education, and football and identity in postapartheid South Africa. He has published in the *African Historical Review*, *Soccer and Society*, the *International Journal of the History of Sport*, the *Bulletin of Latin American Research*, and the *South African Labour Bulletin*, among other journals.

Thabo Dladla is director of soccer at the University of KwaZulu-Natal, Pieter-maritzburg campus. A former professional footballer, Dladla has coached at the SAFA Transnet School of Excellence and served as an assistant coach for the South African Under-Twenty men's national team at the 1997 U-20 World Cup. He is the founder and technical director of the Izichwe Youth Football Program in Pieter-maritzburg.

Killian Doherty holds a master's degree in architecture from the Royal Techni-cal College (KTH) in Stockholm, Sweden. He has worked in Stockholm, Dublin, and London and volunteered with a grassroots organization on the post-Katrina reconstruction of New Orleans. A visiting studio tutor at the KTH in Stockholm and Gothenburg and at the Kigali Institute of Science and Technology in Kigali, Rwanda, Doherty has exhibited his work internationally and is currently designing and constructing a community sports facility in Kigali.

Jennifer Doyle teaches at the University of California, Riverside. Her soccer blog is *From a Left Wing* (http://fromaleftwing.blogspot.com). She is the author of *Sex Objects: Art and the Dialectics of Desire* (2006) and is completing a book on difficulty, emotion, and contemporary art. Her current projects include a collection of essays exploring the margins of football culture and a book about art and sport.

Laurent Dubois is Marcello Lotti Professor of Romance Studies and History at Duke University and the author of several books, including *Soccer Empire: The World Cup and the Future of France* (2010).

Marc Fletcher holds a PhD in African studies from the University of Edinburgh and is an honorary research fellow at the School of Geography, Archaeology, and Environmental Sciences, University of the Witwatersrand. His research examines the multiple divisions in football fandom in Johannesburg, especially race, ethnic-ity, and class.

Albert Grundlingh is a professor and chair of the history department at the Uni-versity of Stellenbosch. He has published numerous articles on South African his-tory and historiography. His books include *The Dynamics of Treason: Boer Collabora-tion in the South African War of 1899–1902* (2006) and, with André Odendaal and Burridge Spies, *Beyond the Tryline: Rugby and South African Society* (1995).

Andrew M. Guest teaches in the Department of Social and Behavioral Sciences at the University of Portland, Oregon. He spent much of the World Cup year draw-ing on experiences as a soccer player, coach, and scholar in locales ranging from Ohio and Illinois to Malawi and Angola to write about both American and African soccer for *PitchInvasion.net*. His general academic interests focus on child, youth, and life-span development, particularly in relation to sports.

John Samuel Harpham earned a bachelor's degree from Duke University in 2010. He is currently traveling and writing before he begins his doctoral studies in political theory. His research interests include the aesthetic of crime in early detective fiction and the idea of contradiction in the philosophy of slavery. His research on soccer in France was made possible by a Benenson Award from Duke University.

Sergio Varela Hernández holds a doctoral degree in social anthropology from the Universidad Iberoamericana. His research focuses on sports fans. Based in Johannesburg during the 2010 World Cup, Varela conducted a two-month ethnographic study of Mexican World Cup fans funded by the Research and Graduate Program in Social Anthropology at the Universidad Iberoamericana and the National Council of Science and Technology. This research also benefited from the support of the Department of Anthropology at the University of the Witwatersrand.

Daniel Herwitz is the Mary Fair Croushore Professor of Humanities and director of the Institute for the Humanities at the University of Michigan. He has written extensively on the aesthetics of film, music, and visual art, and his monograph on Indian painter M. F. Husain won a National Book Award in India. Herwitz is the author of *Race and Reconciliation* (2003), based on his experiences in South Africa, and of short stories that have appeared in the *Michigan Quarterly Review*. A philosopher by training, Herwitz is also the coeditor, with Lydia Goehr, of *The Don Giovanni Moment: Essays on the Legacy of an Opera* (2006). He is an honorary research associate at the University of Cape Town.

Anna Mayumi Kerber is an Austrian freelance journalist and photographer. Since completing her master's degree in journalism and media management in 2007, she has been working as a reporter in South Africa and West Africa and in the Netherlands for various media. During the Road to 2010 project, she wrote a six-month series of articles for the Austrian newspaper *Die Presse* and kept a feature blog for the Austrian radio station FM4.

David Patrick Lane provided podcast analysis and content on Uruguay for the *Guardian* (United Kingdom) during the World Cup in South Africa. He contributes to the *Football Is Coming Home* blog (http://www.footballiscominghome.info) and the *Africa Is a Country* blog, and is working on a book on the African diaspora and football.

Mohlomi Kekeletso Maubane is a Soweto-based writer and an independent soccer researcher. His work has been published in the *Mail and Guardian* weekly newspaper and in *Hype* magazine. Maubane has also done research and scriptwriting for several South African TV programs, including *Siyaya 2010*. He plans to return to university to conduct research on South African football history.

John Nauright is director of the Academy of International Sport, Provost's Fellow for International Programs, and a professor in the School of Recreation, Health, and Tourism at George Mason University. He is also visiting professor of cultural studies at the University of the West Indies, Cave Hill. He is the author of many works on sports in South Africa and on global sport, including *Long Run to Free-*

dom: Sport, Cultures, and Identities in South Africa (2010), *The Routledge Companion to Sports History* (coedited with S. W. Pope, 2010), and *Sport around the World: History, Culture, Practice* (4 vols., forthcoming).

Mark Perryman is a writer and commentator on Englishness and football and a research fellow in sport and leisure culture at the University of Brighton. He is convenor of *LondonEnglandFans.com*, cofounder of *PhilosophyFootball.com*, and author of several books, including *Ingerland: Travels with a Football Nation* (2006).

Niels Posthumus is a sports editor at the *Trouw* newspaper in the Netherlands. He studied political science at the Free University of Amsterdam and newspaper journalism at Erasmus University. He has worked as an Africa correspondent for several Dutch and Belgian newspapers and contributed to the soccer magazine *Hard Gras* as well as the soccer blog *11apen.nl*. In 2008, he was a reporter for the *Star* in Johannesburg.

Fiona Rankin-Smith is special projects curator at the Wits Art Museum, University of the Witwatersrand. She was the curator of *Halakasha!* at the Standard Bank Gallery in Johannesburg during June and July 2010.

Rodney Reiners played professional football with Santos in Cape Town in the 1980s and 1990s. Since hanging up his boots, he has worked as a reporter for *Kick Off* magazine and Cape Talk Radio before taking up his current position as chief soccer writer for the *Cape Argus* newspaper.

David Roberts holds a doctoral degree in Geography and Planning from the University of Toronto. His research focuses on the social implications for marginalized members of South African society from the intense securitization of public space during the 2010 South African World Cup. His research in South Africa was conducted while he was a visiting research associate at the Centre for Critical Research on Race and Identity at the University of KwaZulu-Natal with funding from FIFA's João Havelange Scholarship.

Meg Vandermerwe is a lecturer in English literature and creative writing at the University of the Western Cape. She is the author of a short story collection, *This Place I Call Home* (2010), and is currently writing a novel, set in Cape Town during the 2010 World Cup, that explores the issue of South African xenophobia toward immigrants.

Craig Waite is a doctoral candidate in history at Indiana University. He was a Fulbright Scholar in Ghana in 2007–8 and is completing his dissertation, "Representing the Nation: Football, Politics, and Masculinity in Gold Coast/Ghana, 1945–1966."

Solomon Waliaula is a lecturer in the Department of English and Theatre at Moi University. He recently completed a doctoral dissertation on football culture and performance in contemporary Kenya.

Index